AN IRANIAN
METAMORPHOSIS

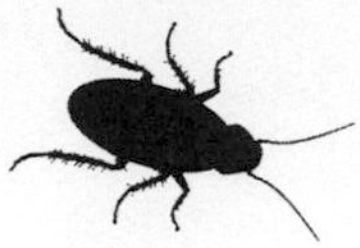

An Iranian Metamorphosis

Originally published as *Une Métamorphose Iranienne* by Çà et Là.

Translated by Ghazal Mosadeq

Editor: Tom Kaczynski

Copy editors: Cassidy Wilson & Alec Berry

Art Direction: Tom Kaczynski
Production assistants: Madeline McGrane & Rachel Topka

Uncivilized Books
P.O. Box 6434
Minneapolis, MN 55406
USA

uncivilizedbooks.com

First Edition, October 2014
10 9 8 7 6 5 4 3 2 1

ISBN 978-0-9889014-4-5

DISTRIBUTED TO THE TRADE BY:

Consortium Book Sales & Distribution, LLC.
34 Thirteenth Avenue NE,
Suite 101 Minneapolis,
MN 55413-1007
Orders: (800) 283-3572

Printed in the USA

AN IRANIAN METAMORPHOSIS

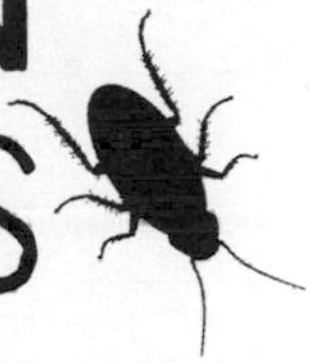

MANA NEYESTANI

Uncivilized Books, Publisher

This translation is by Ghazal Mosadeq, to whom I'm indebted, for her moral support and her unfailing friendship.

MANA NEYESTANI

WRITE DOWN THE WHOLE STORY!

THE WHOLE STORY... HOW CAN I FIT IN ALL THE DETAILS?

SUMMARIZE! MAKE SURE YOU STAY INSIDE THE FRAME.

HOW CAN I SUMMARIZE THE LAST FIVE MONTHS INSIDE A SMALL RECTANGLE?

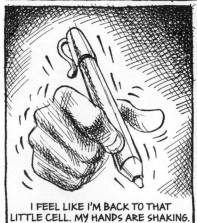

I FEEL LIKE I'M BACK TO THAT LITTLE CELL. MY HANDS ARE SHAKING.

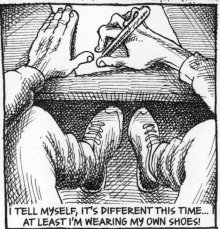

I TELL MYSELF, IT'S DIFFERENT THIS TIME... AT LEAST I'M WEARING MY OWN SHOES!

A TINY RECTANGLE FOR THE WHOLE STORY...

...FIVE MONTHS AGO I HAD SEVERAL PAGES.

MR. NEYESTANI, WRITE THE WHOLE STORY. ALL THE DETAILS PLEASE.

WELL, WRITE EVERYTHING DOWN TO CONVINCE THE JUDGE OF YOUR INNOCENCE.

BUT... I KEEP TELLING YOU IT WAS ALL A MISUNDERSTANDING. THERE'S NOTHING TO TELL.

I STARTED WRITING. I HAD TO FILL SEVERAL PAGES AND THE STORY WAS HARDLY A PARAGRAPH LONG, BUT NOW...

...ERAL THREAT ...LOSS... ...ING PHONE CALLS AND ALSO THE RISK OF A SEVERE VERDICT FROM THE REVOLU- TIONARY COURT WE DECIDED TO LEAVE THE COUNTRY. WE WENT TO DUBAI (EMIRATE) A FRIEND IN DUBAI SUGGESTED TO COME TO LANCHR OFFICE

... IT'S TOO LONG!

DED TO
OUNTRY. WE
UBAI (EMIRATE).
UBAI SUGGEST
UNCHR OFFICE
N ANKARA
DIDN'T I TELL YOU TO STAY INSIDE THE FRAME?
HIS ACCUSATORY TONE TAKES ME BACK FIVE MONTHS TO THAT ROOM...
UNCHR OFFICE, ANKARA, TURKEY, NOVEMBER 2006
DIDN'T I TELL YOU TO STAY INSIDE THE FRAME? WHY DON'T YOU LISTEN?
I HAVE TO REMEMBER IT'S DIFFERENT THIS TIME. THIS GUY ISN'T MY INTERROGATOR. HE'S HERE TO HELP.
SEE, IN IRAN THEY BRUTALLY DISCRIMINATE AGAINST GAYS...

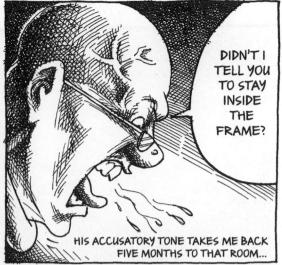

CHAPTER ONE

IT ALL STARTED WITH A COCKROACH...

ONE MORNING GREGOR SAMSA WOKE UP FROM AN ANXIOUS DREAM AND DISCOVERED...

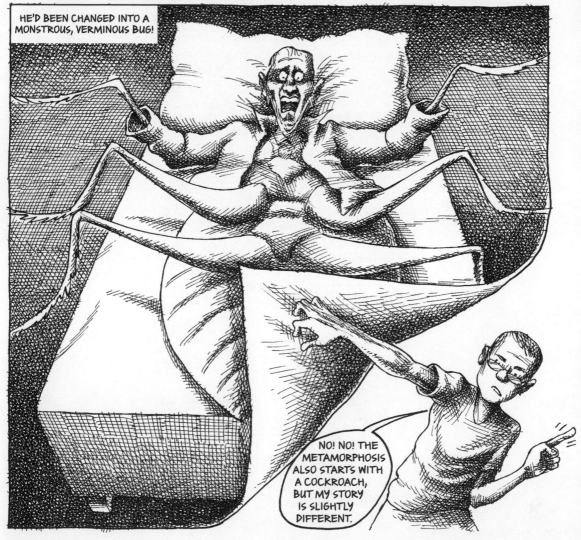

HE'D BEEN CHANGED INTO A MONSTROUS, VERMINOUS BUG!

NO! NO! THE METAMORPHOSIS ALSO STARTS WITH A COCKROACH, BUT MY STORY IS SLIGHTLY DIFFERENT.

I STARTED AS AN EDITORIAL CARTOONIST WHEN I WAS 16. AFTER THAT, I DREW CARTOONS FOR MANY POLITICAL, REFORMIST, AND OPPOSITION NEWSPAPERS. AFTER 17 REFORMIST NEWSPAPERS WERE BANNED IN THE SPRING OF 2000, I WAS OUT OF A JOB. I QUIT DRAWING POLITICAL CARTOONS AND STARTED WORKING FOR YOUR READER MAGAZINES. SOME OF MY COLLEAGUES WHO ENDURED INTERROGATIONS WARNED ME THAT MY NAME CAME UP A FEW TIMES. WORKING FOR CHILDREN'S PUBLICATIONS LIFTED MY SPIRITS AND IT SEEMED LESS RISKY... BOY WAS I WRONG! IN 2004 THE CHIEF EDITOR OF IRAN JOMEH, THE WEEKEND LEISURE SECTION OF THE IRAN NEWSPAPER, APPOINTED ME EDITOR OF THE CHILDREN'S PAGES. FOR TWO YEARS EVERYTHING WENT WELL. THEN IN 2005 THE GOVERNMENT (WHICH FUNDED OUR NEWSPAPER) GOT RADICALLY RELIGIOUS AND OUR MANAGEMENT GOT REALLY STRICT. BUT IT COULD'VE BEEN WORSE. WE DEALT WITH LEISURE NOT POLITICS. EVERY SATURDAY MORNING I'D COME UP WITH A TOPIC FOR SATIRE OR SCIENCE ARTICLE. ON SUNDAY I'D DRAW THE ILLUSTRATIONS AND SEND THEM TO THE LAYOUT DESIGNER. THAT FATEFUL SATURDAY DIDN'T SEEM ANY DIFFERENT FROM THE OTHERS...

IDIOT! YOU'VE GONE OUTSIDE THE FRAME AGAIN!

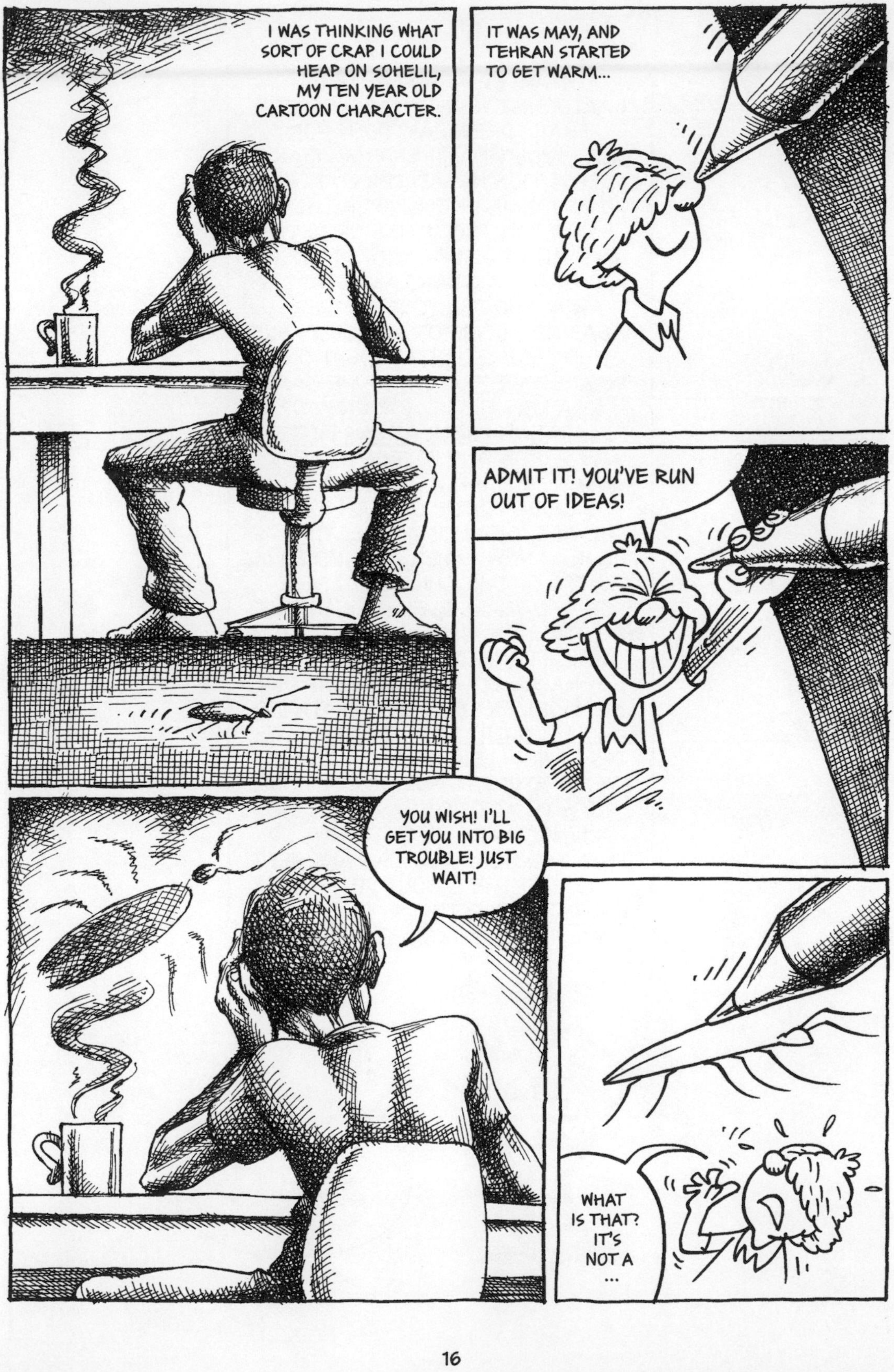
I WAS THINKING WHAT SORT OF CRAP I COULD HEAP ON SOHELIL, MY TEN YEAR OLD CARTOON CHARACTER.
IT WAS MAY, AND TEHRAN STARTED TO GET WARM...
ADMIT IT! YOU'VE RUN OUT OF IDEAS!
YOU WISH! I'LL GET YOU INTO BIG TROUBLE! JUST WAIT!
WHAT IS THAT? IT'S NOT A ...

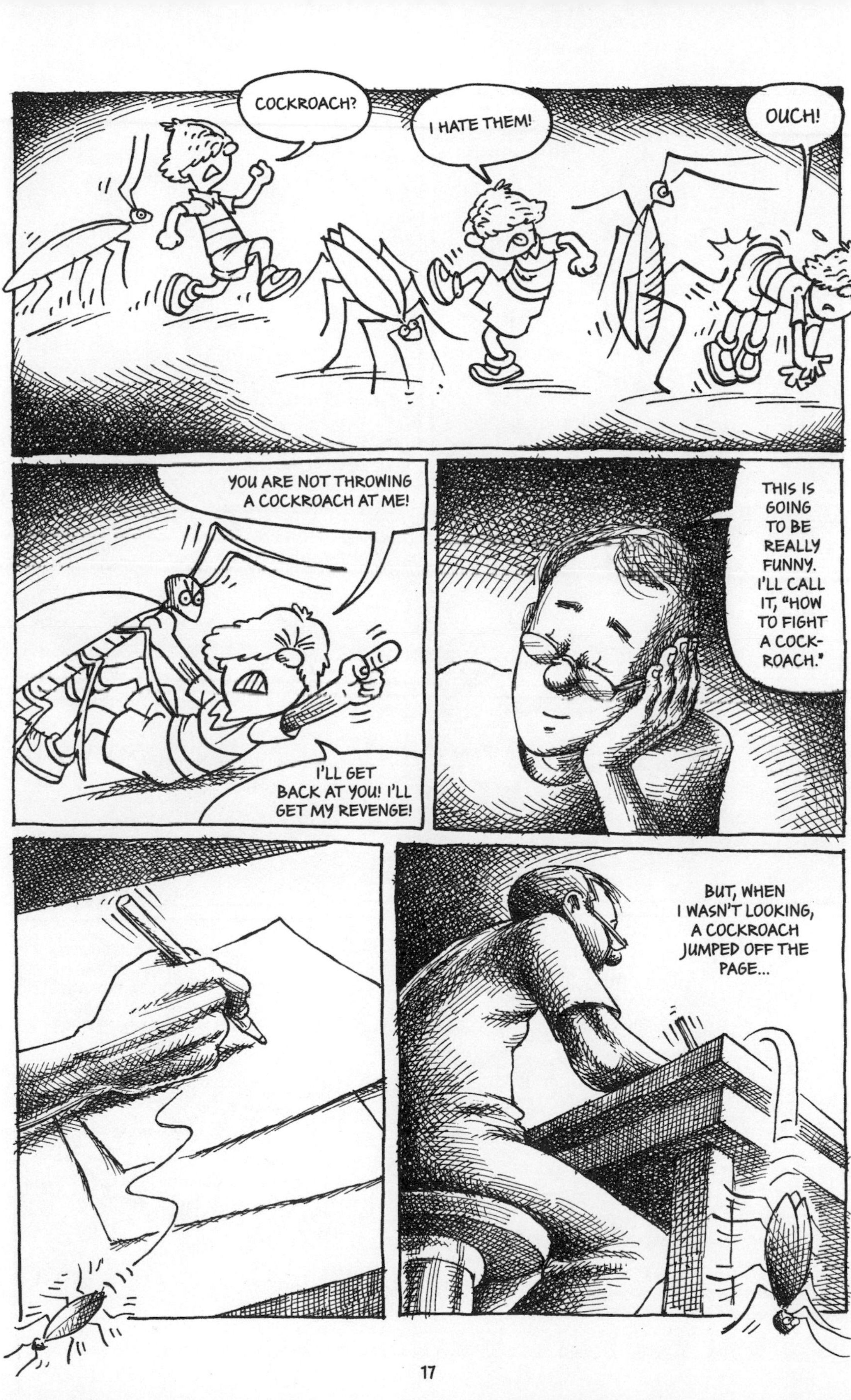
COCKROACH?
I HATE THEM!
OUCH!
YOU ARE NOT THROWING A COCKROACH AT ME!
I'LL GET BACK AT YOU! I'LL GET MY REVENGE!
THIS IS GOING TO BE REALLY FUNNY. I'LL CALL IT, "HOW TO FIGHT A COCK-ROACH."
BUT, WHEN I WASN'T LOOKING, A COCKROACH JUMPED OFF THE PAGE...

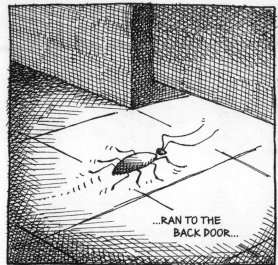

...RAN TO THE BACK DOOR...
...SKITTERED DOWNSTAIRS...
...GOT ON THE STREET...
...AND HIKED ALL THE WAY TO THE CITIES OF TABRIZ AND ARDEBIL IN THE AZERI PROVINCES – TO INFLUENCE MY FUTURE WITHOUT MY KNOWLEDGE.
CASPIAN SEA
TABRIZ
ARDABIL
RASHT
ZANJAN
SARI
TEHRAN
SEMNAN
SANANDAJ
HAMADAN
DASHT-E-
Jolfa
Khoy
Kaleybar
Marand
Ahar
Astara
Salmas
Shabestar
Heris
Sarab
Hashtpar
Bostan Abad
Azarshahr
Khalkhal
Maragheh
Miyaneh
Sowme'eh Sara
Masuleh
Fuman
Rudsar
Bonab
Hashtrud
Miyandoab
Naqadeh
Mahabad
Piranshahr
Shahin Dezh
Bukan
Takab
Soltaniyeh
Abhar
Sardasht
Baneh
Divandarreh
Bijar
Marivan
Paveh
Kamyaran
Qorveh
Javanrud
Alisadr
Razan
Kabudrahang
Bahar
Tafresh
Saveh
Qom
Shahriyar
Karaj
Tajrish
Damavand
Firuzkuh
Pol-e-Sefid
Garmsar
Varamin
Tonekabon
Nowshahr
Chalus
Nur
Amol
Babol
Qa'emshahr
Kordkuy
Gorgan
Shahrud
Damghan
Dizin

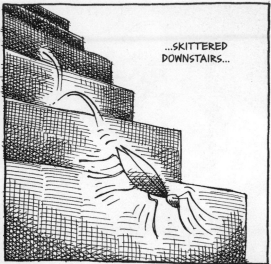

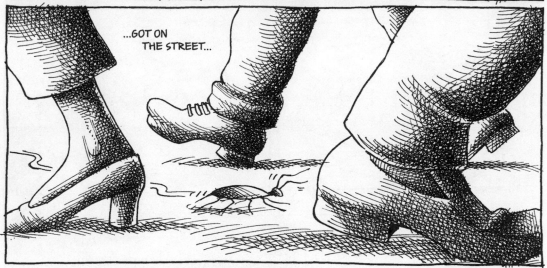

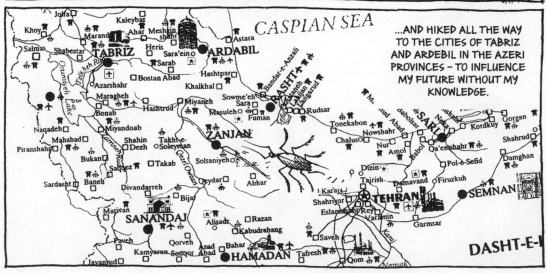

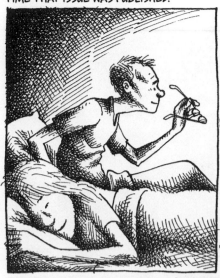

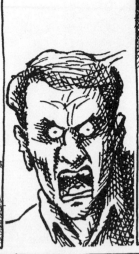

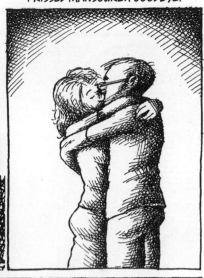

A WEEK HAD PASSED FROM THE TIME THAT ISSUE WAS PUBLISHED.
I KISSED MANSOUREH GOODBYE.
I PUT A WEEK'S WORK ON CD AND RAN TO THE IRAN-JOMEH OFFICE.
I FELT GREAT!
AT THE OFFICE, MEHRDAD, THE EDITOR, CALLED ME.
MANA! BEFORE YOU GO TO LAYOUT, I WANT TO HAVE A WORD.
SURE!

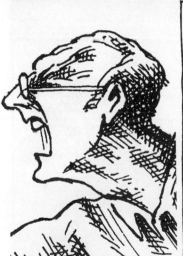

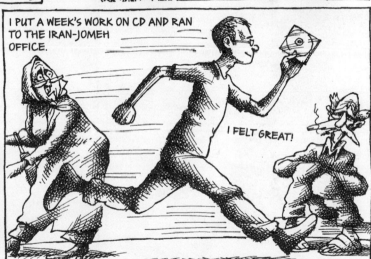

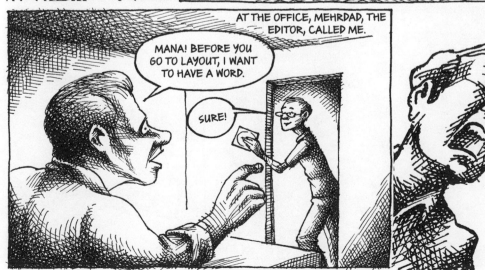

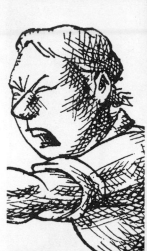

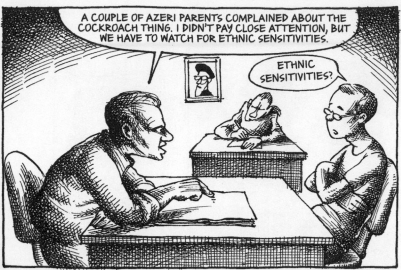

A COUPLE OF AZERI PARENTS COMPLAINED ABOUT THE COCKROACH THING. I DIDN'T PAY CLOSE ATTENTION, BUT WE HAVE TO WATCH FOR ETHNIC SENSITIVITIES.
ETHNIC SENSITIVITIES?
YES. IN ONE OF THE CARTOONS, A COCK-ROACH USES AN AZERI WORD.
سوسک ها سوسک نشید!
SooSoo SooSking sisko
SooSKI SooSKung
Namana?
اول باید
گفت وگو کنیم
که سوسک،
نمی شه. دستور
YOU CAN'T MEAN "NAMANA"? ARE YOU KIDDING ME? I OFTEN USE IT. WHENEVER I CAN'T THINK OF SOMETHING I SAY: NAMANA.
I KNOW. IT HAPPENS. JUST BE AWARE OF IT FROM NOW ON.

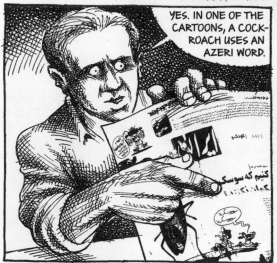

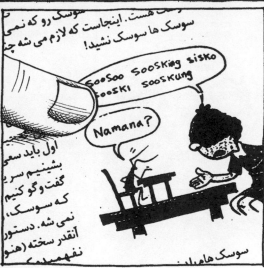

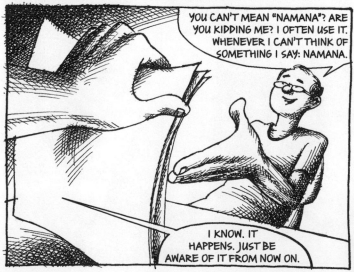

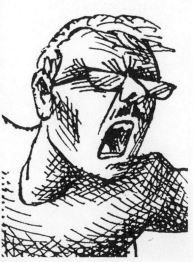

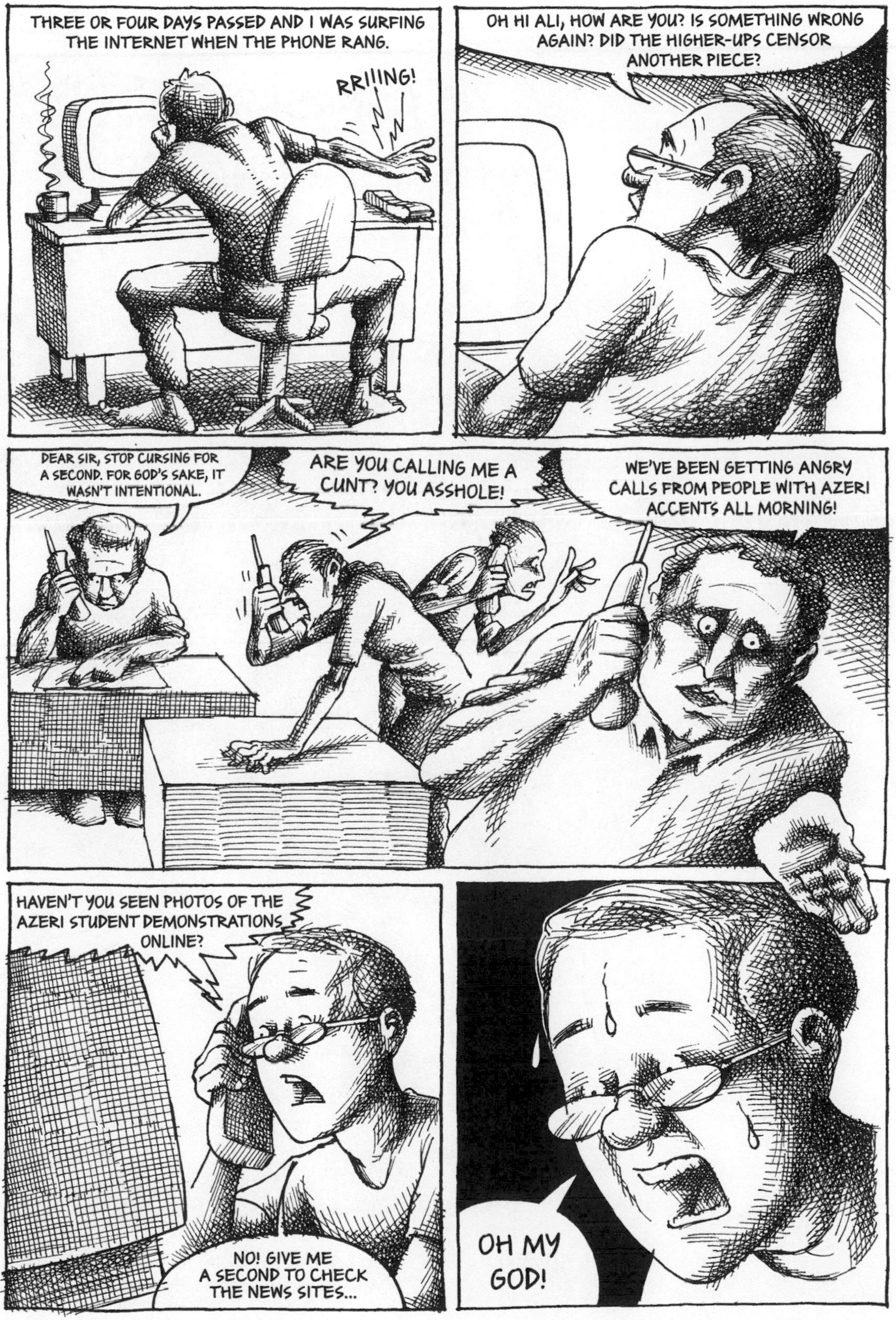
THREE OR FOUR DAYS PASSED AND I WAS SURFING THE INTERNET WHEN THE PHONE RANG.
RRIIING!
OH HI ALI, HOW ARE YOU? IS SOMETHING WRONG AGAIN? DID THE HIGHER-UPS CENSOR ANOTHER PIECE?
DEAR SIR, STOP CURSING FOR A SECOND. FOR GOD'S SAKE, IT WASN'T INTENTIONAL.
ARE YOU CALLING ME A CUNT? YOU ASSHOLE!
WE'VE BEEN GETTING ANGRY CALLS FROM PEOPLE WITH AZERI ACCENTS ALL MORNING!
HAVEN'T YOU SEEN PHOTOS OF THE AZERI STUDENT DEMONSTRATIONS ONLINE?
NO! GIVE ME A SECOND TO CHECK THE NEWS SITES...
OH MY GOD!

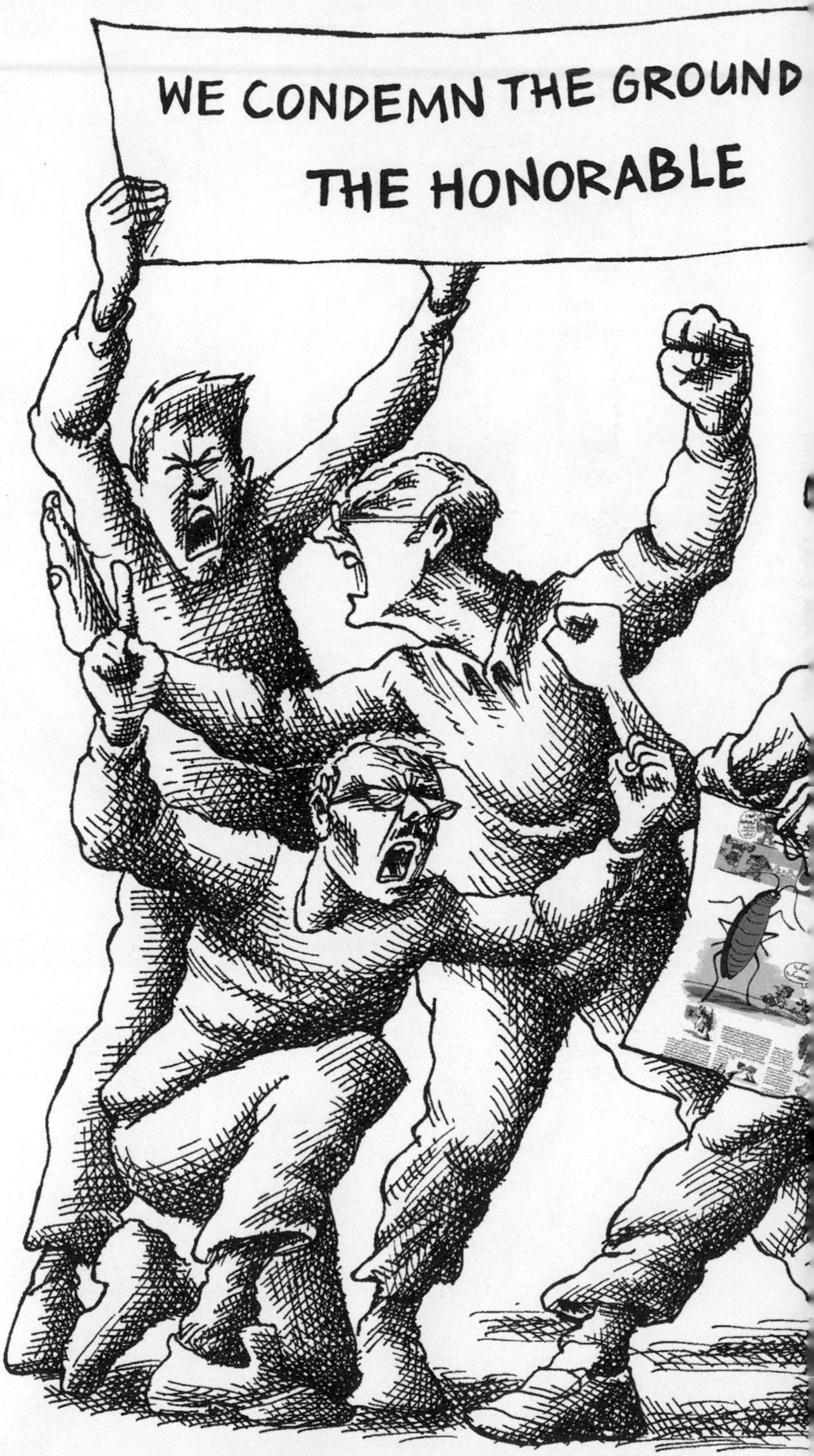
WE CONDEMN THE GROUND
THE HONORABLE

I COULD NOT BELIEVE THAT PEOPLE WERE DEMONSTRATING AGAINST THE IRANIAN NEWSPAPER...

* IN IRAN AZERBAIJANIS SOMETIMES REFER TO THEMSELVES AS TURKS.

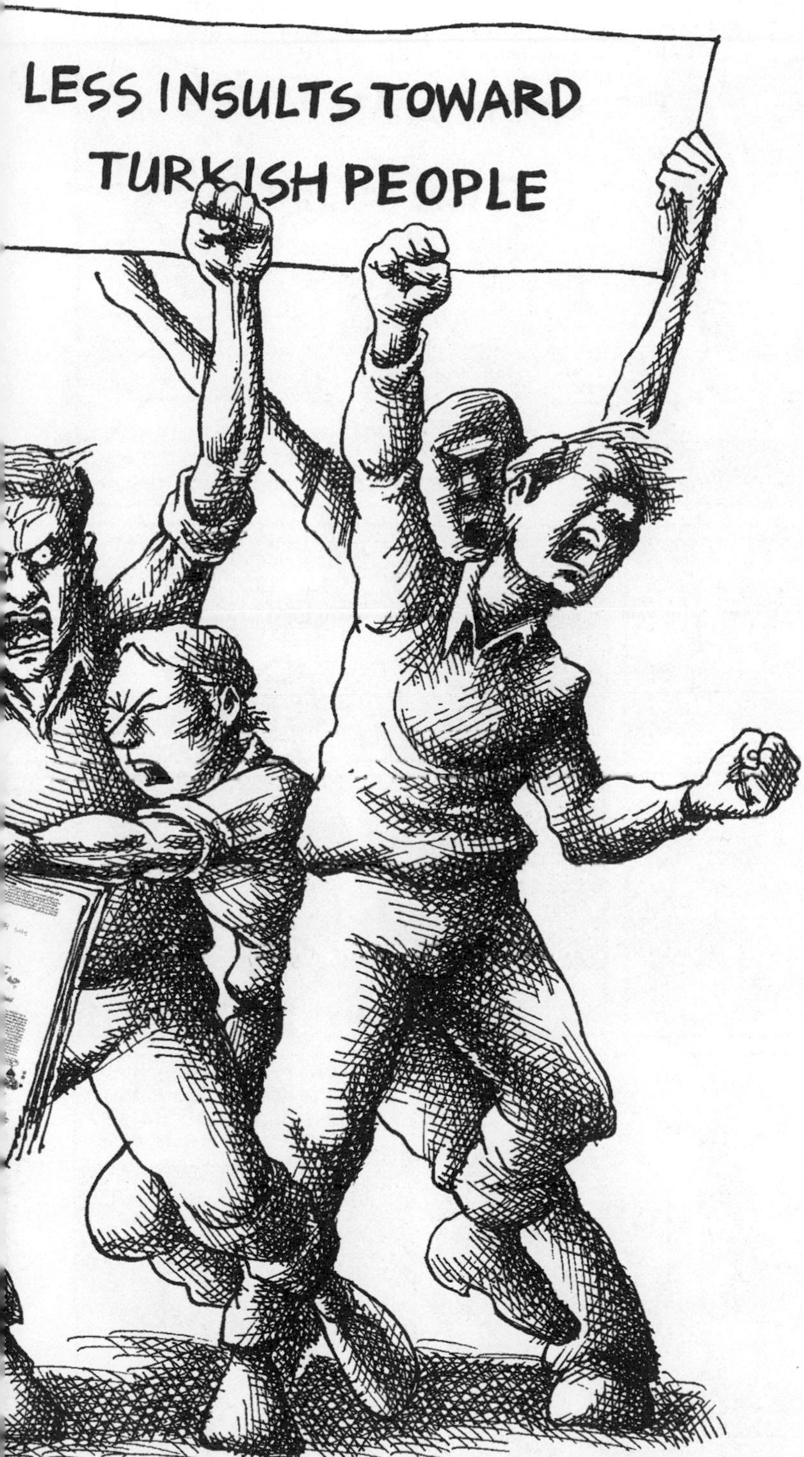
LESS INSULTS TOWARD TURKISH PEOPLE

AND THEY WERE DOING IT BECAUSE OF A SINGLE WORD IN MY CARTOON: NAMANA!
THE DEMONSTRATIONS WERE GROWING BY THE HOUR.

WE HAD A MEETING AT IRAN-JOMEH'S OFFICE.

UNFORTUNATELY, THE CARTOON HAS BEEN PHOTOCOPIED AND DISTRIBUTED IN AZERI CITIES. NOW THE AZERIES ARE OFFENDED BECAUSE THEY MISTAKENLY THINK THEY HAVE BEEN CALLED COCKROACHES.

I AM TERRIBLY SORRY. IT NEVER OCCURRED TO ME THAT IT WAS OFFENSIVE. IF IT HELPS I CAN RESIGN.

NO! RESIGNING WILL CONFIRM THAT I THINK IT WAS AN INSULT. WE ALREADY APOLOGIZED TWICE, FORMALLY AND INFORMALLY.

I WILL PUBLISH MY THIRD APOLOGY IN THIS WEEK. I HOPE IT WILL CALM THINGS DOWN.

AGAIN, I'M REALLY SORRY.

I WAS ABOUT TO LEAVE WHEN REZA THE NEWS PHOTO-GRAPHER STOPPED ME.

BY THE WAY...

... JUST TO BE SAFE, HIDE ANY ALCOHOL YOU MIGHT HAVE... IN CASE OF A POLICE RAID...

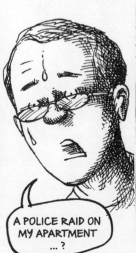

A POLICE RAID ON MY APARTMENT ... ?

I DON'T WANT TO SCARE YOU. HOPEFULLY ALL WILL GO WELL. BUT REALISTICALLY THE CASE WILL PROBABLY BECOME A MATTER OF STATE SECURITY.

IN THE FOLLOWING DAYS, DEMONSTRATIONS SPREAD FROM UNIVERSITIES TO THE STREETS.

TABRIZ BAZAAR WENT ON STRIKE. SITUATION WAS WORSENING.

HELLO? MANA? I GOT A CALL FROM THE INTELLIGENCE MINISTRY.

THEY WANT US TO COME IN FOR QUESTIONING TOMORROW MORNING.

SOMETHING WRONG?

NO... NOTHING IMPORTANT.

LIKE EVERY OTHER NIGHT, MANSOUREH AND I WENT FOR A WALK.

HAD I KNOWN WHAT WAS IN STORE FOR ME, I WOULD HAVE CARVED A PICTURE OF THE MOON INTO MY BRAIN...

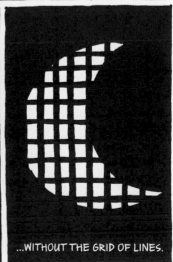

...WITHOUT THE GRID OF LINES.

25

CHAPTER TWO

WELCOME TO 209

THE NEXT DAY MEHRDAD CALLED TO LET ME KNOW THAT THE LOCATION OF THE QUESTIONING MOVED FROM THE INTELLIGENCE MINISTRY TO THE MAIN PROSECUTION OFFICE.

MANSOUREH, THROW OUT ALL THE BOOZE...OR GIVE IT TO SOMEONE.

I'M SCARED.

OH SWEETHEART, IT'S NOTHING.

I WAS LYING. THEY WOULDN'T HAVE CALLED US IN FOR "NOTHING." I KNEW A SUMMONS WAS BAD NEWS.

BY THE WAY, THEY SUGGESTED TO SAY THAT YOU HAVE AZERI BLOOD FROM ONE OF YOUR PARENTS. THAT MIGHT CALM THE AZERIS DOWN A BIT.

SURE. IT'S WELL-KNOWN MY FATHER IS A FAMOUS POET FROM KERMAN.* I CAN SAY MY MOTHER IS AZERI.

FUCK THIS TRAFFIC JAM.

WE GOT THERE AN HOUR LATE.

OFFICE OF THE ATTORNEY GENERAL

WE'RE HERE.

*KERMAN IS ONE OF THE NON-AZERI CITIES IN IRAN.

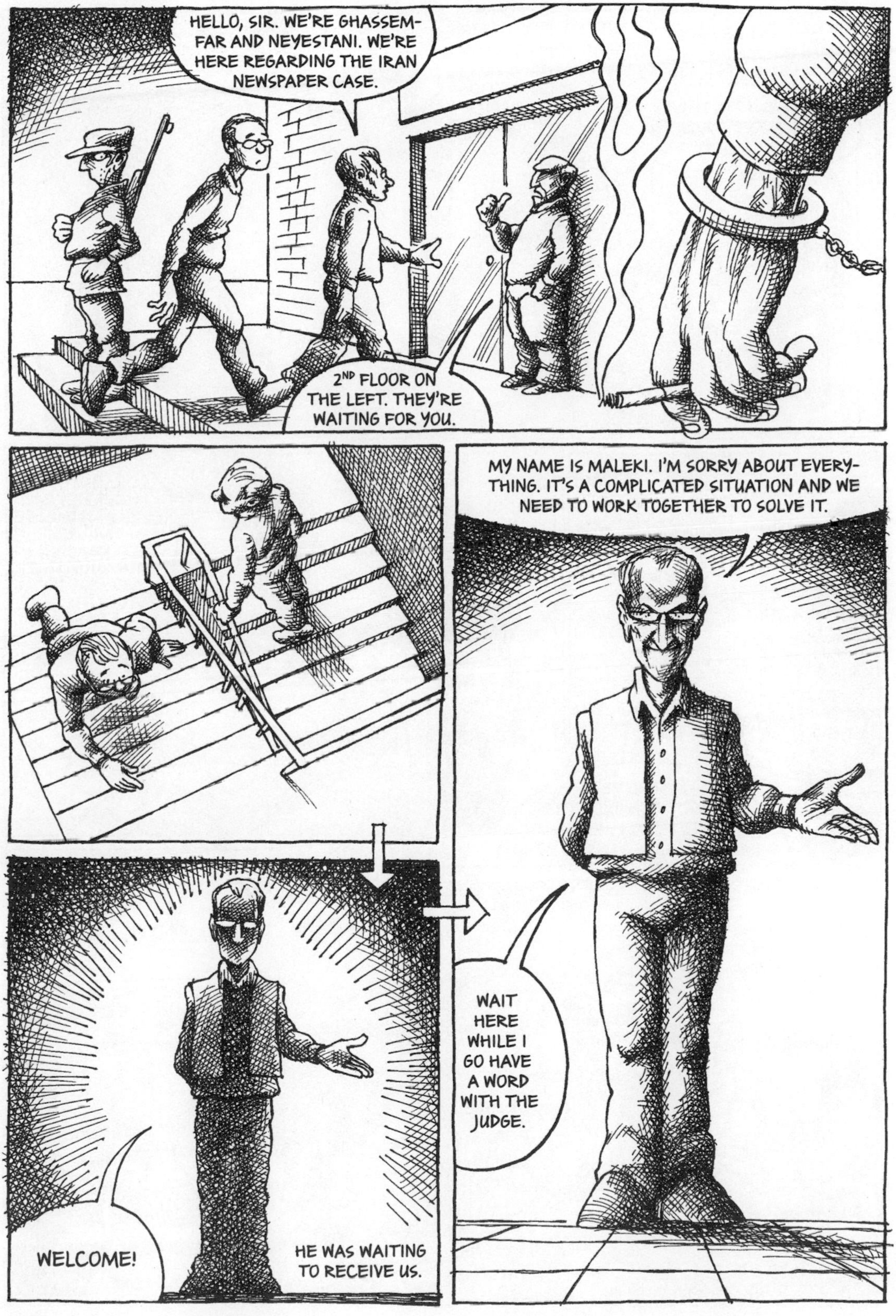
HELLO, SIR. WE'RE GHASSEMFAR AND NEYESTANI. WE'RE HERE REGARDING THE IRAN NEWSPAPER CASE.
2ND FLOOR ON THE LEFT. THEY'RE WAITING FOR YOU.
MY NAME IS MALEKI. I'M SORRY ABOUT EVERYTHING. IT'S A COMPLICATED SITUATION AND WE NEED TO WORK TOGETHER TO SOLVE IT.
WELCOME!
HE WAS WAITING TO RECEIVE US.
WAIT HERE WHILE I GO HAVE A WORD WITH THE JUDGE.

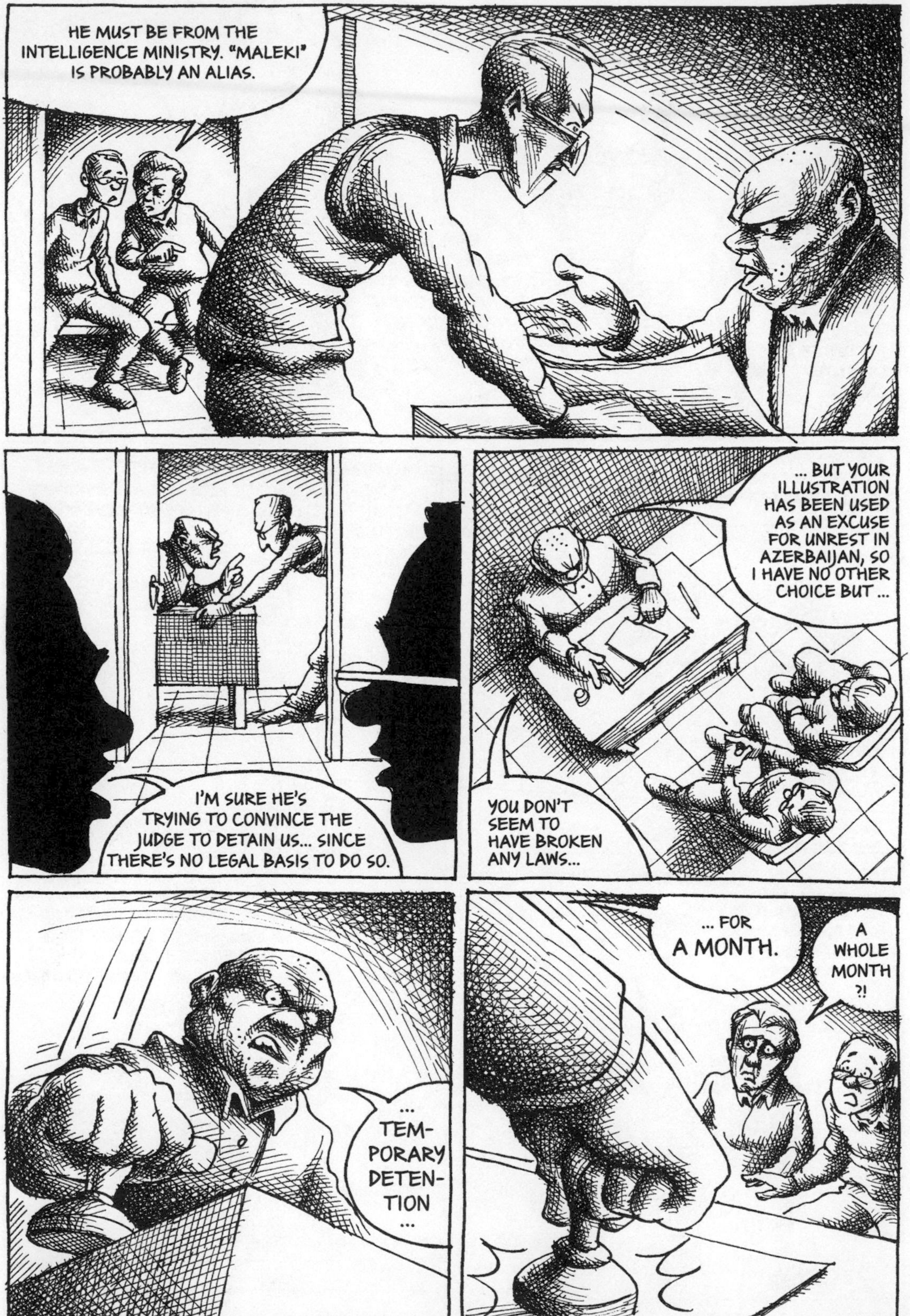
HE MUST BE FROM THE INTELLIGENCE MINISTRY. "MALEKI" IS PROBABLY AN ALIAS.
I'M SURE HE'S TRYING TO CONVINCE THE JUDGE TO DETAIN US... SINCE THERE'S NO LEGAL BASIS TO DO SO.
YOU DON'T SEEM TO HAVE BROKEN ANY LAWS...
... BUT YOUR ILLUSTRATION HAS BEEN USED AS AN EXCUSE FOR UNREST IN AZERBAIJAN, SO I HAVE NO OTHER CHOICE BUT ...
... TEMPORARY DETENTION ...
... FOR A MONTH.
A WHOLE MONTH ?!

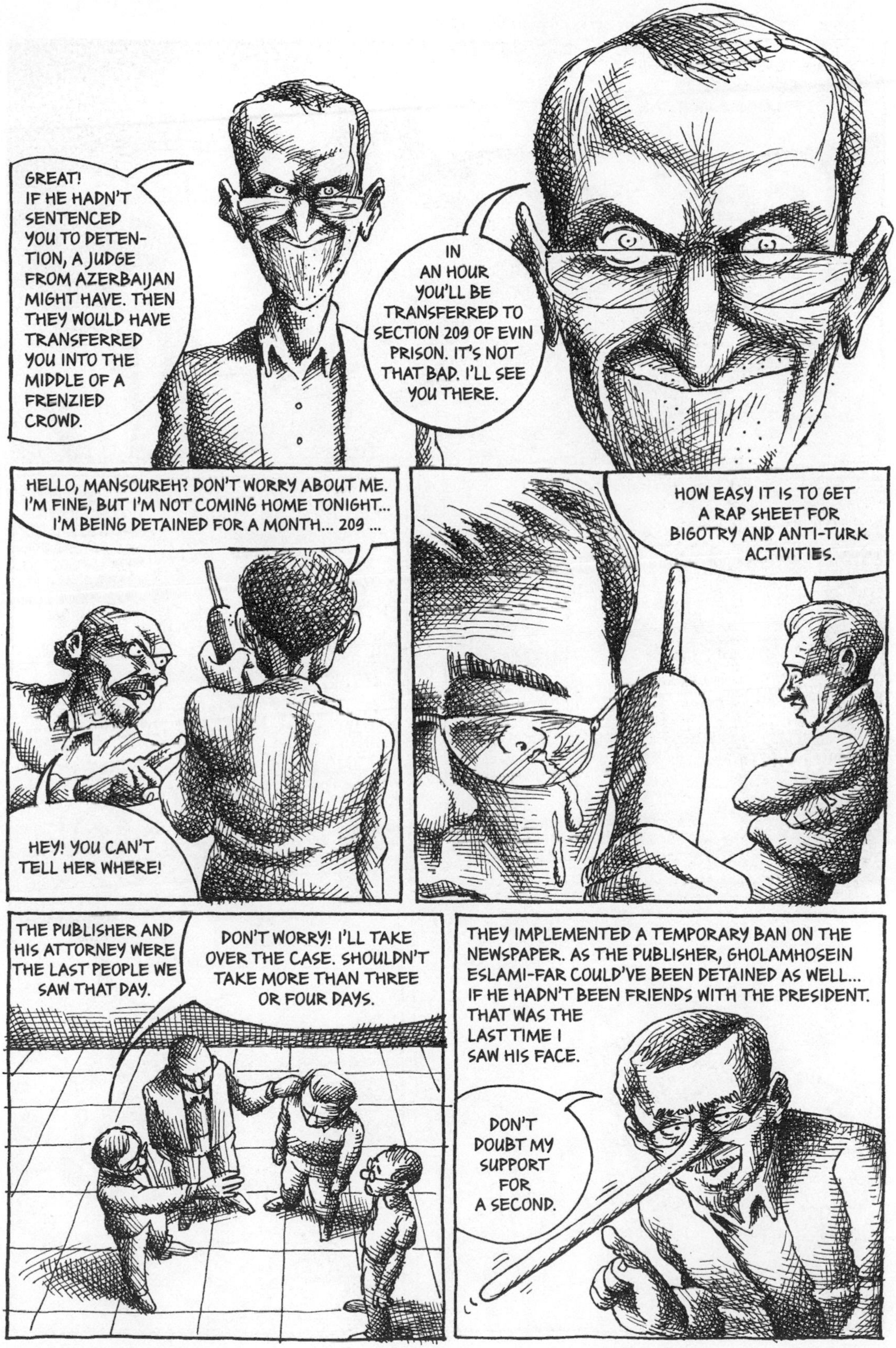
GREAT!
IF HE HADN'T SENTENCED YOU TO DETENTION, A JUDGE FROM AZERBAIJAN MIGHT HAVE. THEN THEY WOULD HAVE TRANSFERRED YOU INTO THE MIDDLE OF A FRENZIED CROWD.
IN AN HOUR YOU'LL BE TRANSFERRED TO SECTION 209 OF EVIN PRISON. IT'S NOT THAT BAD. I'LL SEE YOU THERE.
HELLO, MANSOUREH? DON'T WORRY ABOUT ME. I'M FINE, BUT I'M NOT COMING HOME TONIGHT... I'M BEING DETAINED FOR A MONTH... 209 ...
HEY! YOU CAN'T TELL HER WHERE!
HOW EASY IT IS TO GET A RAP SHEET FOR BIGOTRY AND ANTI-TURK ACTIVITIES.
THE PUBLISHER AND HIS ATTORNEY WERE THE LAST PEOPLE WE SAW THAT DAY.
DON'T WORRY! I'LL TAKE OVER THE CASE. SHOULDN'T TAKE MORE THAN THREE OR FOUR DAYS.
THEY IMPLEMENTED A TEMPORARY BAN ON THE NEWSPAPER. AS THE PUBLISHER, GHOLAMHOSEIN ESLAMI-FAR COULD'VE BEEN DETAINED AS WELL... IF HE HADN'T BEEN FRIENDS WITH THE PRESIDENT.
THAT WAS THE LAST TIME I SAW HIS FACE.
DON'T DOUBT MY SUPPORT FOR A SECOND.

AN HOUR LATER WE WERE ON THE WAY TO EVIN PRISON NORTH OF TEHRAN.
WE PASSED THE MAIN GATE ...
AND ARRIVED AT BUILDING 209, THE DETENTION CENTER OF THE MINISTRY OF INTELLIGENCE.
TAKE THIS BEFORE YOU ENTER.
PUT ON THIS BLINDFOLD. IT'S THE RULE.
!

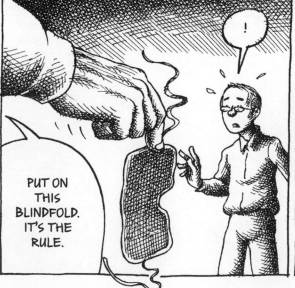

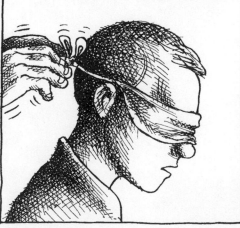

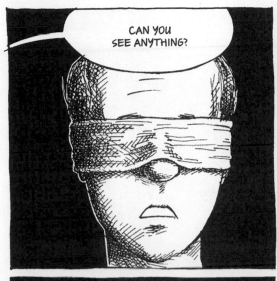

CAN YOU SEE ANYTHING?

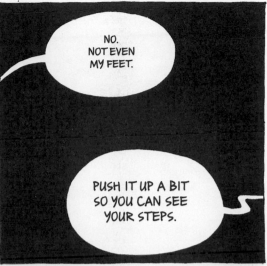

NO. NOT EVEN MY FEET.

PUSH IT UP A BIT SO YOU CAN SEE YOUR STEPS.

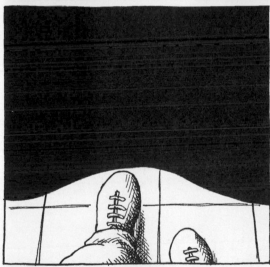

KEEP WALKING. NOW TURN RIGHT.

THEN FOR A MOMENT OUR BLINDFOLDS WERE REMOVED. WE WERE IN A SMALL ROOM. THEY STARTED SOME PAPERWORK, TOOK AWAY OUR CLOTHES, AND HANDED US THE BLUE UNIFORMS OF BUILDING 209.

WE WALKED DOWN A CORRIDOR.

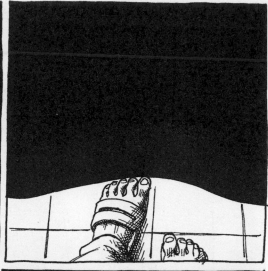

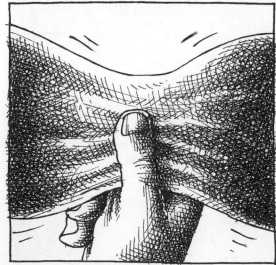

THEY SEPARATED MEHRDAD AND ME.

OKAY, YOU ARE HERE. ENTER. TAKE YOUR BLINDFOLD OFF.

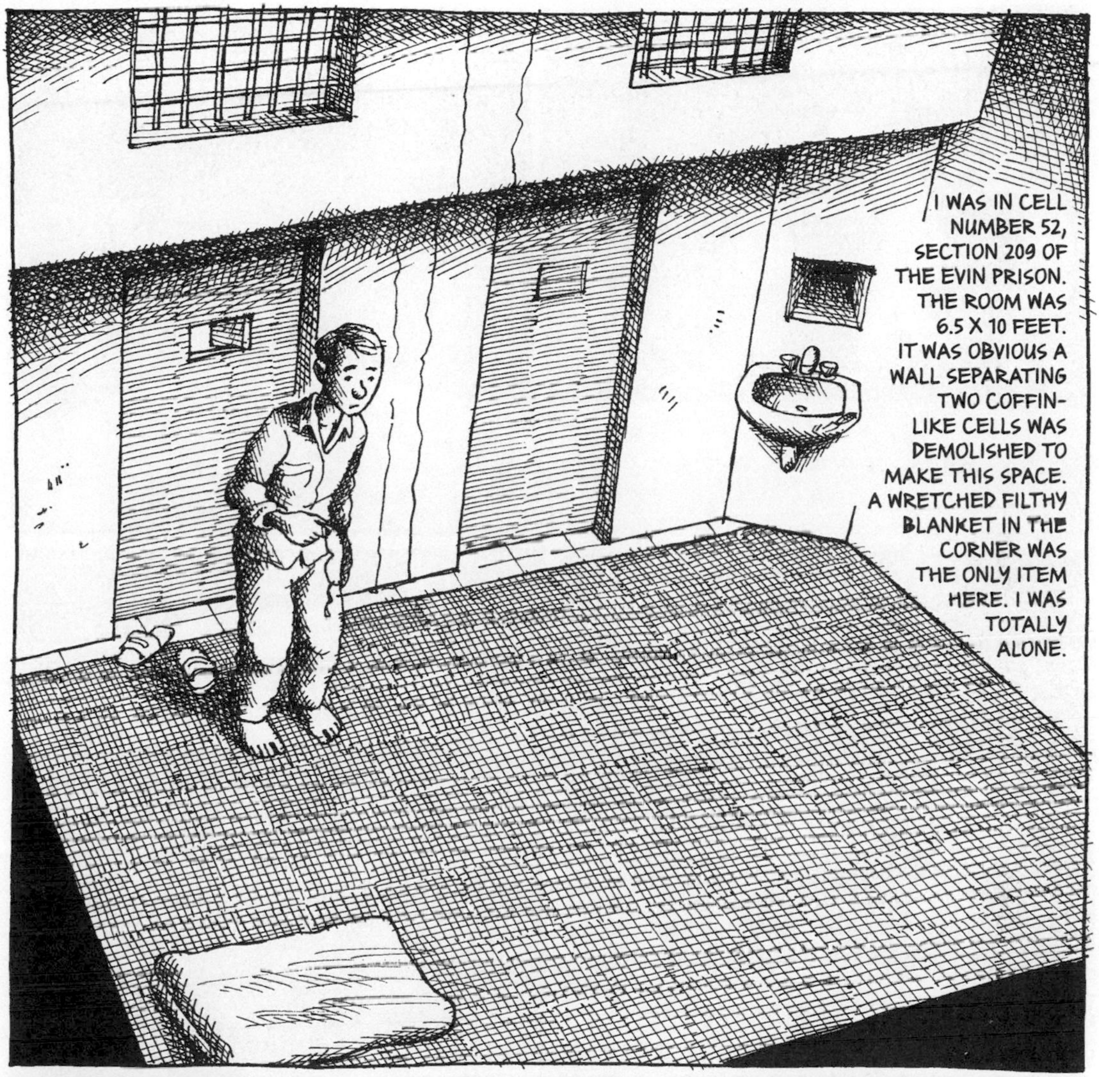
I WAS IN CELL NUMBER 52, SECTION 209 OF THE EVIN PRISON. THE ROOM WAS 6.5 X 10 FEET. IT WAS OBVIOUS A WALL SEPARATING TWO COFFIN-LIKE CELLS WAS DEMOLISHED TO MAKE THIS SPACE. A WRETCHED FILTHY BLANKET IN THE CORNER WAS THE ONLY ITEM HERE. I WAS TOTALLY ALONE.

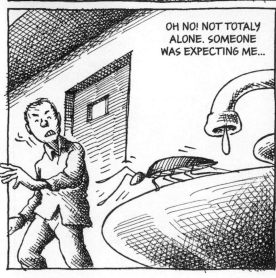

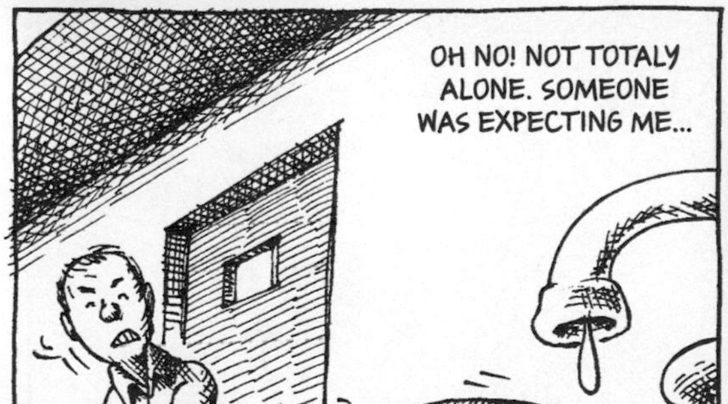
OH NO! NOT TOTALY ALONE. SOMEONE WAS EXPECTING ME...

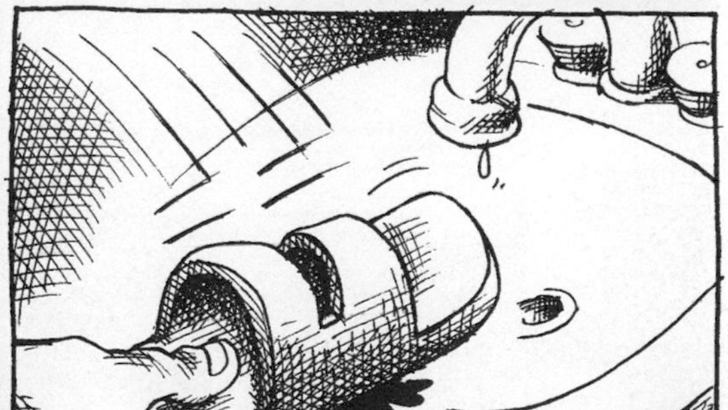
SPLAT

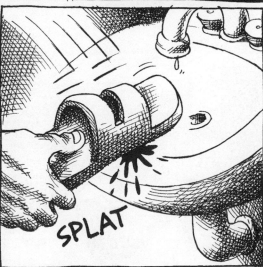

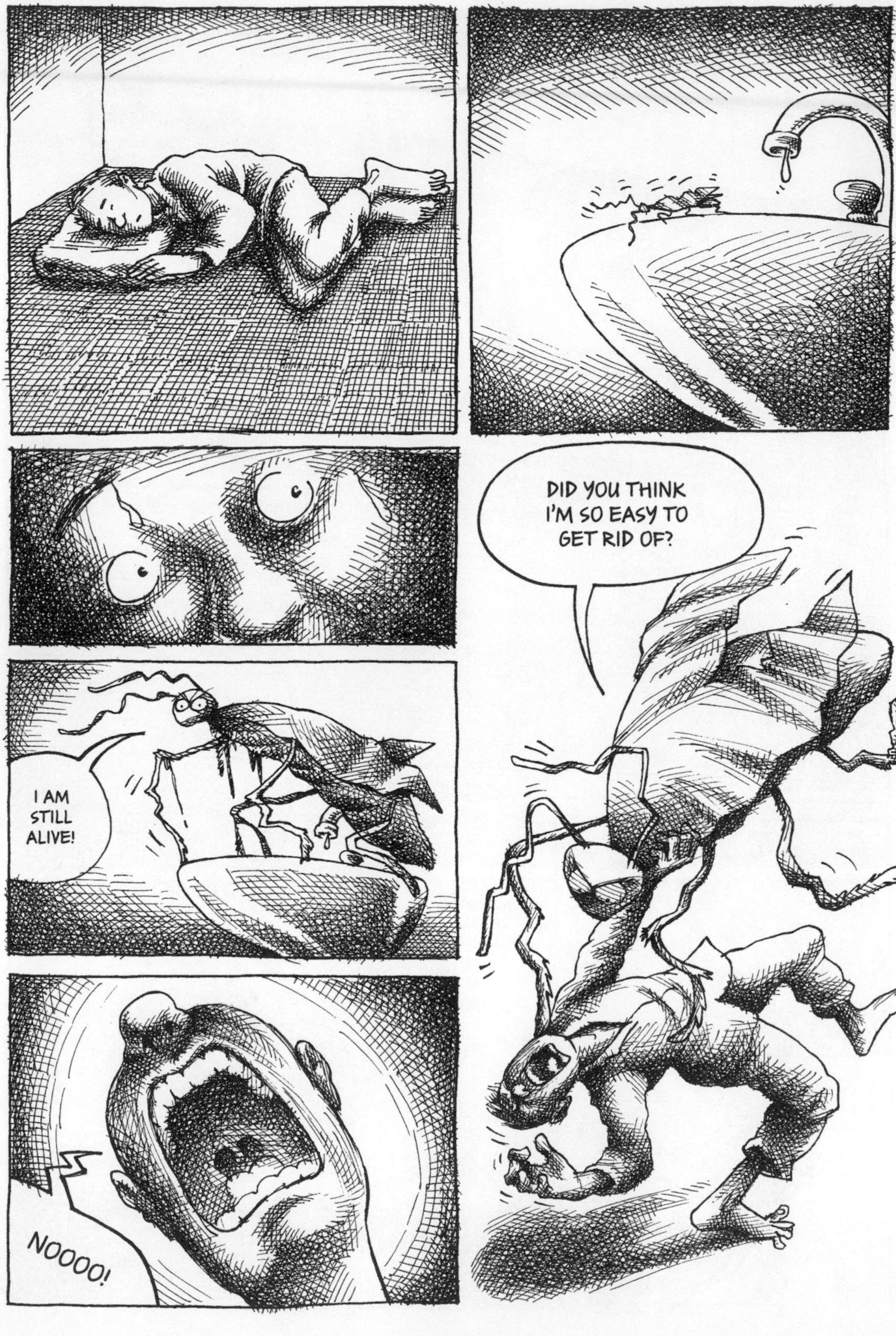
I AM STILL ALIVE!
NOOOO!
DID YOU THINK I'M SO EASY TO GET RID OF?

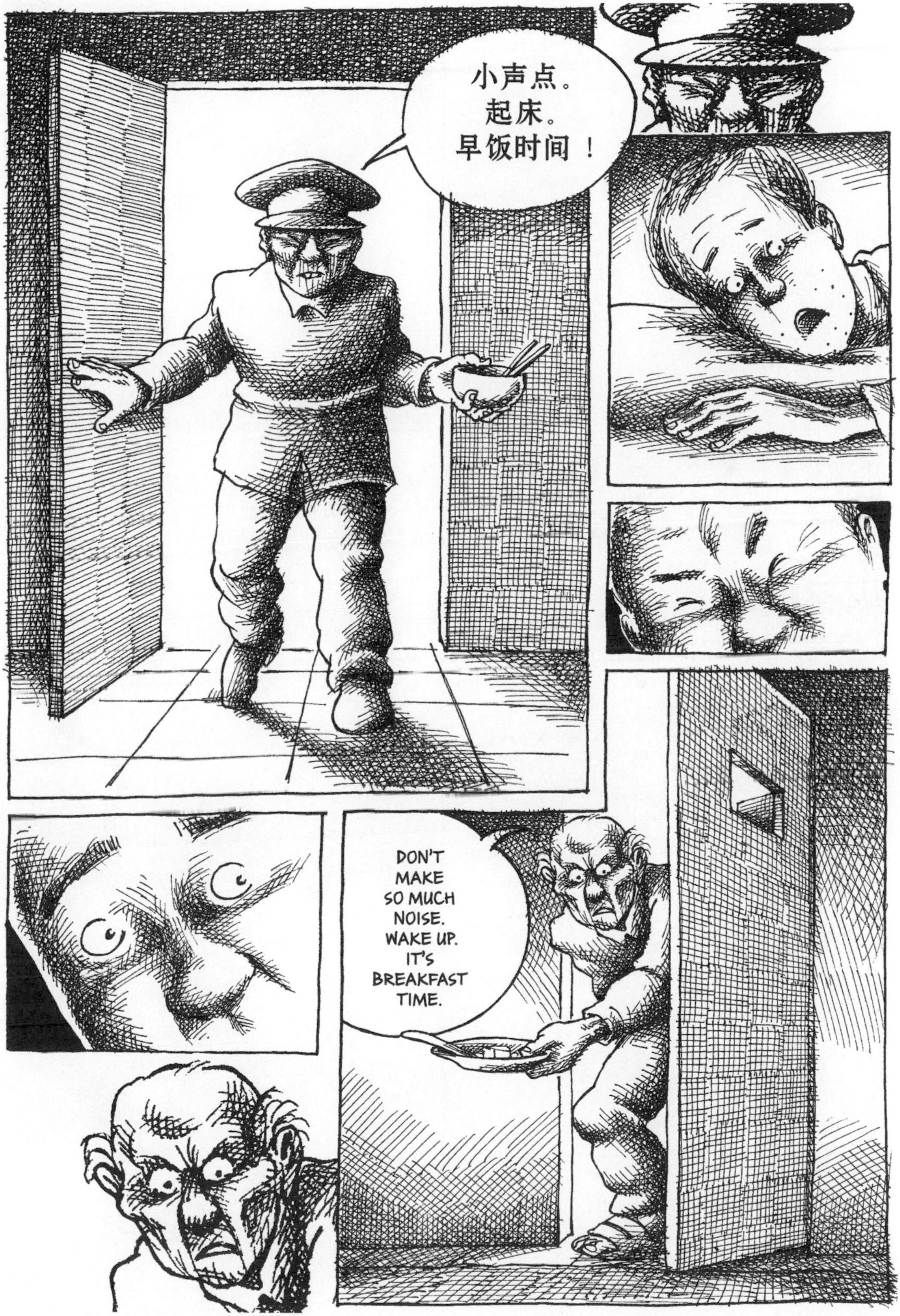
小声点。
起床。
早饭时间！
DON'T MAKE SO MUCH NOISE. WAKE UP. IT'S BREAKFAST TIME.

CHAPTER THREE

CONFESSIONS

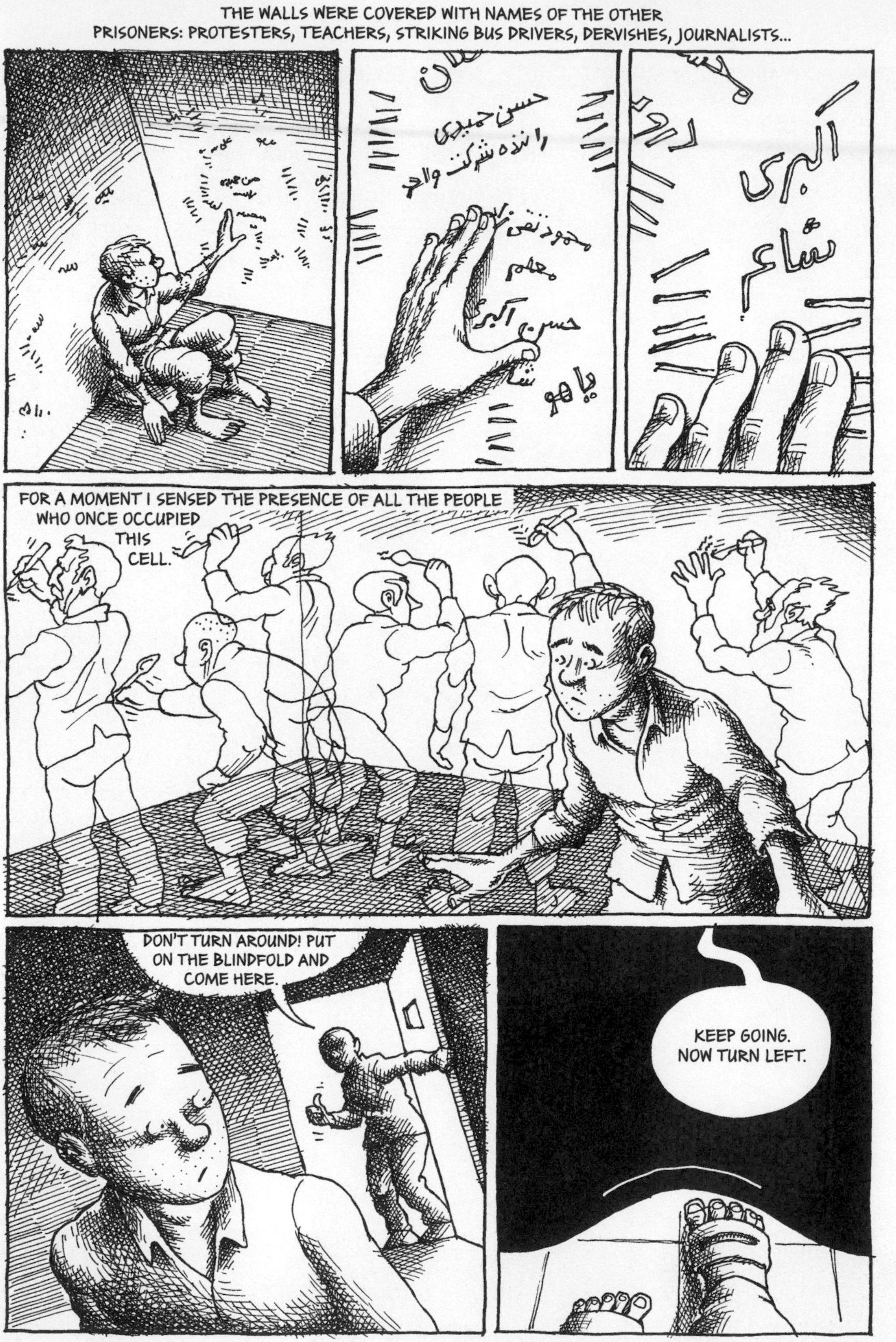
THE WALLS WERE COVERED WITH NAMES OF THE OTHER PRISONERS: PROTESTERS, TEACHERS, STRIKING BUS DRIVERS, DERVISHES, JOURNALISTS...
حسن حمیدی
راننده شرکت واحد
معلم
یاهو
FOR A MOMENT I SENSED THE PRESENCE OF ALL THE PEOPLE WHO ONCE OCCUPIED THIS CELL.
DON'T TURN AROUND! PUT ON THE BLINDFOLD AND COME HERE.
KEEP GOING. NOW TURN LEFT.

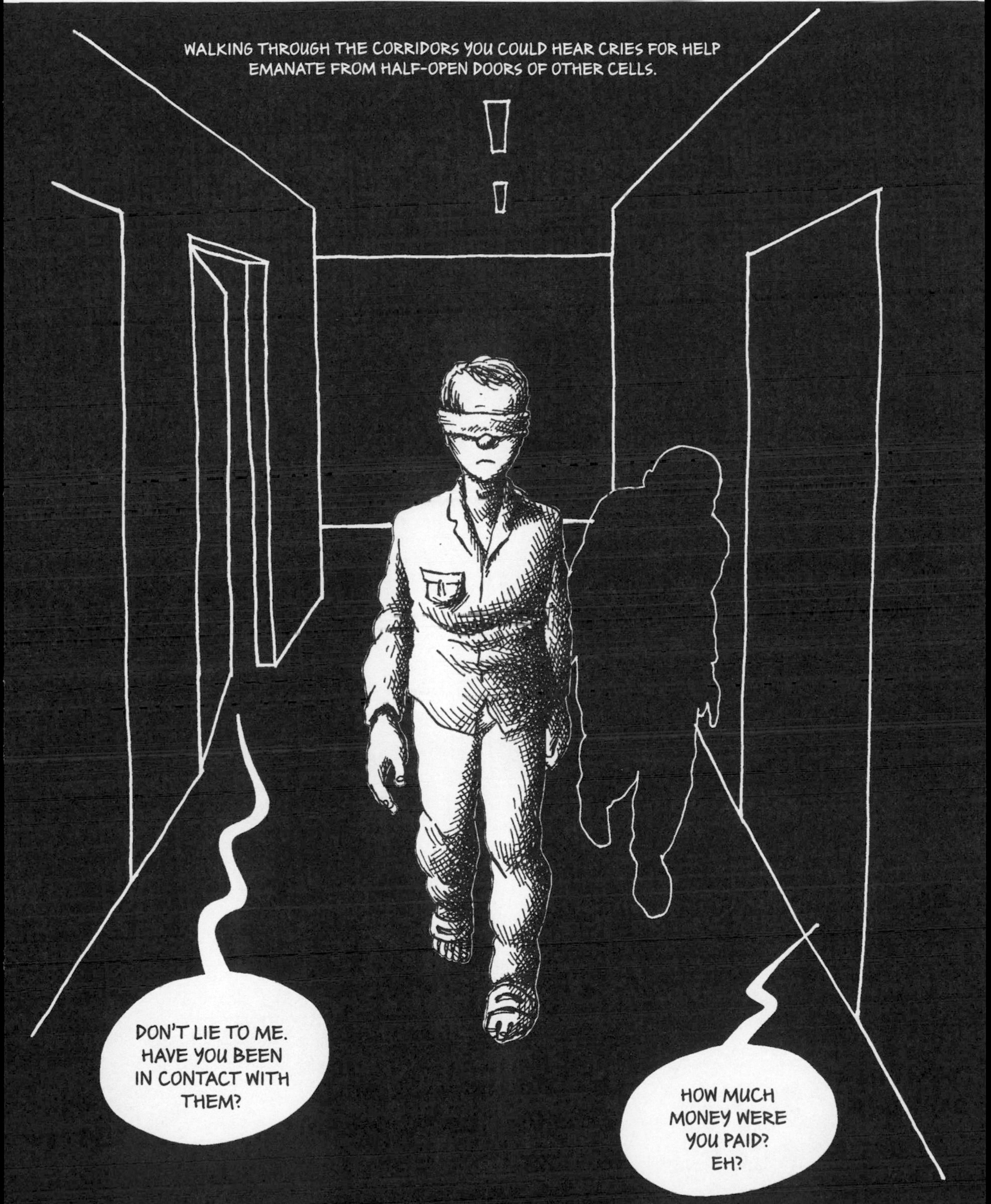
WALKING THROUGH THE CORRIDORS YOU COULD HEAR CRIES FOR HELP EMANATE FROM HALF-OPEN DOORS OF OTHER CELLS.
DON'T LIE TO ME. HAVE YOU BEEN IN CONTACT WITH THEM?
HOW MUCH MONEY WERE YOU PAID? EH?

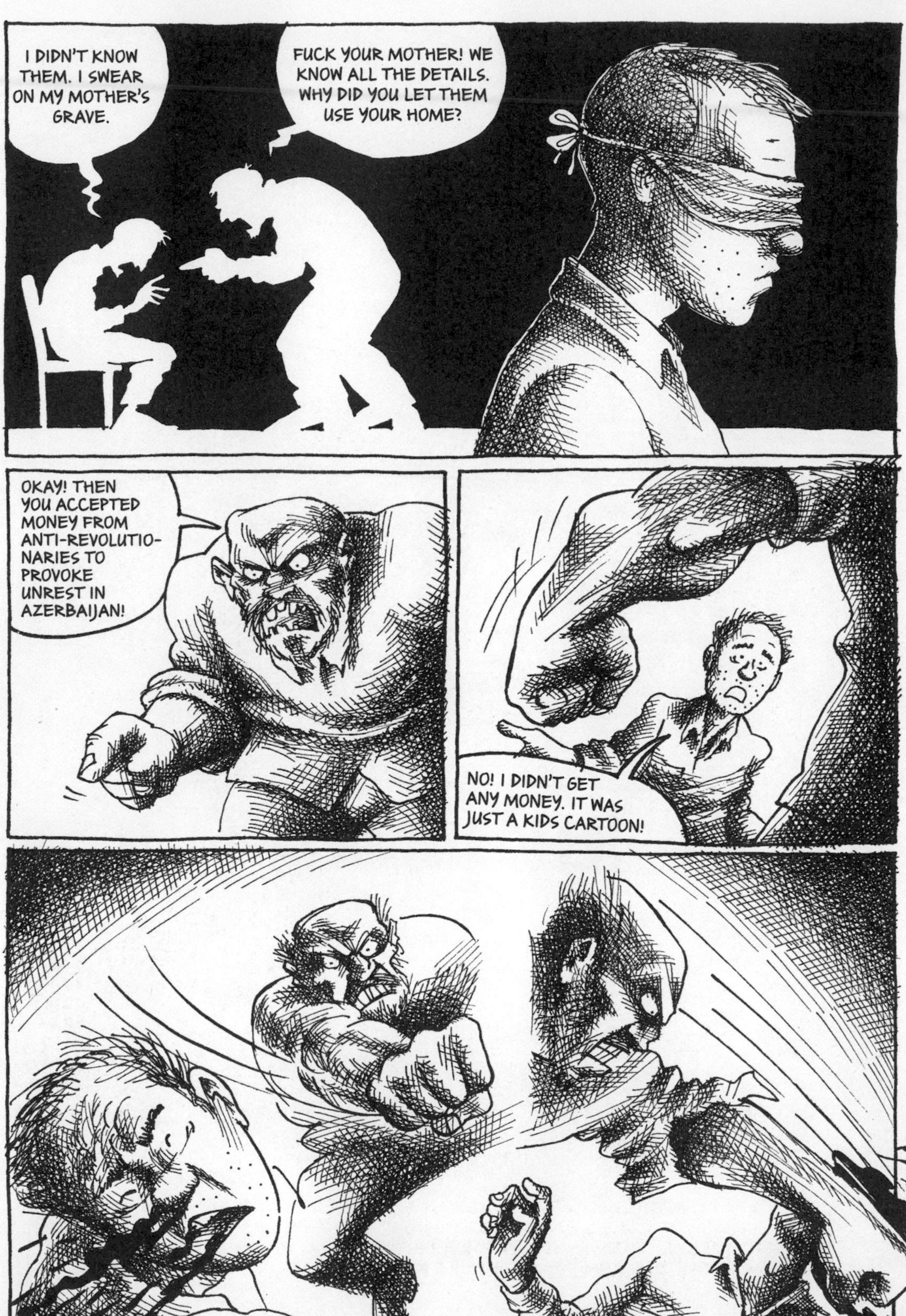
I DIDN'T KNOW THEM. I SWEAR ON MY MOTHER'S GRAVE.
FUCK YOUR MOTHER! WE KNOW ALL THE DETAILS. WHY DID YOU LET THEM USE YOUR HOME?
OKAY! THEN YOU ACCEPTED MONEY FROM ANTI-REVOLUTIONARIES TO PROVOKE UNREST IN AZERBAIJAN!
NO! I DIDN'T GET ANY MONEY. IT WAS JUST A KIDS CARTOON!

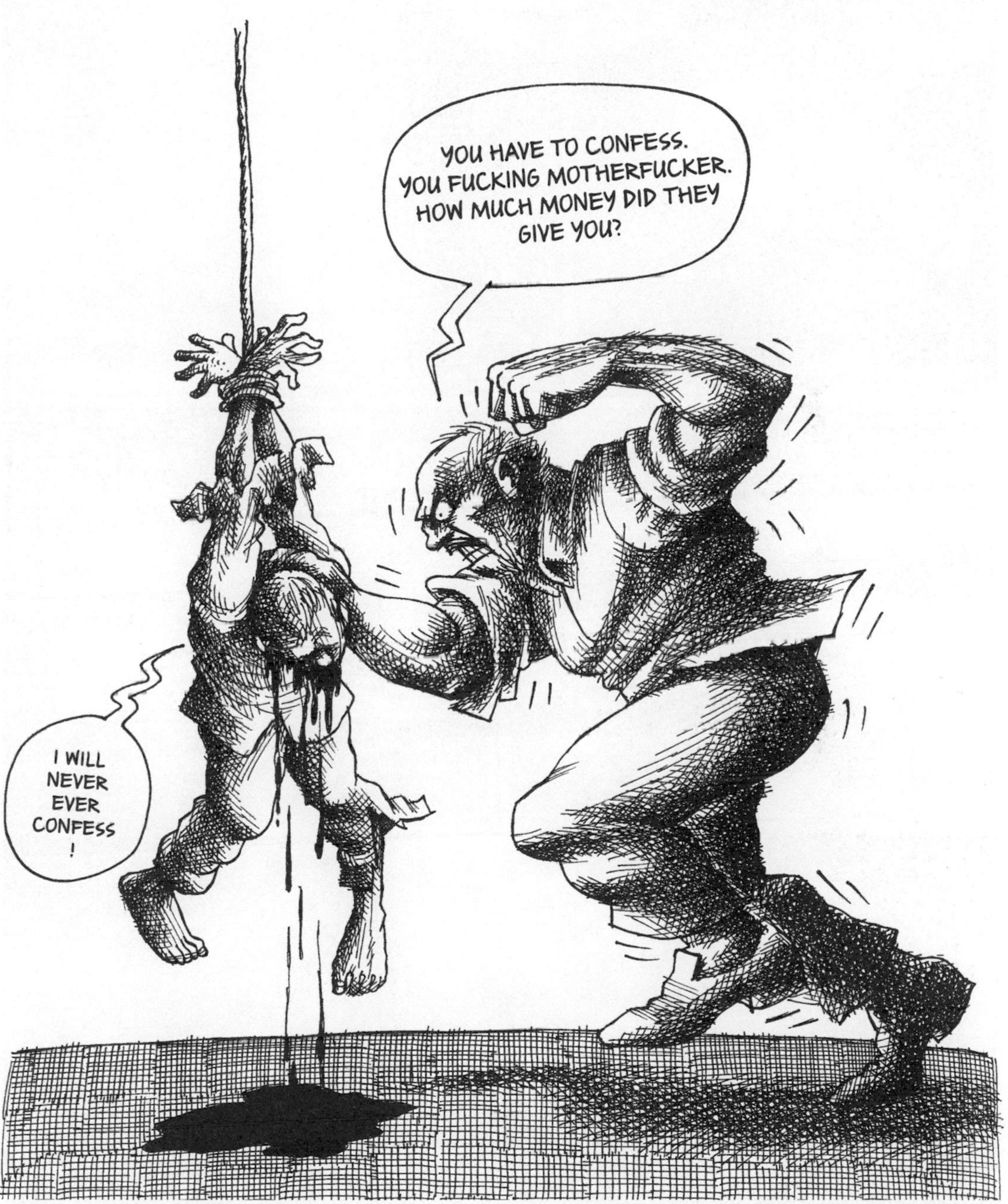
YOU HAVE TO CONFESS. YOU FUCKING MOTHERFUCKER. HOW MUCH MONEY DID THEY GIVE YOU?
I WILL NEVER EVER CONFESS !

IF THE SCENE FROM THE LAST TWO PAGES WERE REAL, THE STORY WOULD HAVE BEEN MORE INTERESTING (AND, OF COURSE, MORE SUCCESSFUL). BUT I'D RATHER TELL YOU EXACTLY WHAT HAPPENED. AFTER ALL, IT WAS MY FATE, HOWEVER BORING. I HAVE TO ADMIT THAT THE LAST TWO PAGES WERE WHAT I WAS AFRAID OF WHILE WAITING IN THE INTERROGATION ROOM.

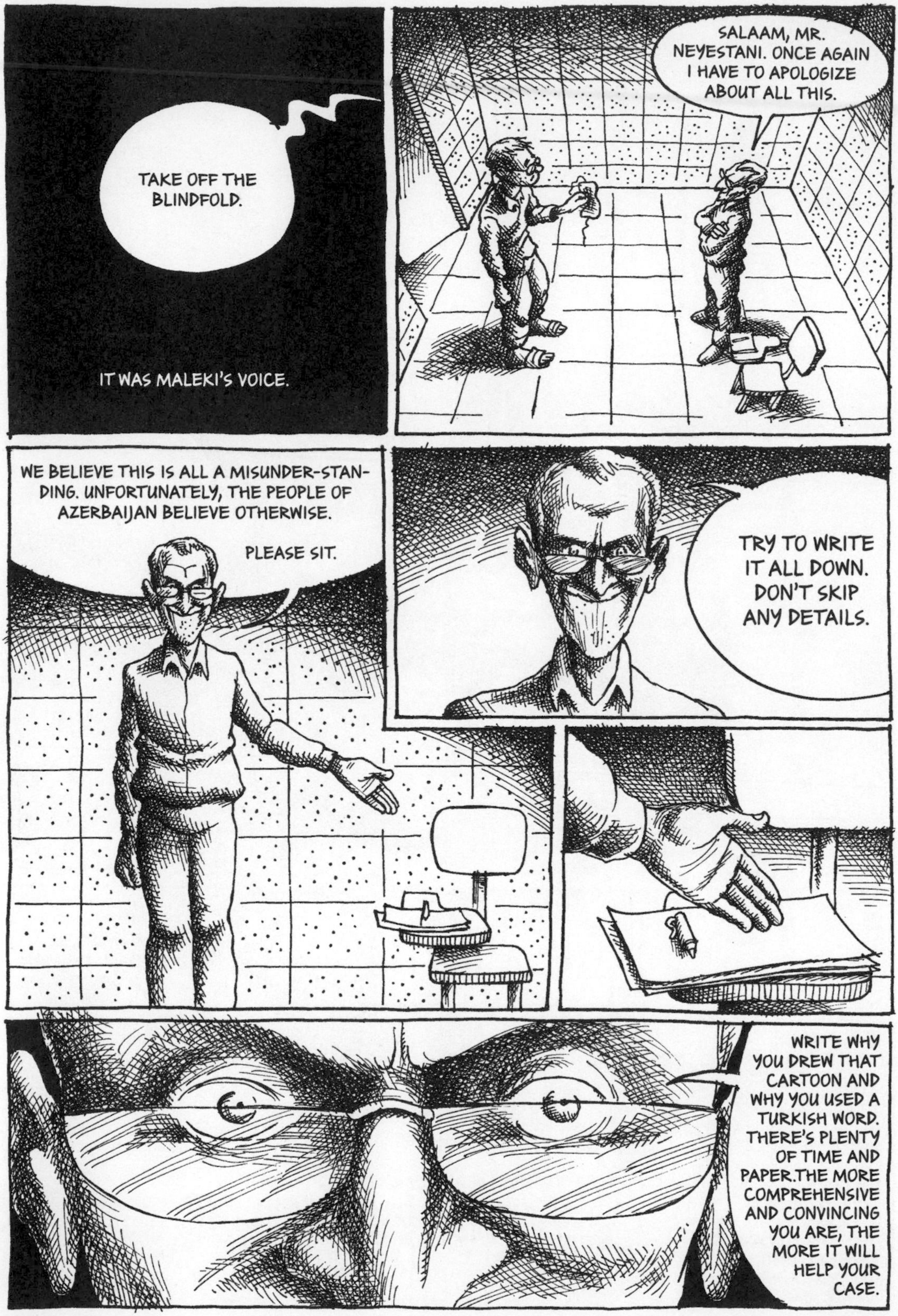
TAKE OFF THE BLINDFOLD.
IT WAS MALEKI'S VOICE.
SALAAM, MR. NEYESTANI. ONCE AGAIN I HAVE TO APOLOGIZE ABOUT ALL THIS.
WE BELIEVE THIS IS ALL A MISUNDER-STANDING. UNFORTUNATELY, THE PEOPLE OF AZERBAIJAN BELIEVE OTHERWISE.
PLEASE SIT.
TRY TO WRITE IT ALL DOWN. DON'T SKIP ANY DETAILS.
WRITE WHY YOU DREW THAT CARTOON AND WHY YOU USED A TURKISH WORD. THERE'S PLENTY OF TIME AND PAPER.THE MORE COMPREHENSIVE AND CONVINCING YOU ARE, THE MORE IT WILL HELP YOUR CASE.

... SINCE SUMMER WAS APPROACHING AND THE WEATHER WAS GETTING WARMER OUR HOUSE FILLED WITH COCKROACHES. I DECIDED TO USE THE BUG AS THE THEME FOR THAT ISSUE OF THE KID'S MAGAZINE.

"NAMANA" IS USED OFTEN IN FARSI. I DIDN'T HAVE ITS TURKISH ROOTS IN MIND.

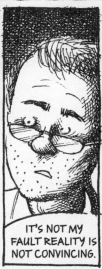

MR. NEYESTANI, WE'RE NOT AGAINST YOU; THE PEOPLE OF AZERBAIJAN ARE.

YOUR STORY IS NOT VERY CONVINCING, MR. NEYESTANI.

IT'S NOT MY FAULT REALITY IS NOT CONVINCING.

THEY BELIEVE THIS WAS DESIGNED TO HUMILIATE THEM AND THEIR CULTURE. THEY WON'T ACCEPT ANYTHING LESS.

THIS IS A UNIQUE OPPORTUNITY TO VERIFY YOUR INFORMATION AND COMPLETE OUR RECORDS.

WE'LL CONTINUE TOMORROW. TRY TO FIND BETTER REASONS. TAKE THE PEN AND PAPER WITH YOU. YOU... AND KEEP YOUR GLASSES.

WHAT SHOULD I WRITE?

WRITE ABOUT IRANIAN CARTOONISTS YOU KNOW; EVERYTHING ABOUT THEM.

45

KEEP WALKING...
TURN RIGHT. WE'R HERE.

REMOVE THE BLIND-
FOLD. DON'T TURN AROUND.
DON'T LOOK AT MY FACE!

HI !

THOUGHT I'D PAY YOU A VISIT,
IF YOU'RE ALONE.

GET OUT OF MY SIGHT!
YOU AND THAT CLUMSY
COCKROACH CAUSED ALL
THIS NONSENSE!

MY FAULT? I TOLD YOU TO
LEAVE ME ALONE, BUT YOU
DIDN'T LISTEN.

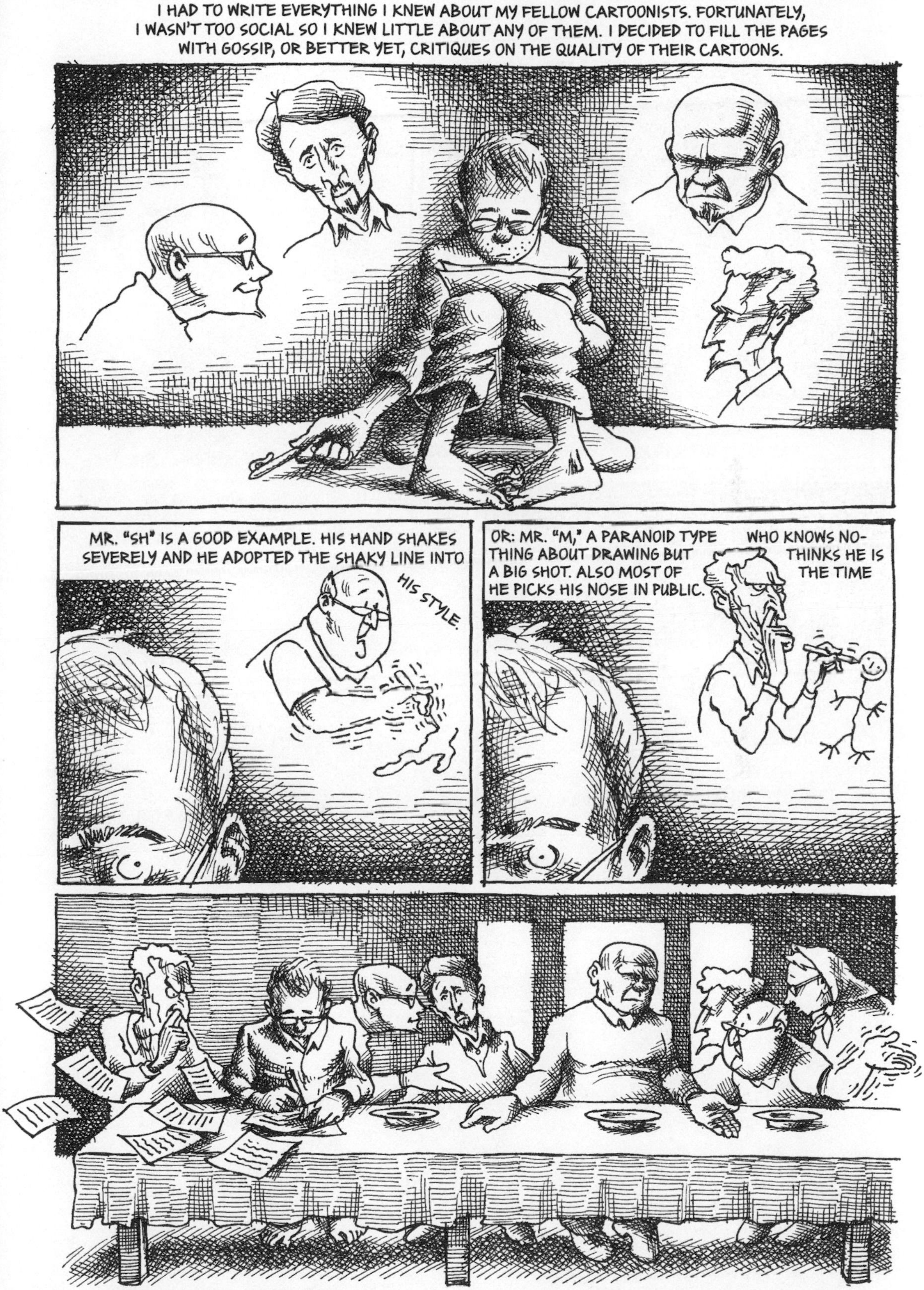
I HAD TO WRITE EVERYTHING I KNEW ABOUT MY FELLOW CARTOONISTS. FORTUNATELY, I WASN'T TOO SOCIAL SO I KNEW LITTLE ABOUT ANY OF THEM. I DECIDED TO FILL THE PAGES WITH GOSSIP, OR BETTER YET, CRITIQUES ON THE QUALITY OF THEIR CARTOONS.
MR. "SH" IS A GOOD EXAMPLE. HIS HAND SHAKES SEVERELY AND HE ADOPTED THE SHAKY LINE INTO
HIS STYLE.
OR: MR. "M," A PARANOID TYPE WHO KNOWS NOTHING ABOUT DRAWING BUT THINKS HE IS A BIG SHOT. ALSO MOST OF THE TIME HE PICKS HIS NOSE IN PUBLIC.
I DIDN'T FEEL LIKE A TRAITOR BECAUSE I WROTE NOTHING OF ANY IMPORTANCE ABOUT MY PEERS.

CHAPTER FOUR

THE WHEELS OF CHANGE

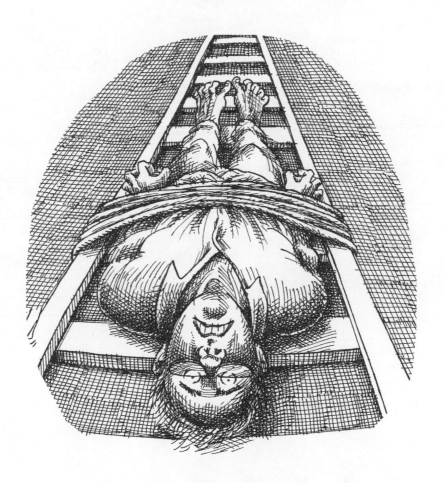

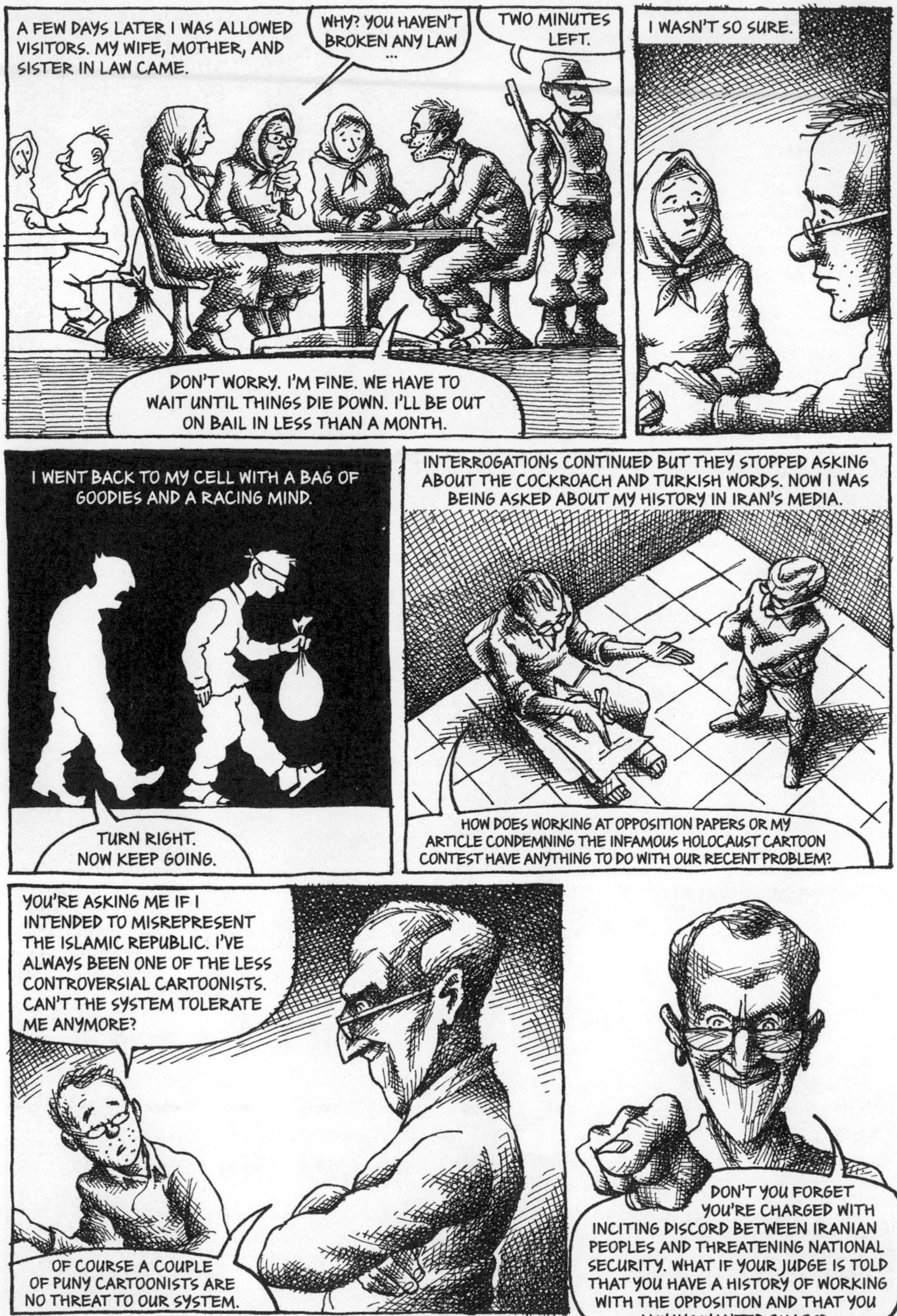
A FEW DAYS LATER I WAS ALLOWED VISITORS. MY WIFE, MOTHER, AND SISTER IN LAW CAME.
WHY? YOU HAVEN'T BROKEN ANY LAW ...
TWO MINUTES LEFT.
DON'T WORRY. I'M FINE. WE HAVE TO WAIT UNTIL THINGS DIE DOWN. I'LL BE OUT ON BAIL IN LESS THAN A MONTH.
I WASN'T SO SURE.
I WENT BACK TO MY CELL WITH A BAG OF GOODIES AND A RACING MIND.
TURN RIGHT. NOW KEEP GOING.
INTERROGATIONS CONTINUED BUT THEY STOPPED ASKING ABOUT THE COCKROACH AND TURKISH WORDS. NOW I WAS BEING ASKED ABOUT MY HISTORY IN IRAN'S MEDIA.
HOW DOES WORKING AT OPPOSITION PAPERS OR MY ARTICLE CONDEMNING THE INFAMOUS HOLOCAUST CARTOON CONTEST HAVE ANYTHING TO DO WITH OUR RECENT PROBLEM?
YOU'RE ASKING ME IF I INTENDED TO MISREPRESENT THE ISLAMIC REPUBLIC. I'VE ALWAYS BEEN ONE OF THE LESS CONTROVERSIAL CARTOONISTS. CAN'T THE SYSTEM TOLERATE ME ANYMORE?
OF COURSE A COUPLE OF PUNY CARTOONISTS ARE NO THREAT TO OUR SYSTEM.
DON'T YOU FORGET YOU'RE CHARGED WITH INCITING DISCORD BETWEEN IRANIAN PEOPLES AND THREATENING NATIONAL SECURITY. WHAT IF YOUR JUDGE IS TOLD THAT YOU HAVE A HISTORY OF WORKING WITH THE OPPOSITION AND THAT YOU ALWAYS WANTED CHAOS?

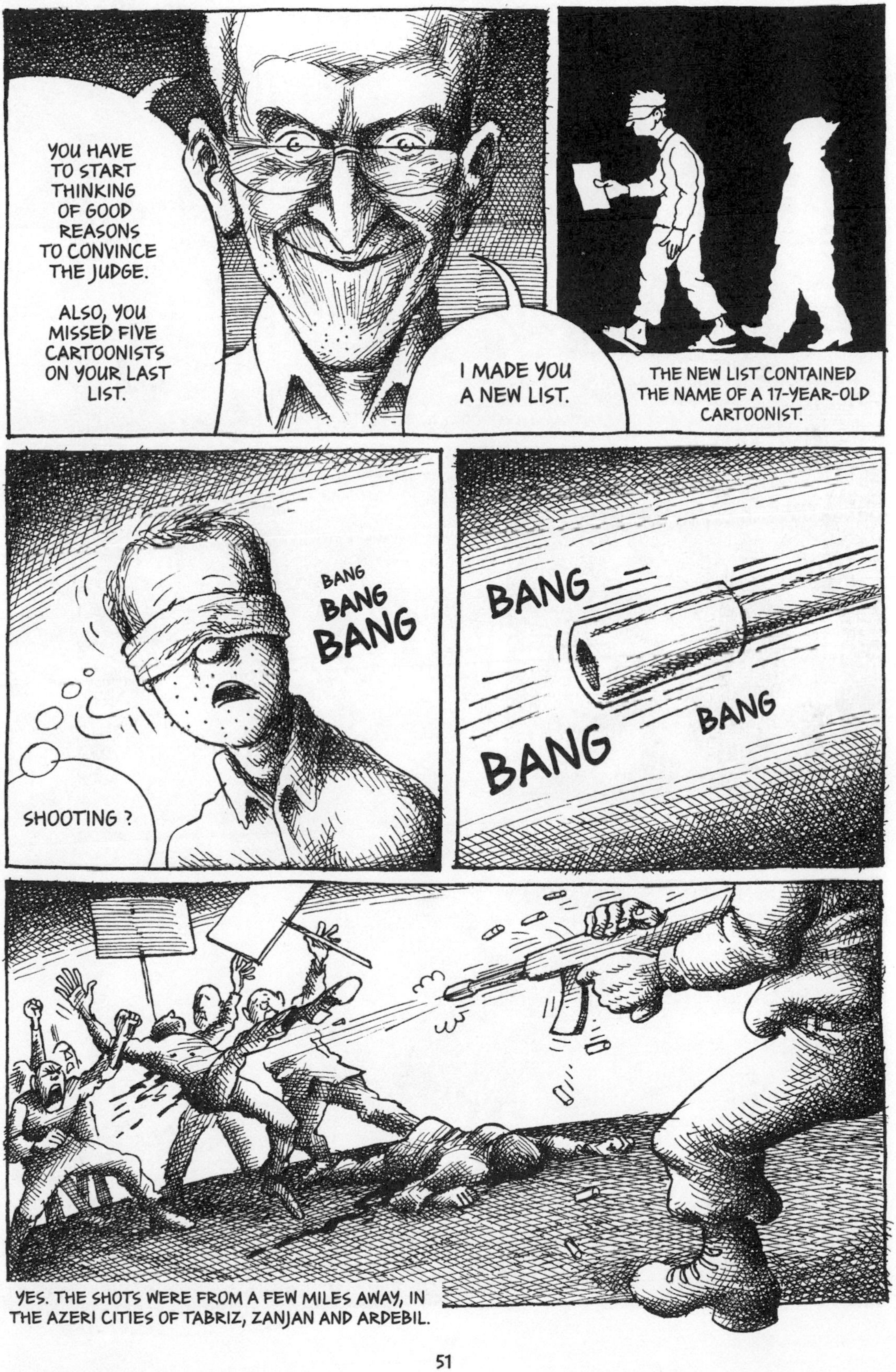

YOU HAVE TO START THINKING OF GOOD REASONS TO CONVINCE THE JUDGE.
ALSO, YOU MISSED FIVE CARTOONISTS ON YOUR LAST LIST.
I MADE YOU A NEW LIST.
THE NEW LIST CONTAINED THE NAME OF A 17-YEAR-OLD CARTOONIST.
BANG
BANG
BANG
SHOOTING ?
BANG
BANG
BANG
YES. THE SHOTS WERE FROM A FEW MILES AWAY, IN THE AZERI CITIES OF TABRIZ, ZANJAN AND ARDEBIL.

THE GOVERNMENT FORCES OPENED FIRE ON ANGRY PROTESTERS. THERE WAS BLOODSHED...

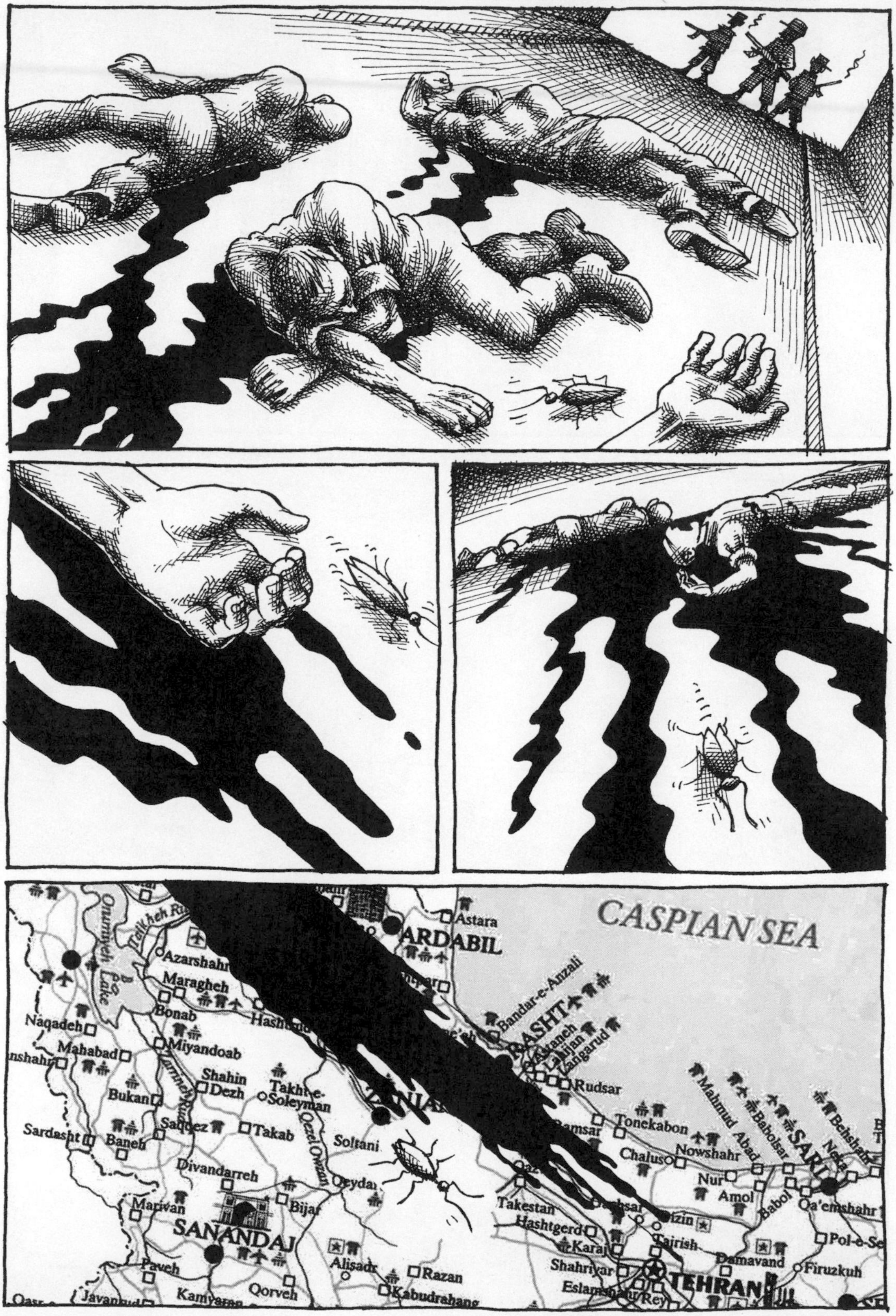
CASPIAN SEA
Astara
ARDABIL
Azarshahr
Maragheh
Bonab
Naqadeh
Mahabad
Miyandoab
Shahin Dezh
Takht-e-Soleyman
Bukan
Saqqez
Takab
Sardasht
Baneh
Soltani
Divandarreh
Marivan
SANANDAJ
Bijar
Paveh
Alisadr
Razan
Kabudrahang
Qorveh
Bandar-e-Anzali
Rudsar
Tonekabon
Chalus
Nowshahr
Mahmud Abad
Babolsar
Nur
Amol
Babol
Qa'emshahr
Neka
Takestan
Hashtgerd
Karaj
Tajrish
Shahriyar
TEHRAN
Damavand
Firuzkuh

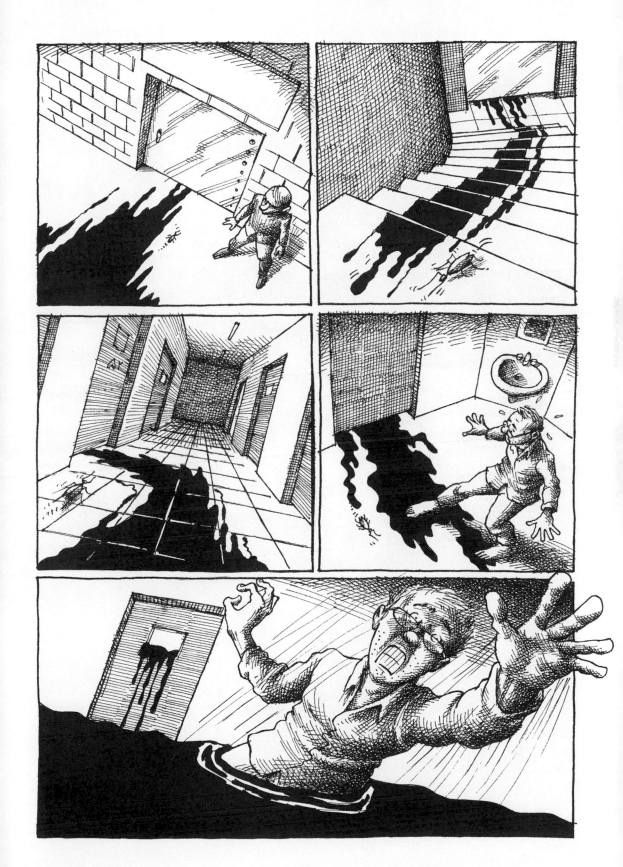

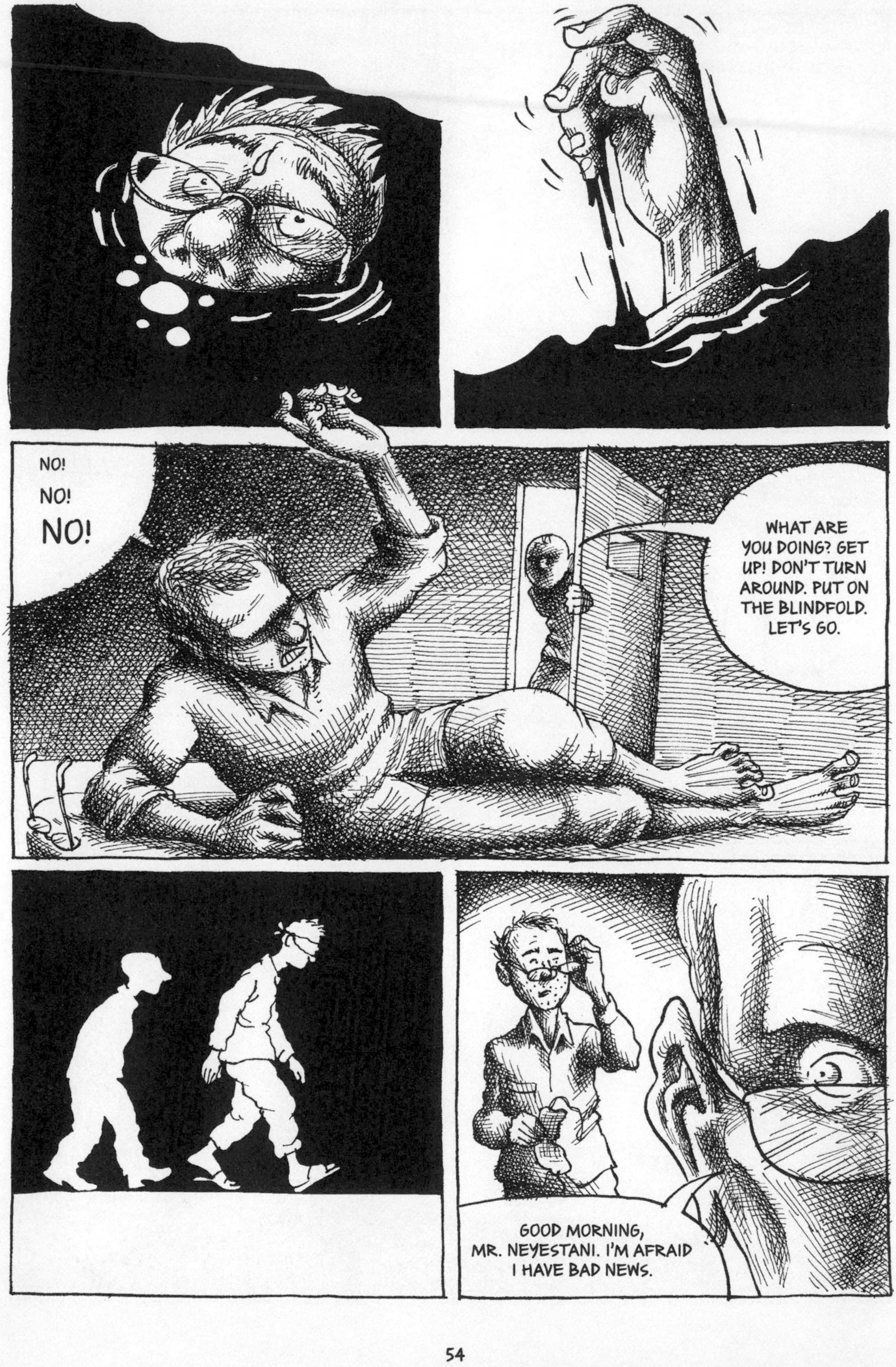

NO!
NO!
NO!
WHAT ARE YOU DOING? GET UP! DON'T TURN AROUND. PUT ON THE BLINDFOLD. LET'S GO.
GOOD MORNING, MR. NEYESTANI. I'M AFRAID I HAVE BAD NEWS.

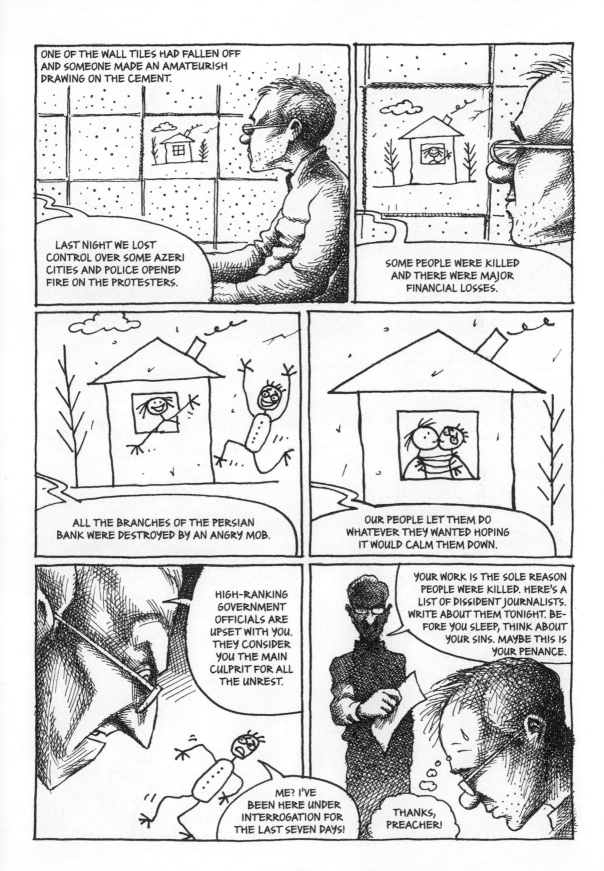

ONE OF THE WALL TILES HAD FALLEN OFF AND SOMEONE MADE AN AMATEURISH DRAWING ON THE CEMENT.

LAST NIGHT WE LOST CONTROL OVER SOME AZERI CITIES AND POLICE OPENED FIRE ON THE PROTESTERS.

SOME PEOPLE WERE KILLED AND THERE WERE MAJOR FINANCIAL LOSSES.

ALL THE BRANCHES OF THE PERSIAN BANK WERE DESTROYED BY AN ANGRY MOB.

OUR PEOPLE LET THEM DO WHATEVER THEY WANTED HOPING IT WOULD CALM THEM DOWN.

HIGH-RANKING GOVERNMENT OFFICIALS ARE UPSET WITH YOU. THEY CONSIDER YOU THE MAIN CULPRIT FOR ALL THE UNREST.

ME? I'VE BEEN HERE UNDER INTERROGATION FOR THE LAST SEVEN DAYS!

YOUR WORK IS THE SOLE REASON PEOPLE WERE KILLED. HERE'S A LIST OF DISSIDENT JOURNALISTS. WRITE ABOUT THEM TONIGHT. BEFORE YOU SLEEP, THINK ABOUT YOUR SINS. MAYBE THIS IS YOUR PENANCE.

THANKS, PREACHER!

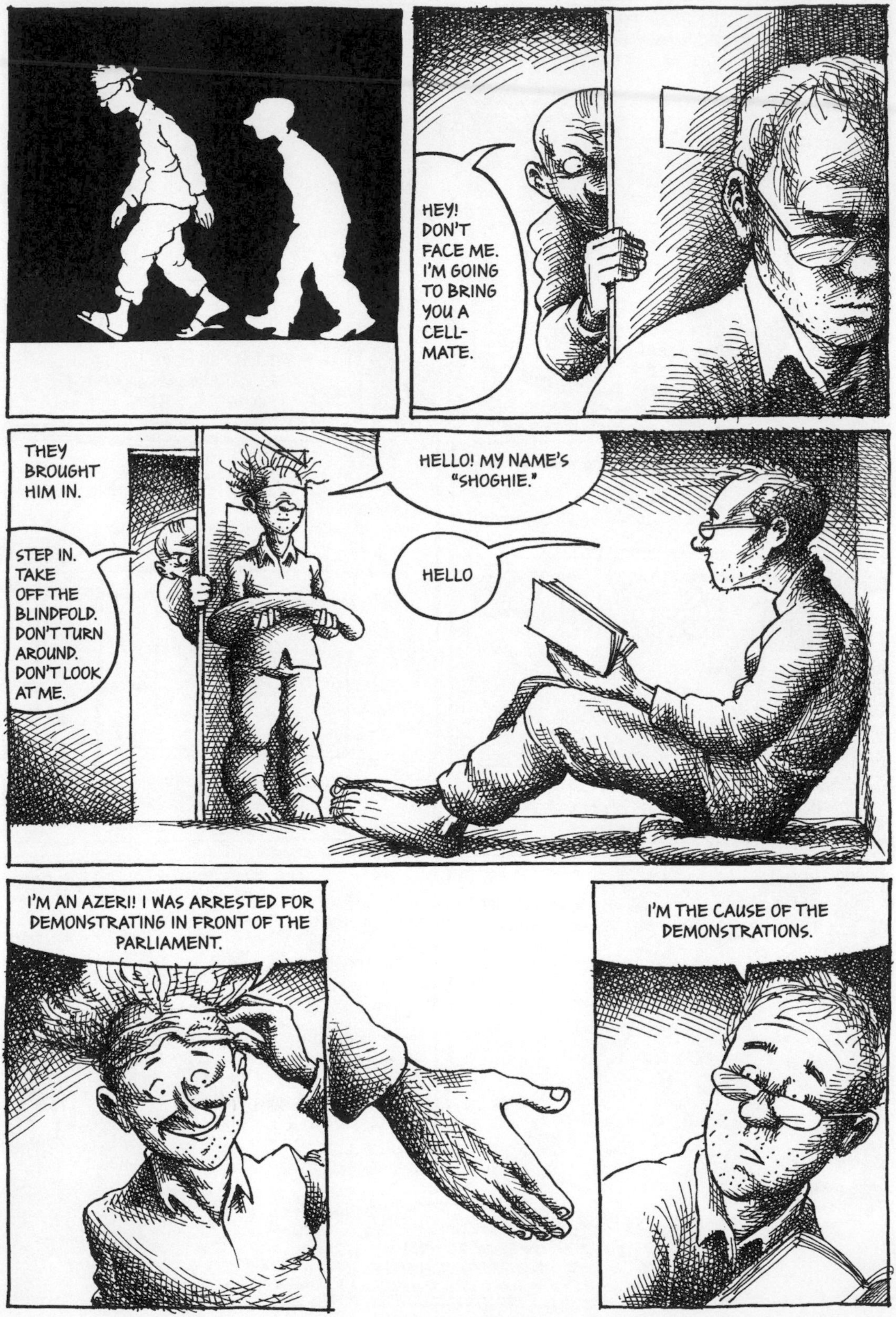
HEY! DON'T FACE ME. I'M GOING TO BRING YOU A CELL-MATE.
THEY BROUGHT HIM IN.
STEP IN. TAKE OFF THE BLINDFOLD. DON'T TURN AROUND. DON'T LOOK AT ME.
HELLO! MY NAME'S "SHOGHIE."
HELLO
I'M AN AZERI! I WAS ARRESTED FOR DEMONSTRATING IN FRONT OF THE PARLIAMENT.
I'M THE CAUSE OF THE DEMONSTRATIONS.

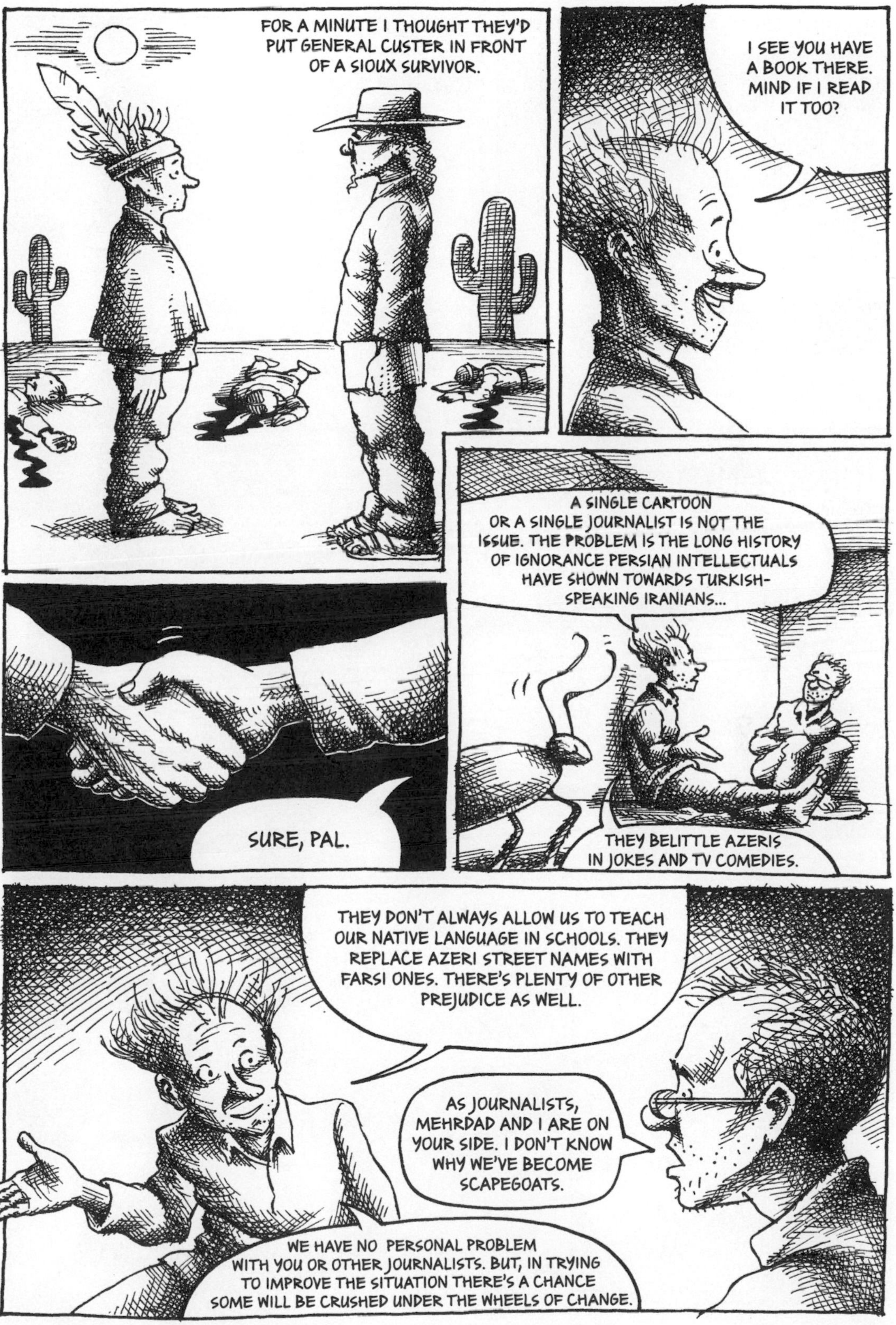
FOR A MINUTE I THOUGHT THEY'D PUT GENERAL CUSTER IN FRONT OF A SIOUX SURVIVOR.
I SEE YOU HAVE A BOOK THERE. MIND IF I READ IT TOO?
SURE, PAL.
A SINGLE CARTOON OR A SINGLE JOURNALIST IS NOT THE ISSUE. THE PROBLEM IS THE LONG HISTORY OF IGNORANCE PERSIAN INTELLECTUALS HAVE SHOWN TOWARDS TURKISH-SPEAKING IRANIANS...
THEY BELITTLE AZERIS IN JOKES AND TV COMEDIES.
THEY DON'T ALWAYS ALLOW US TO TEACH OUR NATIVE LANGUAGE IN SCHOOLS. THEY REPLACE AZERI STREET NAMES WITH FARSI ONES. THERE'S PLENTY OF OTHER PREJUDICE AS WELL.
AS JOURNALISTS, MEHRDAD AND I ARE ON YOUR SIDE. I DON'T KNOW WHY WE'VE BECOME SCAPEGOATS.
WE HAVE NO PERSONAL PROBLEM WITH YOU OR OTHER JOURNALISTS. BUT, IN TRYING TO IMPROVE THE SITUATION THERE'S A CHANCE SOME WILL BE CRUSHED UNDER THE WHEELS OF CHANGE.

I COULDN'T DEAL WITH THAT!

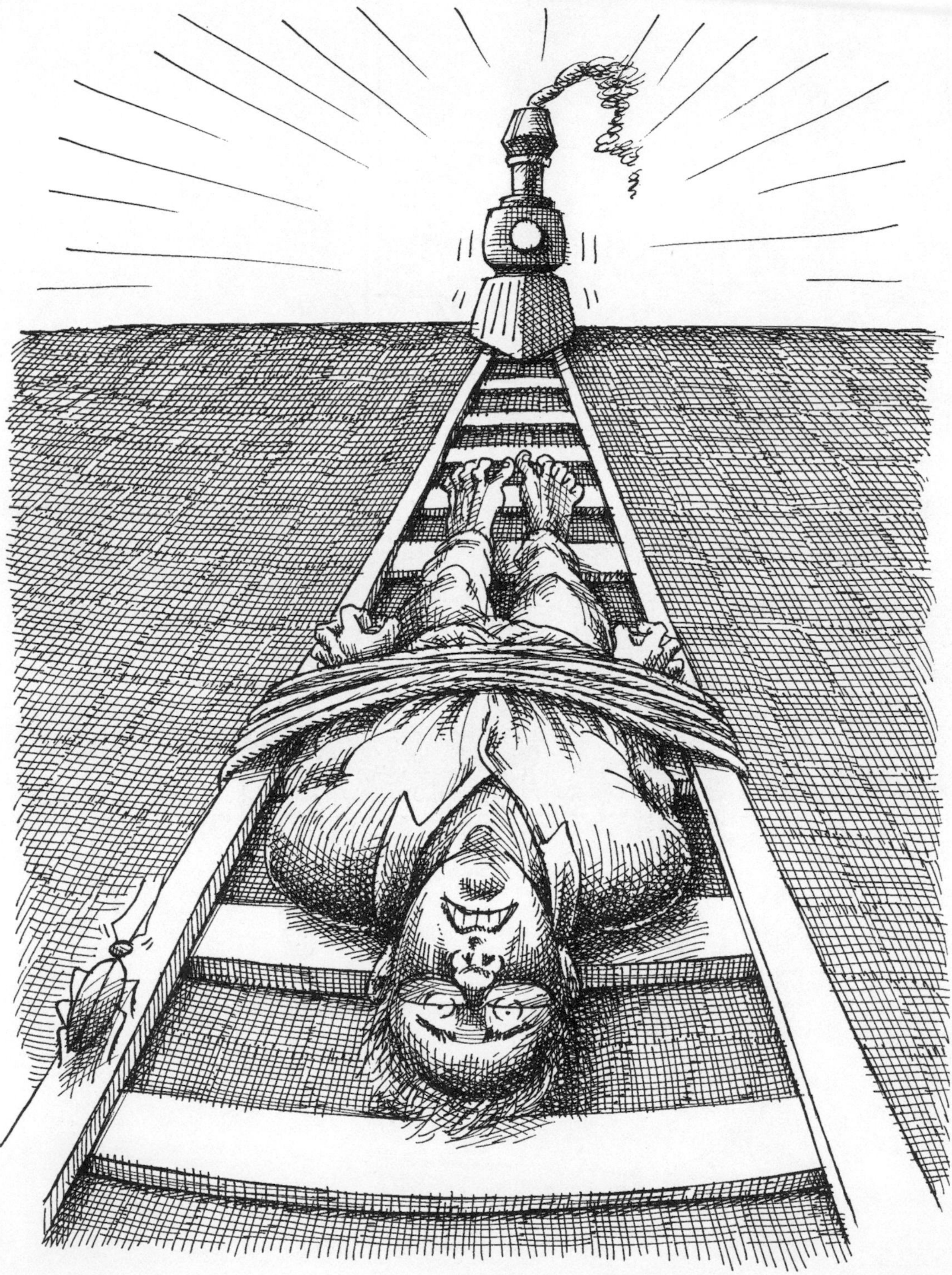

CHAPTER FIVE

MR. PROSECUTOR

AFTER ELEVEN DAYS IN DETENTION.

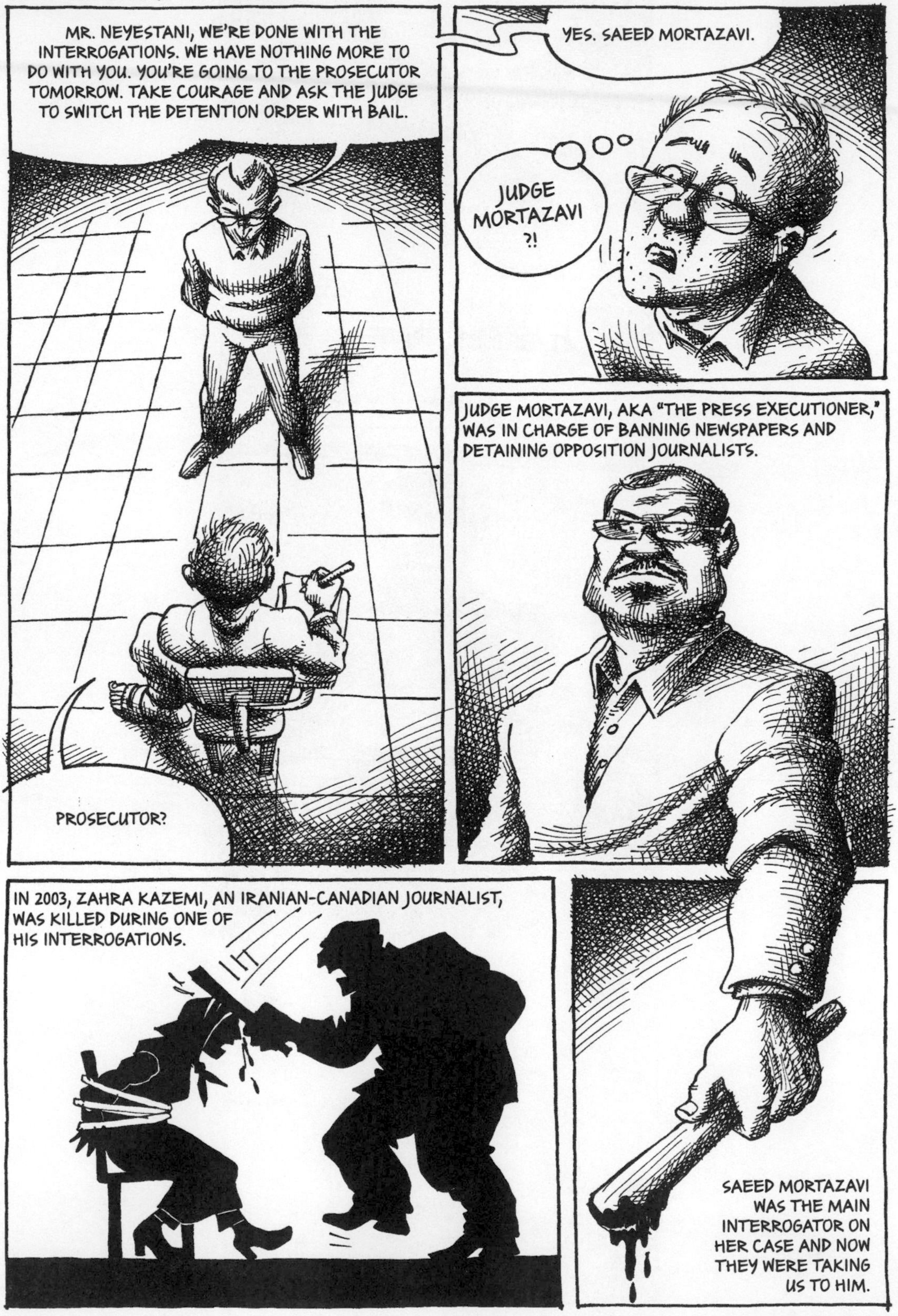
MR. NEYESTANI, WE'RE DONE WITH THE INTERROGATIONS. WE HAVE NOTHING MORE TO DO WITH YOU. YOU'RE GOING TO THE PROSECUTOR TOMORROW. TAKE COURAGE AND ASK THE JUDGE TO SWITCH THE DETENTION ORDER WITH BAIL.
PROSECUTOR?
YES. SAEED MORTAZAVI.
JUDGE MORTAZAVI ?!
JUDGE MORTAZAVI, AKA "THE PRESS EXECUTIONER," WAS IN CHARGE OF BANNING NEWSPAPERS AND DETAINING OPPOSITION JOURNALISTS.
IN 2003, ZAHRA KAZEMI, AN IRANIAN-CANADIAN JOURNALIST, WAS KILLED DURING ONE OF HIS INTERROGATIONS.
SAEED MORTAZAVI WAS THE MAIN INTERROGATOR ON HER CASE AND NOW THEY WERE TAKING US TO HIM.

TWO DAYS LATER, THEY TOOK ME OUT OF MY CELL.

IS THAT YOU, MEHRDAD?
NO TALKING
YES
ALAAM MANA!
SALAAM, MEHRDAD !
HELLO CAT WITH AN EYE-PATCH!

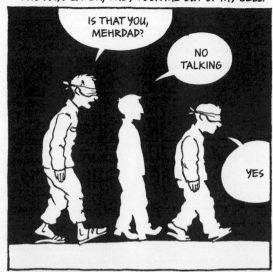

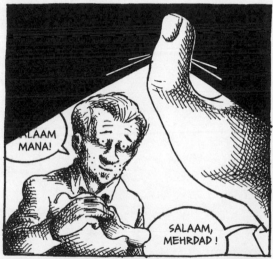

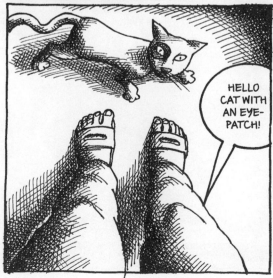

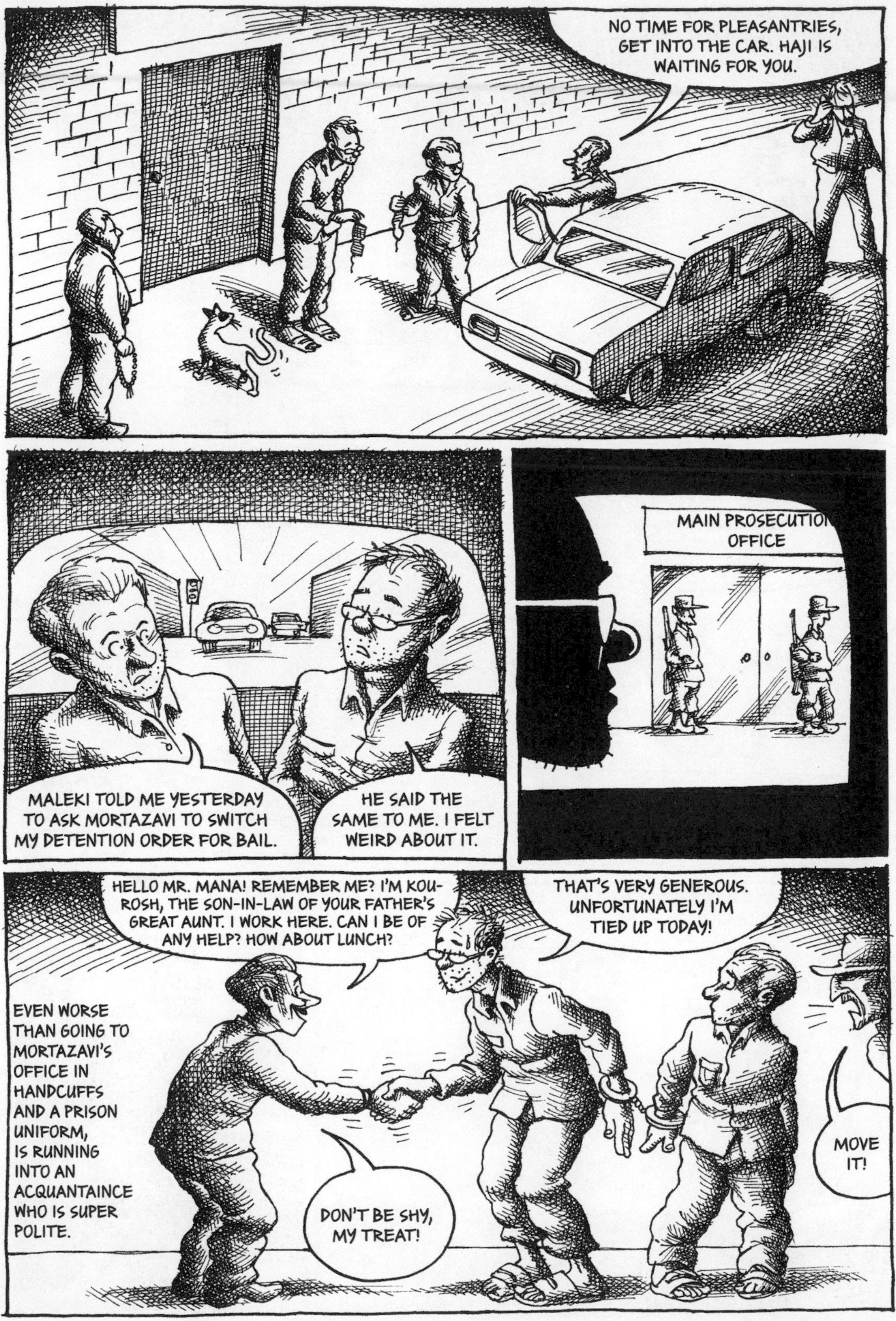
NO TIME FOR PLEASANTRIES, GET INTO THE CAR. HAJI IS WAITING FOR YOU.
MALEKI TOLD ME YESTERDAY TO ASK MORTAZAVI TO SWITCH MY DETENTION ORDER FOR BAIL.
HE SAID THE SAME TO ME. I FELT WEIRD ABOUT IT.
MAIN PROSECUTIO
OFFICE
HELLO MR. MANA! REMEMBER ME? I'M KOUROSH, THE SON-IN-LAW OF YOUR FATHER'S GREAT AUNT. I WORK HERE. CAN I BE OF ANY HELP? HOW ABOUT LUNCH?
THAT'S VERY GENEROUS. UNFORTUNATELY I'M TIED UP TODAY!
EVEN WORSE THAN GOING TO MORTAZAVI'S OFFICE IN HANDCUFFS AND A PRISON UNIFORM, IS RUNNING INTO AN ACQUANTAINCE WHO IS SUPER POLITE.
DON'T BE SHY, MY TREAT!
MOVE IT!

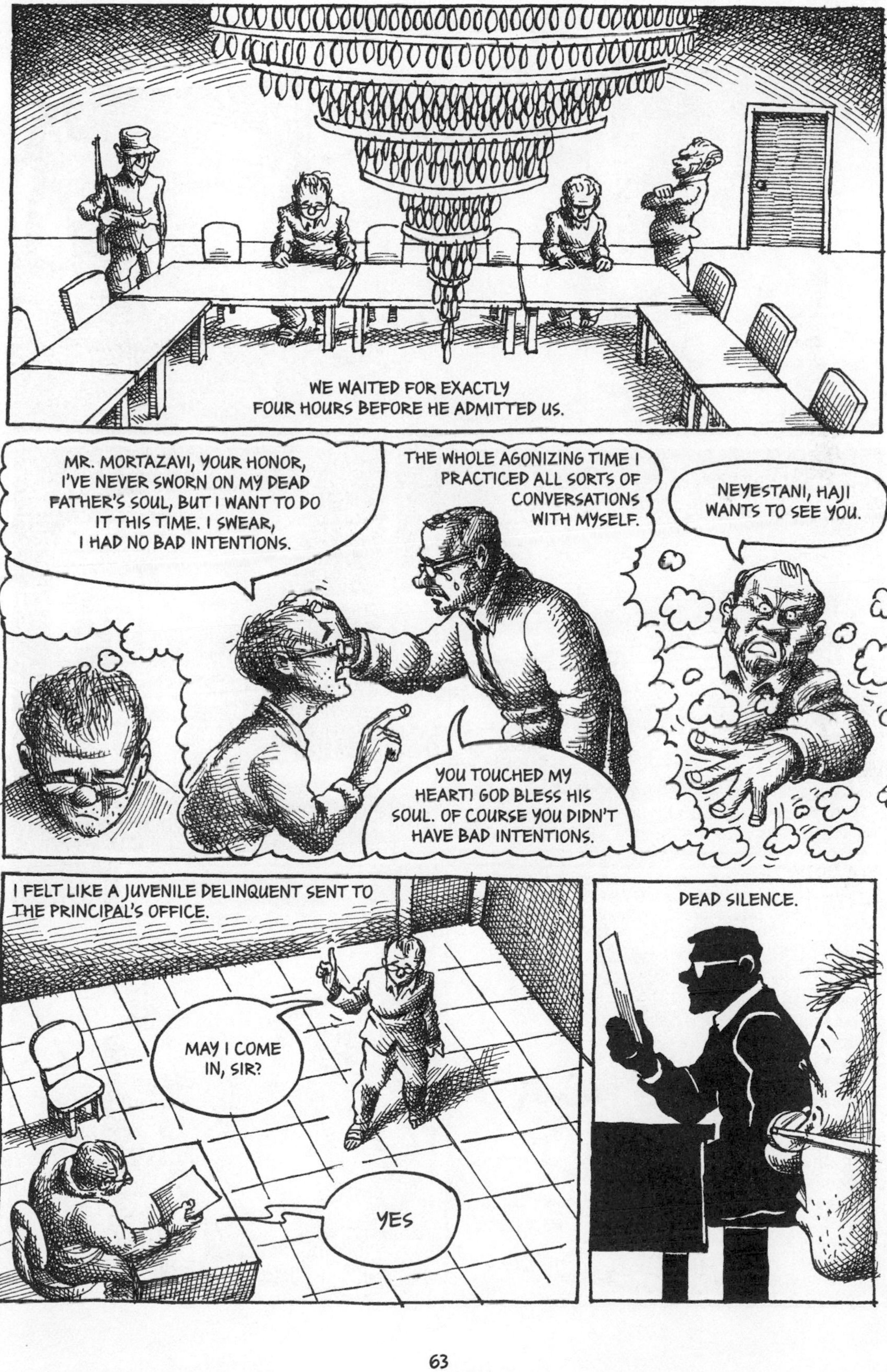
WE WAITED FOR EXACTLY FOUR HOURS BEFORE HE ADMITTED US.
MR. MORTAZAVI, YOUR HONOR, I'VE NEVER SWORN ON MY DEAD FATHER'S SOUL, BUT I WANT TO DO IT THIS TIME. I SWEAR, I HAD NO BAD INTENTIONS.
THE WHOLE AGONIZING TIME I PRACTICED ALL SORTS OF CONVERSATIONS WITH MYSELF.
YOU TOUCHED MY HEART! GOD BLESS HIS SOUL. OF COURSE YOU DIDN'T HAVE BAD INTENTIONS.
NEYESTANI, HAJI WANTS TO SEE YOU.
I FELT LIKE A JUVENILE DELINQUENT SENT TO THE PRINCIPAL'S OFFICE.
MAY I COME IN, SIR?
YES
DEAD SILENCE.

AND THEN ALL OF A SUDDEN:

ARE YOU FINALLY GOING TO COUGH UP A BIT OF TRUTH OR NOT?

HOW DID YOU ACCEPT MONEY FROM AMERICANS TO CAUSE ALL THIS UNREST?

MONEY?? I SWEAR ON MY FATHER'S SOUL I NEVER ...

STOP THE LIES!

TWELVE PEOPLE WERE KILLED IN AZERBAIJAN ...

AND ONE BILLION IN DAMAGES WAS REPORTED. THIS IS 100 PERCENT YOUR FAULT!

DID YOU THINK YOU'D GET AWAY WITH THIS? YOU WILL BE DESTROYED...

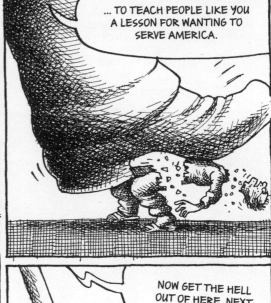

... TO TEACH PEOPLE LIKE YOU A LESSON FOR WANTING TO SERVE AMERICA.

NOW GET THE HELL OUT OF HERE. NEXT TIME YOU COME HERE YOU WILL TELL ME THE TRUTH!

OTHERWISE WE'LL GET EXPERTS IN ENHANCED INTERROGATION TECHNIQUES, TO GET THE TRUTH OUT OF YOU.

HALF AN HOUR LATER, WE WERE ON OUR WAY BACK.

THE STUPID IDIOT MADE UP WHATEVER HE WANTED AND ADDED THAT IF I DON'T CONFESS WHAT HE WANTS TO HEAR HE'D SEND ME TO WHAT HE CALLED "ENHANCED" INTERROGATION!

ENHANCED!
I THINK IT'S MORE ABOUT MARTIAL ARTS THAN INTERROGATION TECHNIQUES.

SUDDENLY THE CAR VEERED IN AN UNFAMILIAR DIRECTION.

THIS IS NOT THE ROAD TO EVIN!

I KNEW THAT THERE WERE HIDDEN DE-TENTION CENTERS WHERE SOME POLITICAL PRISONERS WERE TAKEN TO BE TORTURED. I WAS TERRIFIED.

THIS ISN'T THE ROAD TO EVIN. WHERE ARE THEY TAKING US?

I HAVE NO IDEA... BUT... ISN'T THAT AN EVIN BUILDING?

I NEVER IMAGINED THAT EVIN PRISON WOULD BRING TEARS OF JOY TO MY EYES.

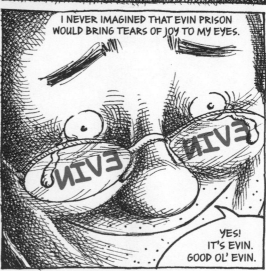

YES!
IT'S EVIN.
GOOD OL' EVIN.

65

AS SOON AS WE GOT THERE, THEY TOOK ME TO MALEKI.

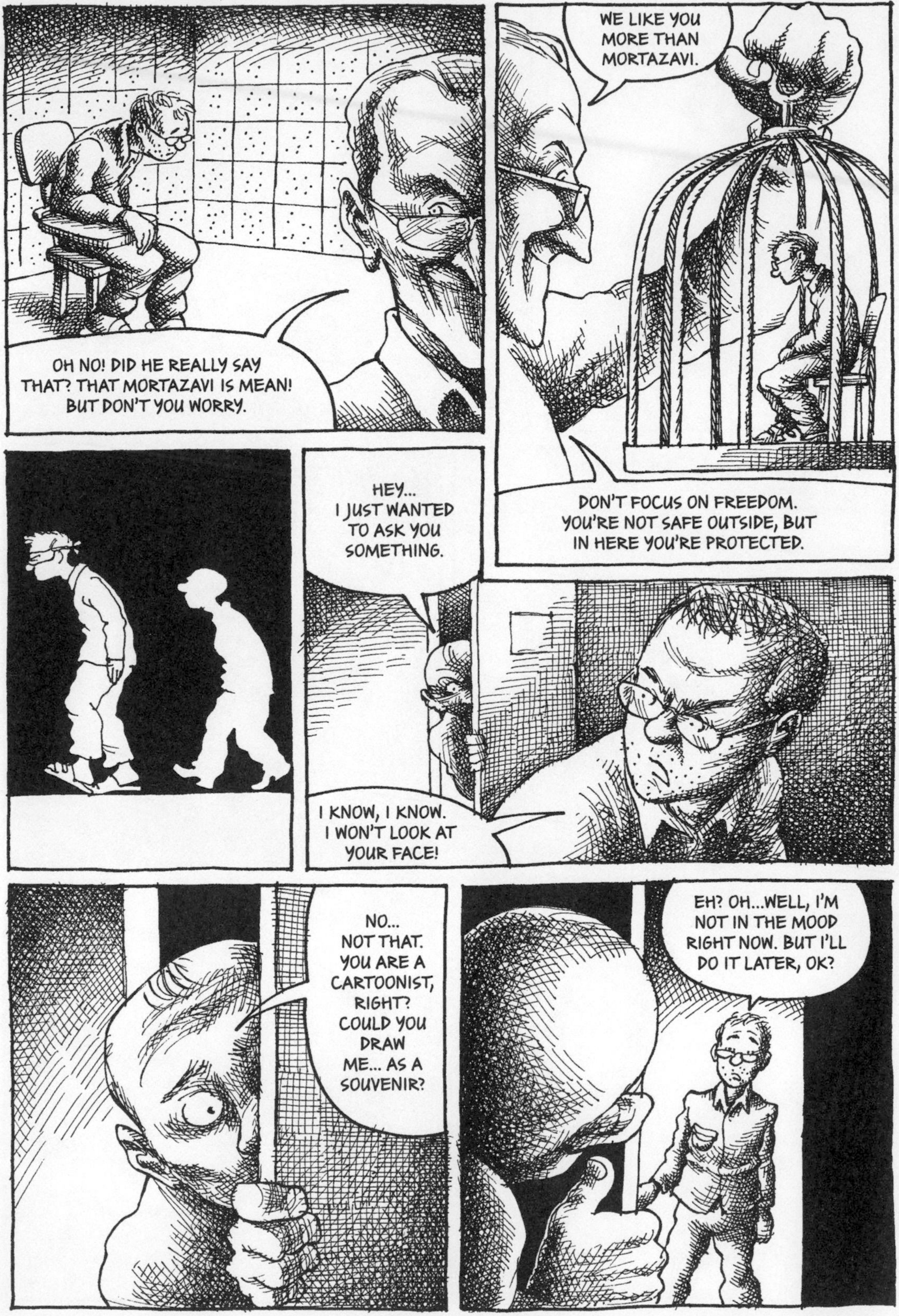
OH NO! DID HE REALLY SAY THAT? THAT MORTAZAVI IS MEAN! BUT DON'T YOU WORRY.
WE LIKE YOU MORE THAN MORTAZAVI.
DON'T FOCUS ON FREEDOM. YOU'RE NOT SAFE OUTSIDE, BUT IN HERE YOU'RE PROTECTED.
HEY... I JUST WANTED TO ASK YOU SOMETHING.
I KNOW, I KNOW. I WON'T LOOK AT YOUR FACE!
NO... NOT THAT. YOU ARE A CARTOONIST, RIGHT? COULD YOU DRAW ME... AS A SOUVENIR?
EH? OH...WELL, I'M NOT IN THE MOOD RIGHT NOW. BUT I'LL DO IT LATER, OK?

SINCE I NEVER GOT THE CHANCE TO DRAW HIM,
I DEDICATE THIS DRAWING TO HIM. I CAN ONLY DRAW
THE PART OF HIM THAT I WAS ABLE TO SEE.

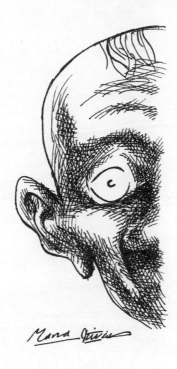

THAT NIGHT THEY BROUGHT MEHRDAD INTO MY CELL. HE WAS A MESS.

I THINK THIS IS ALL JUST A GAME. THEY WANTED TO SHOW US THERE ARE PLACES WORSE THAN 209... SO WE DON'T PROTEST TOO MUCH ABOUT BEING STUCK HERE. ARE YOU OK?

MALEKI TOLD ME THAT THE ONLY WAY TO KEEP MY JOB IS TO COLLABORATE WITH THEM. I TOLD HIM THAT I'M NOT A SPY. SO HE SAID, THAT...

... THEY WON'T LET ME WORK AS A JOURNALIST AGAIN. THAT'S THE ONLY PROFESSION I KNOW. IT'S ALL I'VE EVER DONE. I... LOVE IT.

I'VE NO IDEA WHAT I COULD DO AFTER THIS...

I DIDN'T KNOW WHAT TO SAY TO THIS HONEST AND INNOCENT MAN WHO WENT TO PRISON AND LOST HIS FAVORITE JOB FOREVER... BECAUSE OF ME.

LOOK! YOU CAN SEE THE CRESCENT MOON THROUGH THE BARS...IT'S BEAUTIFUL!

CAN THE MOON SEE US TOO?

CHAPTER SIX:

THE SHIPWRECKED

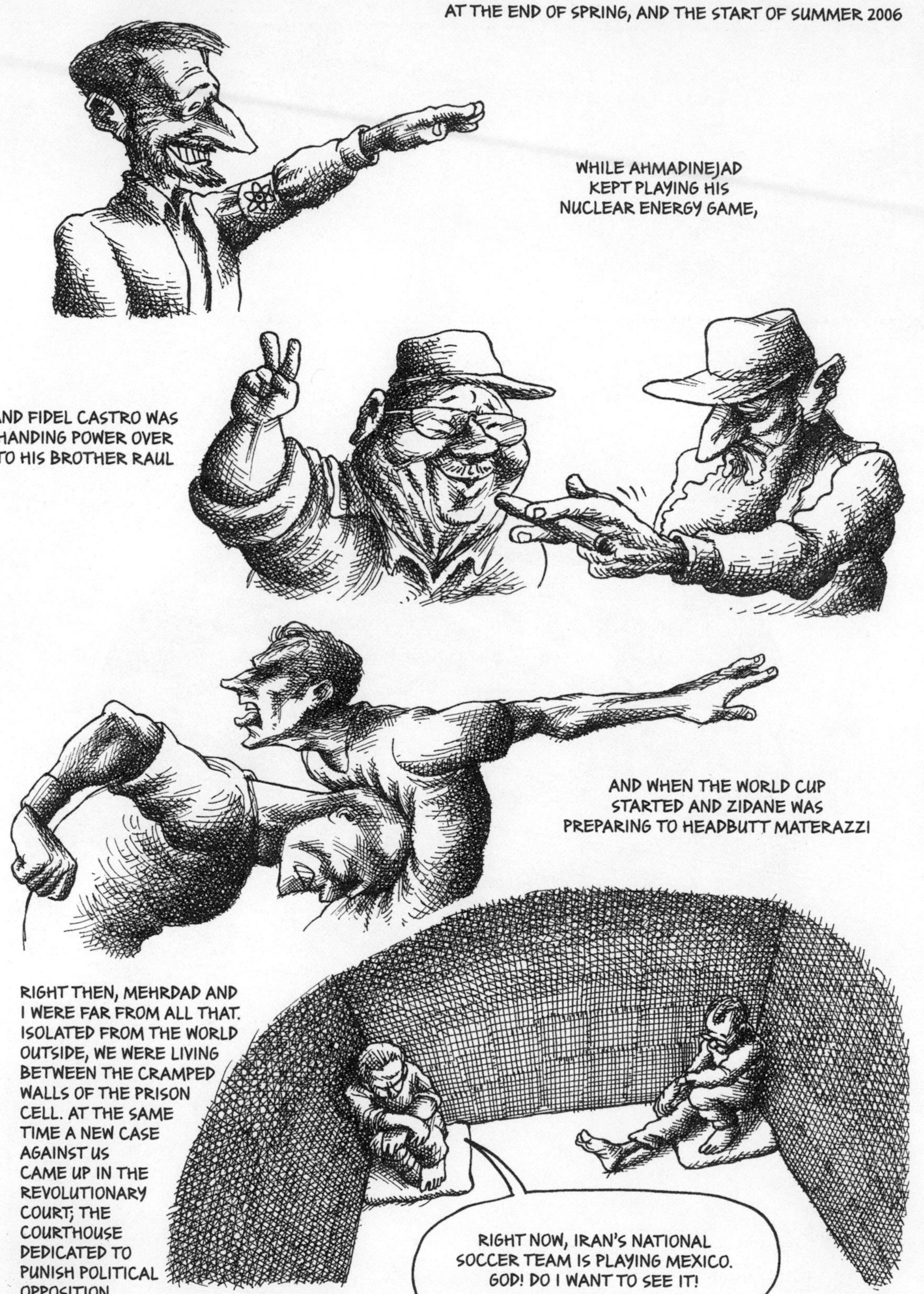
AT THE END OF SPRING, AND THE START OF SUMMER 2006
WHILE AHMADINEJAD KEPT PLAYING HIS NUCLEAR ENERGY GAME,
AND FIDEL CASTRO WAS HANDING POWER OVER TO HIS BROTHER RAUL
AND WHEN THE WORLD CUP STARTED AND ZIDANE WAS PREPARING TO HEADBUTT MATERAZZI
RIGHT THEN, MEHRDAD AND I WERE FAR FROM ALL THAT. ISOLATED FROM THE WORLD OUTSIDE, WE WERE LIVING BETWEEN THE CRAMPED WALLS OF THE PRISON CELL. AT THE SAME TIME A NEW CASE AGAINST US CAME UP IN THE REVOLUTIONARY COURT; THE COURTHOUSE DEDICATED TO PUNISH POLITICAL OPPOSITION.
RIGHT NOW, IRAN'S NATIONAL SOCCER TEAM IS PLAYING MEXICO. GOD! DO I WANT TO SEE IT!

I'D NEVER BEEN A SOCCER FAN, BUT THE GAME NOW GAINED A NEW MEANING FOR ME.

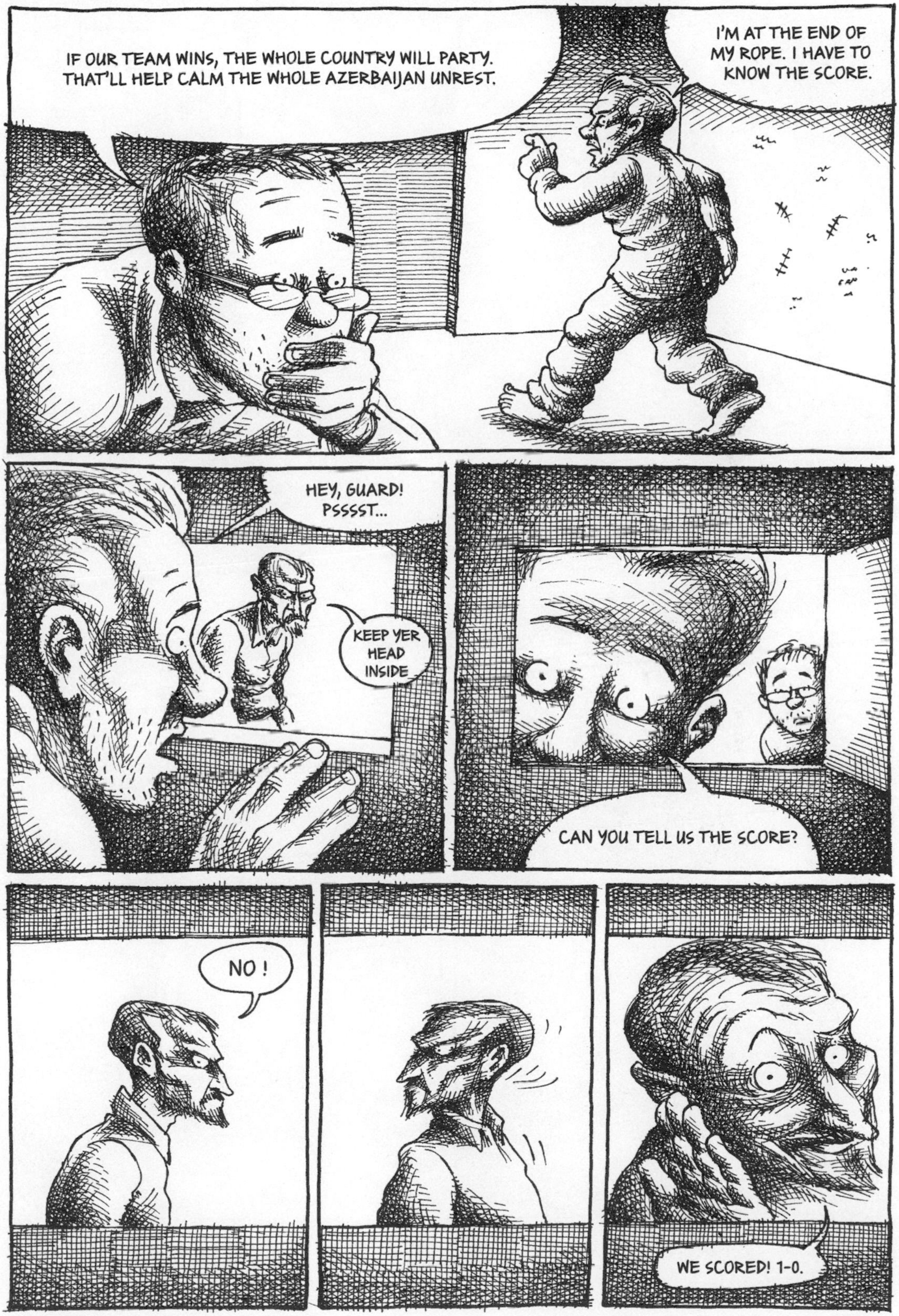
IF OUR TEAM WINS, THE WHOLE COUNTRY WILL PARTY. THAT'LL HELP CALM THE WHOLE AZERBAIJAN UNREST.
I'M AT THE END OF MY ROPE. I HAVE TO KNOW THE SCORE.
HEY, GUARD! PSSSST...
KEEP YER HEAD INSIDE
CAN YOU TELL US THE SCORE?
NO !
WE SCORED! 1-0.

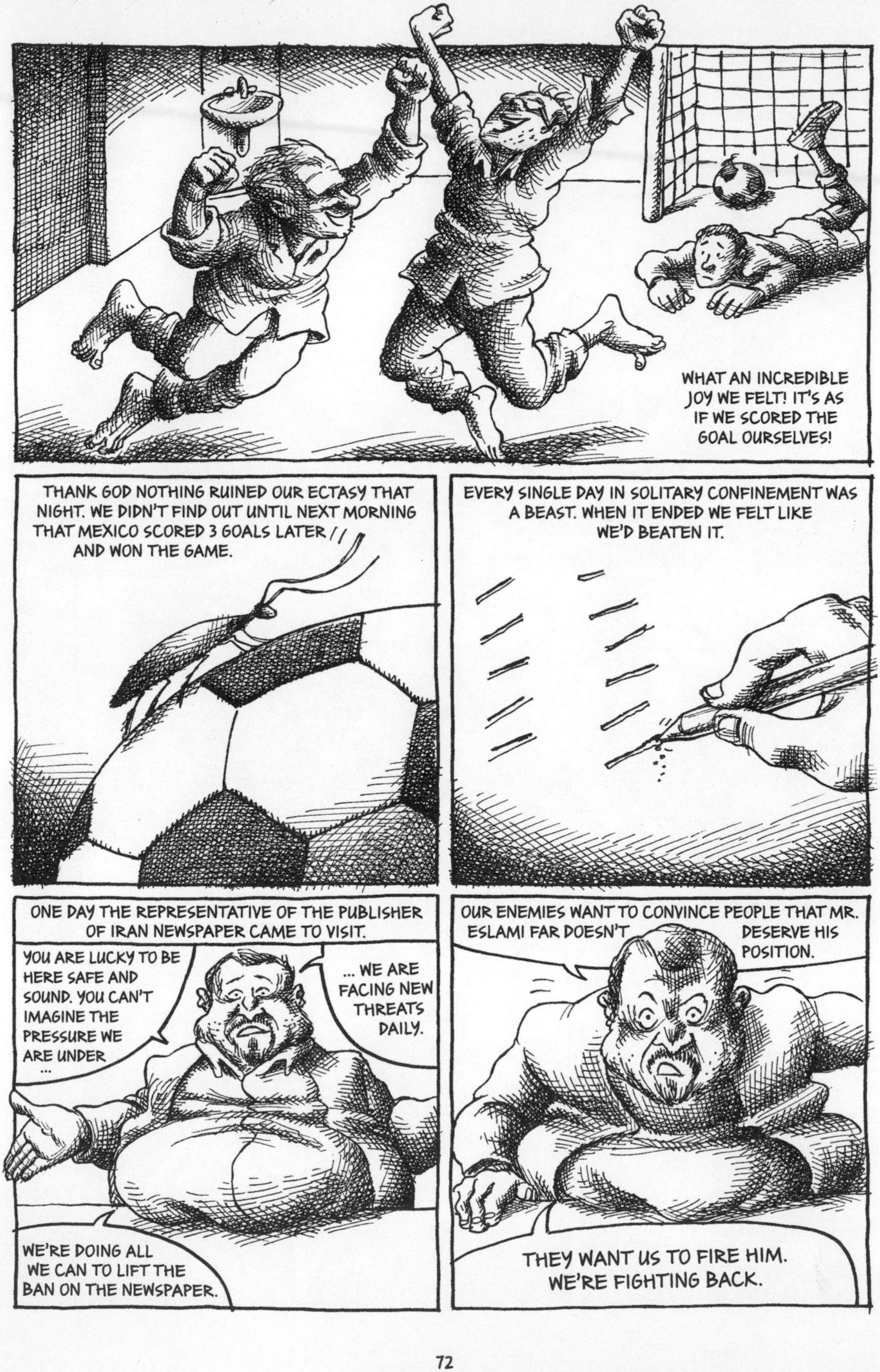

WHAT AN INCREDIBLE JOY WE FELT! IT'S AS IF WE SCORED THE GOAL OURSELVES!
THANK GOD NOTHING RUINED OUR ECTASY THAT NIGHT. WE DIDN'T FIND OUT UNTIL NEXT MORNING THAT MEXICO SCORED 3 GOALS LATER AND WON THE GAME.
EVERY SINGLE DAY IN SOLITARY CONFINEMENT WAS A BEAST. WHEN IT ENDED WE FELT LIKE WE'D BEATEN IT.
ONE DAY THE REPRESENTATIVE OF THE PUBLISHER OF IRAN NEWSPAPER CAME TO VISIT.
YOU ARE LUCKY TO BE HERE SAFE AND SOUND. YOU CAN'T IMAGINE THE PRESSURE WE ARE UNDER ...
... WE ARE FACING NEW THREATS DAILY.
WE'RE DOING ALL WE CAN TO LIFT THE BAN ON THE NEWSPAPER.
OUR ENEMIES WANT TO CONVINCE PEOPLE THAT MR. ESLAMI FAR DOESN'T DESERVE HIS POSITION.
THEY WANT US TO FIRE HIM. WE'RE FIGHTING BACK.

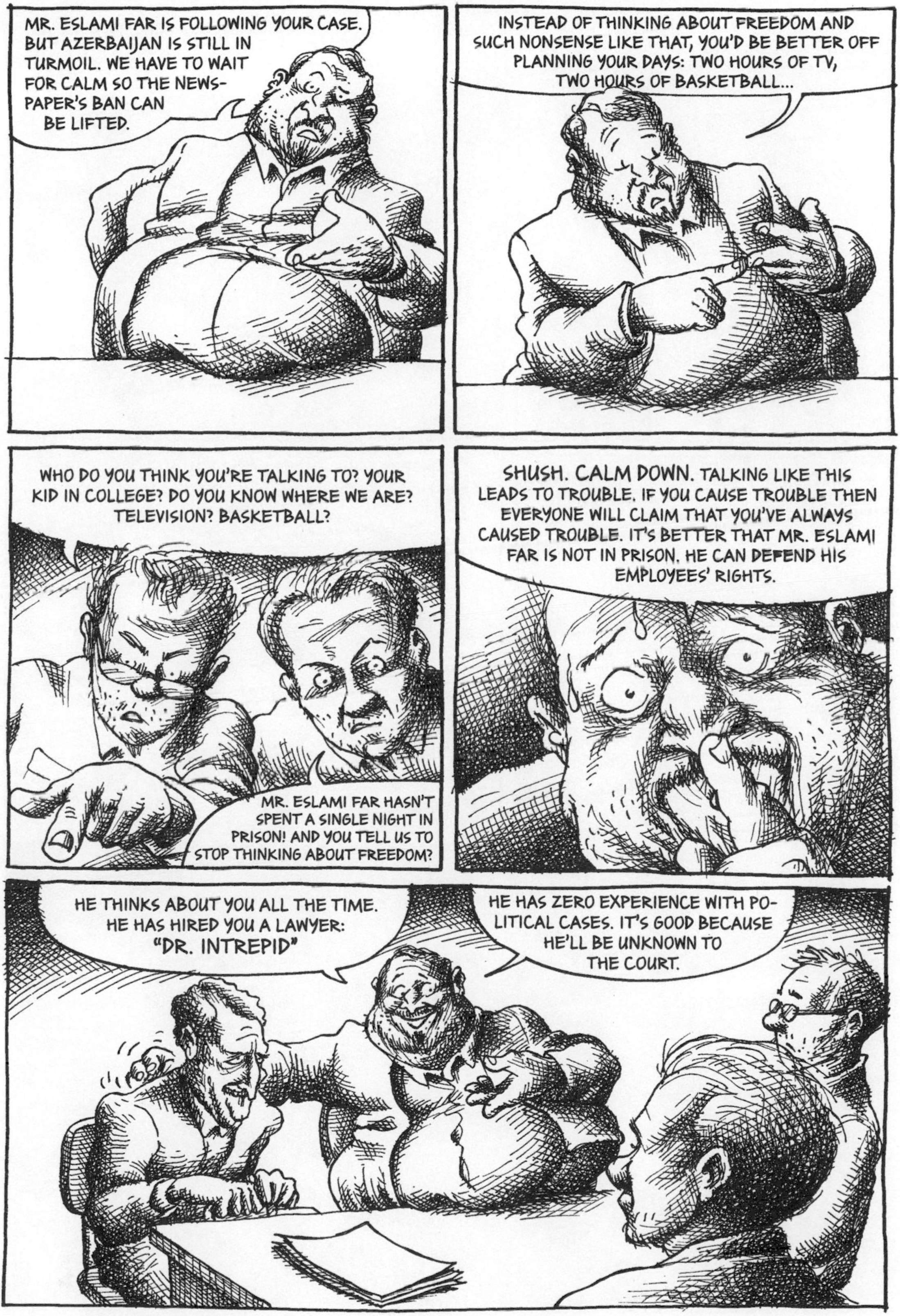
MR. ESLAMI FAR IS FOLLOWING YOUR CASE. BUT AZERBAIJAN IS STILL IN TURMOIL. WE HAVE TO WAIT FOR CALM SO THE NEWSPAPER'S BAN CAN BE LIFTED.
INSTEAD OF THINKING ABOUT FREEDOM AND SUCH NONSENSE LIKE THAT, YOU'D BE BETTER OFF PLANNING YOUR DAYS: TWO HOURS OF TV, TWO HOURS OF BASKETBALL...
WHO DO YOU THINK YOU'RE TALKING TO? YOUR KID IN COLLEGE? DO YOU KNOW WHERE WE ARE? TELEVISION? BASKETBALL?
MR. ESLAMI FAR HASN'T SPENT A SINGLE NIGHT IN PRISON! AND YOU TELL US TO STOP THINKING ABOUT FREEDOM?
SHUSH. CALM DOWN. TALKING LIKE THIS LEADS TO TROUBLE. IF YOU CAUSE TROUBLE THEN EVERYONE WILL CLAIM THAT YOU'VE ALWAYS CAUSED TROUBLE. IT'S BETTER THAT MR. ESLAMI FAR IS NOT IN PRISON. HE CAN DEFEND HIS EMPLOYEES' RIGHTS.
HE THINKS ABOUT YOU ALL THE TIME. HE HAS HIRED YOU A LAWYER: "DR. INTREPID"
HE HAS ZERO EXPERIENCE WITH POLITICAL CASES. IT'S GOOD BECAUSE HE'LL BE UNKNOWN TO THE COURT.

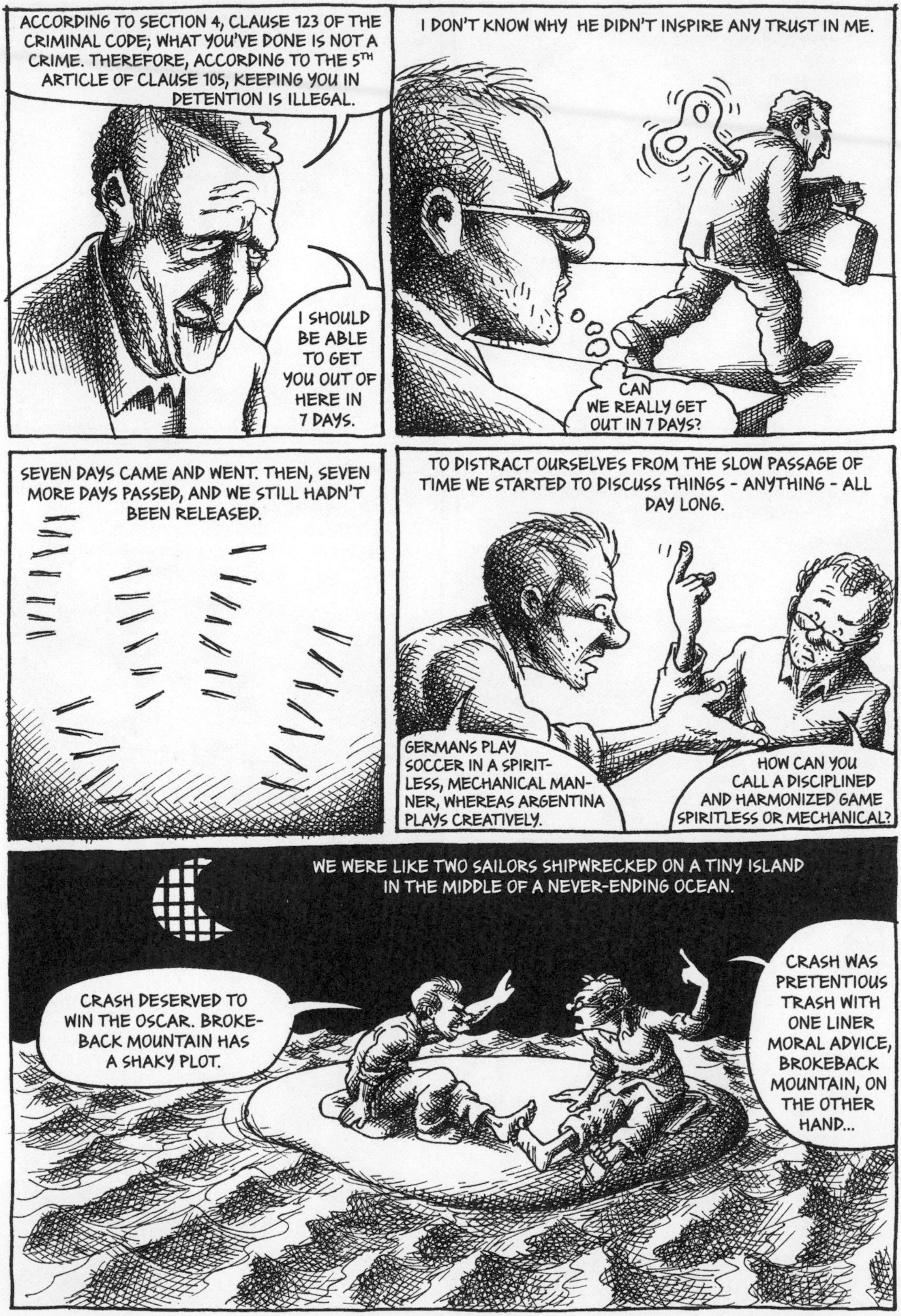

ACCORDING TO SECTION 4, CLAUSE 123 OF THE CRIMINAL CODE; WHAT YOU'VE DONE IS NOT A CRIME. THEREFORE, ACCORDING TO THE 5TH ARTICLE OF CLAUSE 105, KEEPING YOU IN DETENTION IS ILLEGAL.
I SHOULD BE ABLE TO GET YOU OUT OF HERE IN 7 DAYS.
I DON'T KNOW WHY HE DIDN'T INSPIRE ANY TRUST IN ME.
CAN WE REALLY GET OUT IN 7 DAYS?
SEVEN DAYS CAME AND WENT. THEN, SEVEN MORE DAYS PASSED, AND WE STILL HADN'T BEEN RELEASED.
TO DISTRACT OURSELVES FROM THE SLOW PASSAGE OF TIME WE STARTED TO DISCUSS THINGS - ANYTHING - ALL DAY LONG.
GERMANS PLAY SOCCER IN A SPIRIT-LESS, MECHANICAL MAN-NER, WHEREAS ARGENTINA PLAYS CREATIVELY.
HOW CAN YOU CALL A DISCIPLINED AND HARMONIZED GAME SPIRITLESS OR MECHANICAL?
WE WERE LIKE TWO SAILORS SHIPWRECKED ON A TINY ISLAND IN THE MIDDLE OF A NEVER-ENDING OCEAN.
CRASH DESERVED TO WIN THE OSCAR. BROKE-BACK MOUNTAIN HAS A SHAKY PLOT.
CRASH WAS PRETENTIOUS TRASH WITH ONE LINER MORAL ADVICE, BROKEBACK MOUNTAIN, ON THE OTHER HAND...

WE WERE GETTING CLOSE TO 50 DAYS IN SEMI-SOLITARY CONFINEMENT. AFTER 40 DAYS...
WE WERE EXHIBITING SYMPTOMS OF SENSORY DEPRIVATION...
OUR EYES HAD NOTHING TO SEE EXCEPT FOUR EMPTY WALLS AND A TINY WINDOW.
THERE WERE NO SMELLS EXCEPT THE ODOR OF OUR SWEAT.
SINGLE ODOR MOLECULE
THERE WAS NOTHING TO HEAR. DEAD SILENCE.
WE ONLY HEARD AZAN* ...
WHICH WE HEARD EVERY FEW HOURS. AFTER A MONTH I HAD AUDITORY HALLUCINATIONS.
EVEN WHEN THERE WAS NO AZAN WE COULD STIILL HEAR IT IN OUR HEADS.

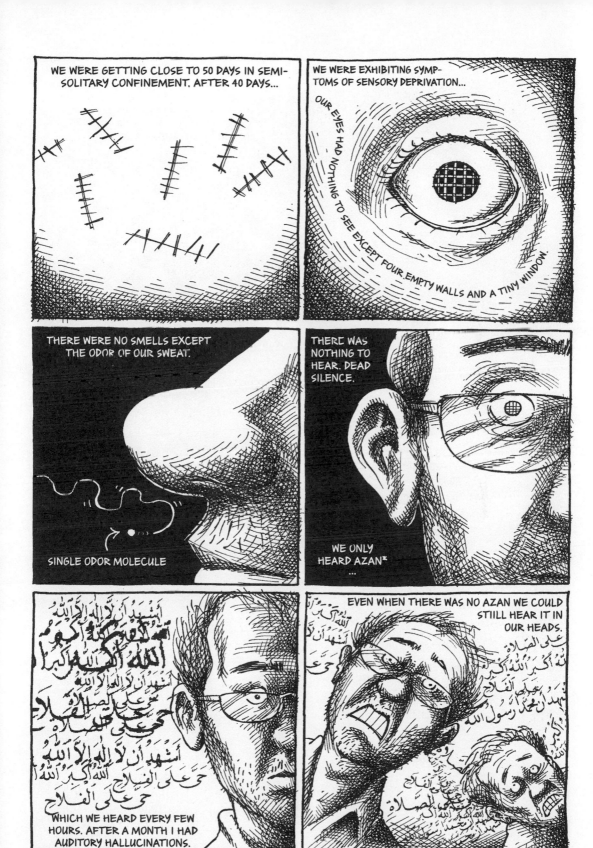

*AZAN OR ADHAN IN ARABIC, IS THE ISLAMIC CALL TO PRAYER.

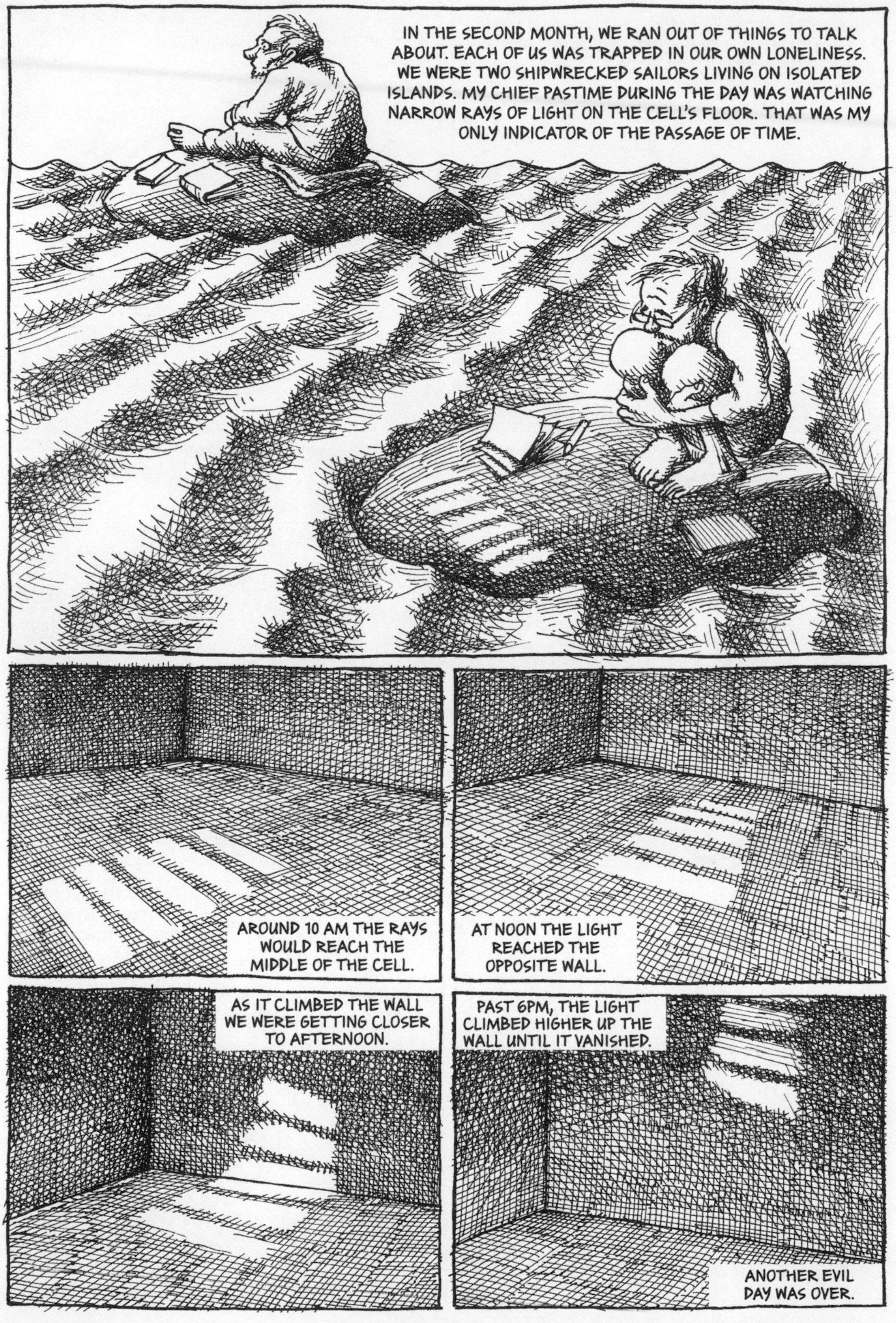
IN THE SECOND MONTH, WE RAN OUT OF THINGS TO TALK ABOUT. EACH OF US WAS TRAPPED IN OUR OWN LONELINESS. WE WERE TWO SHIPWRECKED SAILORS LIVING ON ISOLATED ISLANDS. MY CHIEF PASTIME DURING THE DAY WAS WATCHING NARROW RAYS OF LIGHT ON THE CELL'S FLOOR. THAT WAS MY ONLY INDICATOR OF THE PASSAGE OF TIME.
AROUND 10 AM THE RAYS WOULD REACH THE MIDDLE OF THE CELL.
AT NOON THE LIGHT REACHED THE OPPOSITE WALL.
AS IT CLIMBED THE WALL WE WERE GETTING CLOSER TO AFTERNOON.
PAST 6PM, THE LIGHT CLIMBED HIGHER UP THE WALL UNTIL IT VANISHED.
ANOTHER EVIL DAY WAS OVER.

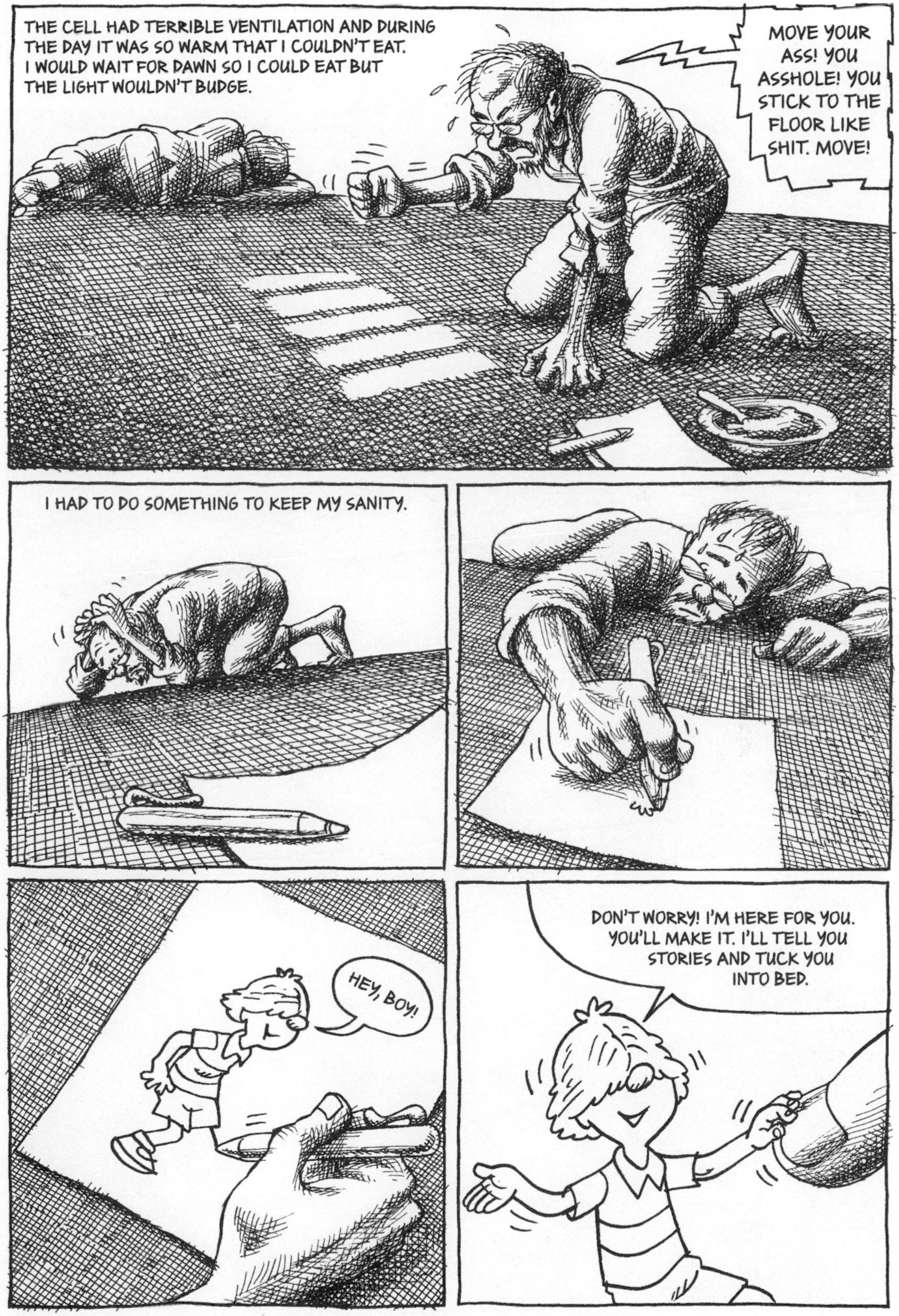
THE CELL HAD TERRIBLE VENTILATION AND DURING THE DAY IT WAS SO WARM THAT I COULDN'T EAT. I WOULD WAIT FOR DAWN SO I COULD EAT BUT THE LIGHT WOULDN'T BUDGE.
MOVE YOUR ASS! YOU ASSHOLE! YOU STICK TO THE FLOOR LIKE SHIT. MOVE!
I HAD TO DO SOMETHING TO KEEP MY SANITY.
HEY, BOY!
DON'T WORRY! I'M HERE FOR YOU. YOU'LL MAKE IT. I'LL TELL YOU STORIES AND TUCK YOU INTO BED.

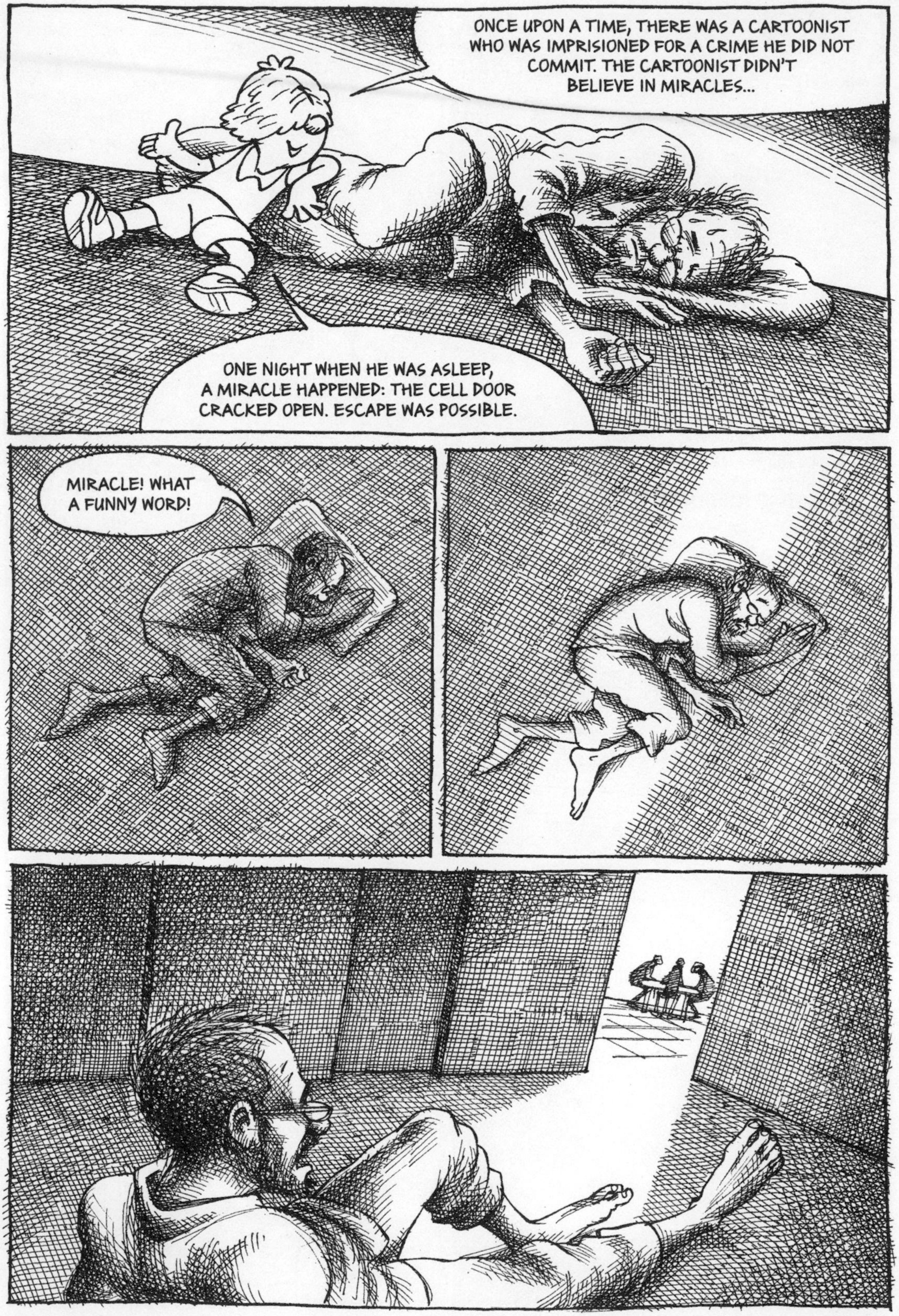

ONCE UPON A TIME, THERE WAS A CARTOONIST WHO WAS IMPRISIONED FOR A CRIME HE DID NOT COMMIT. THE CARTOONIST DIDN'T BELIEVE IN MIRACLES...
ONE NIGHT WHEN HE WAS ASLEEP, A MIRACLE HAPPENED: THE CELL DOOR CRACKED OPEN. ESCAPE WAS POSSIBLE.
MIRACLE! WHAT A FUNNY WORD!

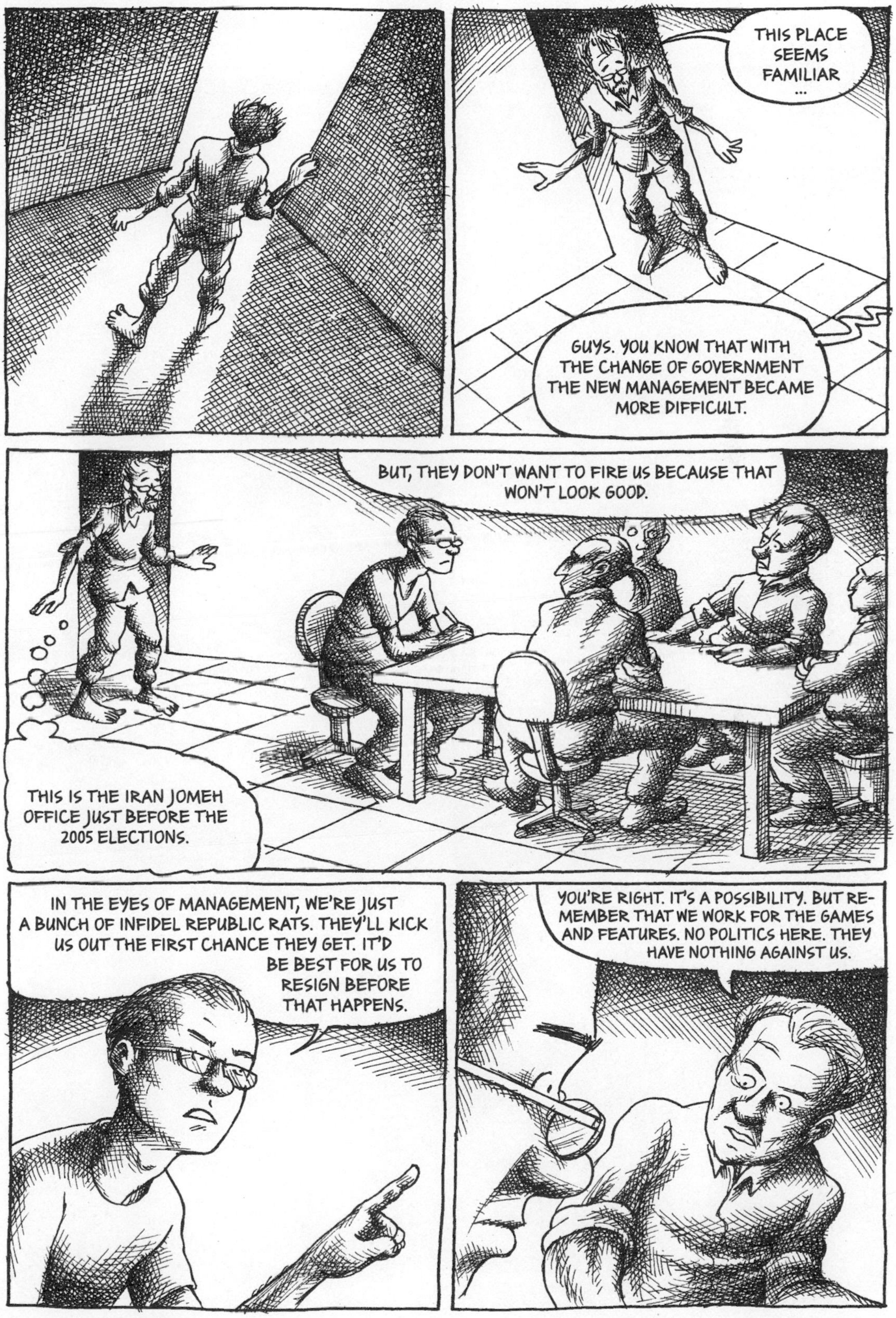
THIS PLACE SEEMS FAMILIAR ...
GUYS. YOU KNOW THAT WITH THE CHANGE OF GOVERNMENT THE NEW MANAGEMENT BECAME MORE DIFFICULT.
BUT, THEY DON'T WANT TO FIRE US BECAUSE THAT WON'T LOOK GOOD.
THIS IS THE IRAN JOMEH OFFICE JUST BEFORE THE 2005 ELECTIONS.
IN THE EYES OF MANAGEMENT, WE'RE JUST A BUNCH OF INFIDEL REPUBLIC RATS. THEY'LL KICK US OUT THE FIRST CHANCE THEY GET. IT'D BE BEST FOR US TO RESIGN BEFORE THAT HAPPENS.
YOU'RE RIGHT. IT'S A POSSIBILITY. BUT REMEMBER THAT WE WORK FOR THE GAMES AND FEATURES. NO POLITICS HERE. THEY HAVE NOTHING AGAINST US.

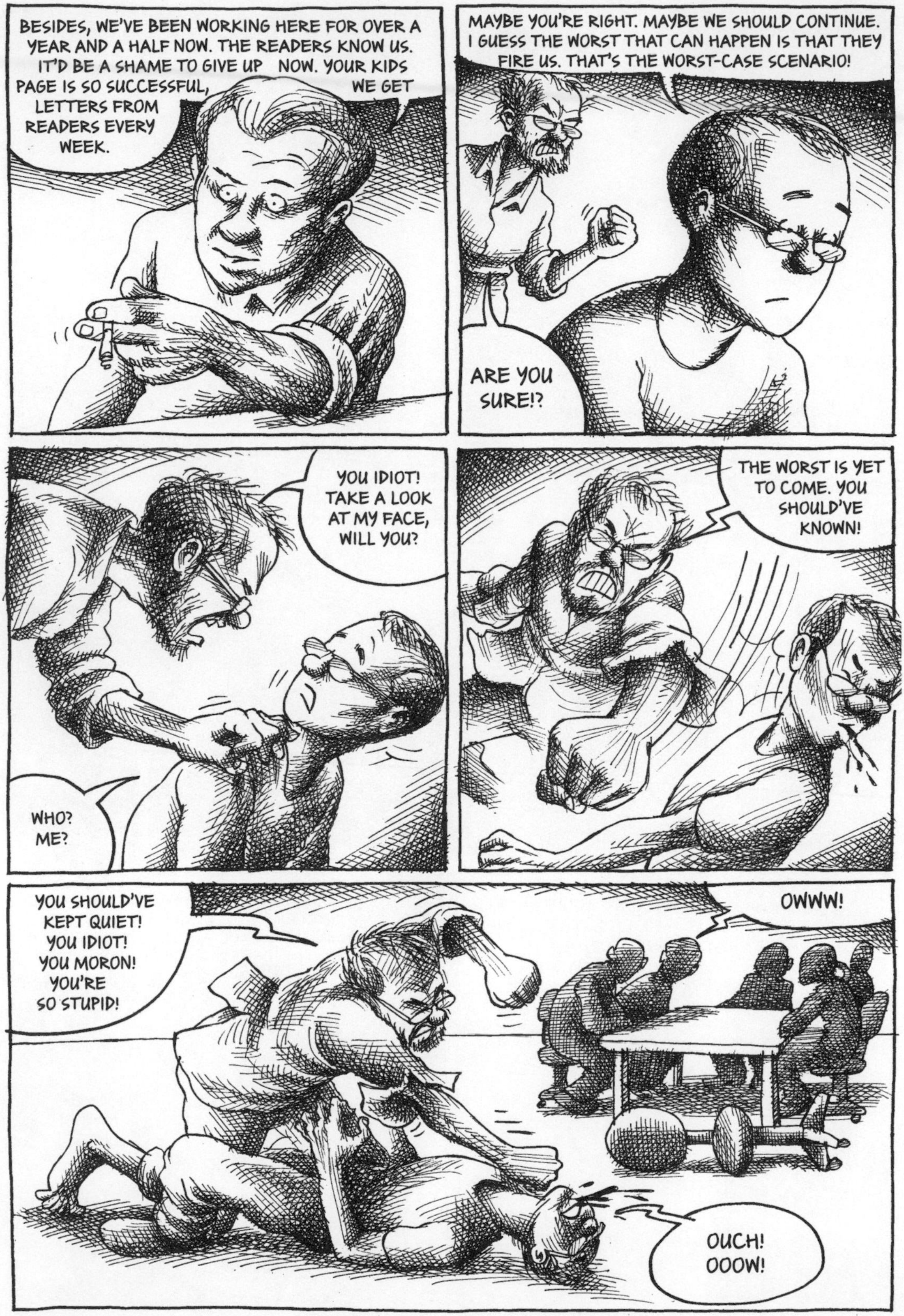

BESIDES, WE'VE BEEN WORKING HERE FOR OVER A YEAR AND A HALF NOW. THE READERS KNOW US. IT'D BE A SHAME TO GIVE UP NOW. YOUR KIDS PAGE IS SO SUCCESSFUL, WE GET LETTERS FROM READERS EVERY WEEK.
MAYBE YOU'RE RIGHT. MAYBE WE SHOULD CONTINUE. I GUESS THE WORST THAT CAN HAPPEN IS THAT THEY FIRE US. THAT'S THE WORST-CASE SCENARIO!
ARE YOU SURE!?
YOU IDIOT! TAKE A LOOK AT MY FACE, WILL YOU?
WHO? ME?
THE WORST IS YET TO COME. YOU SHOULD'VE KNOWN!
YOU SHOULD'VE KEPT QUIET! YOU IDIOT! YOU MORON! YOU'RE SO STUPID!
OWWW!
OUCH! OOOW!

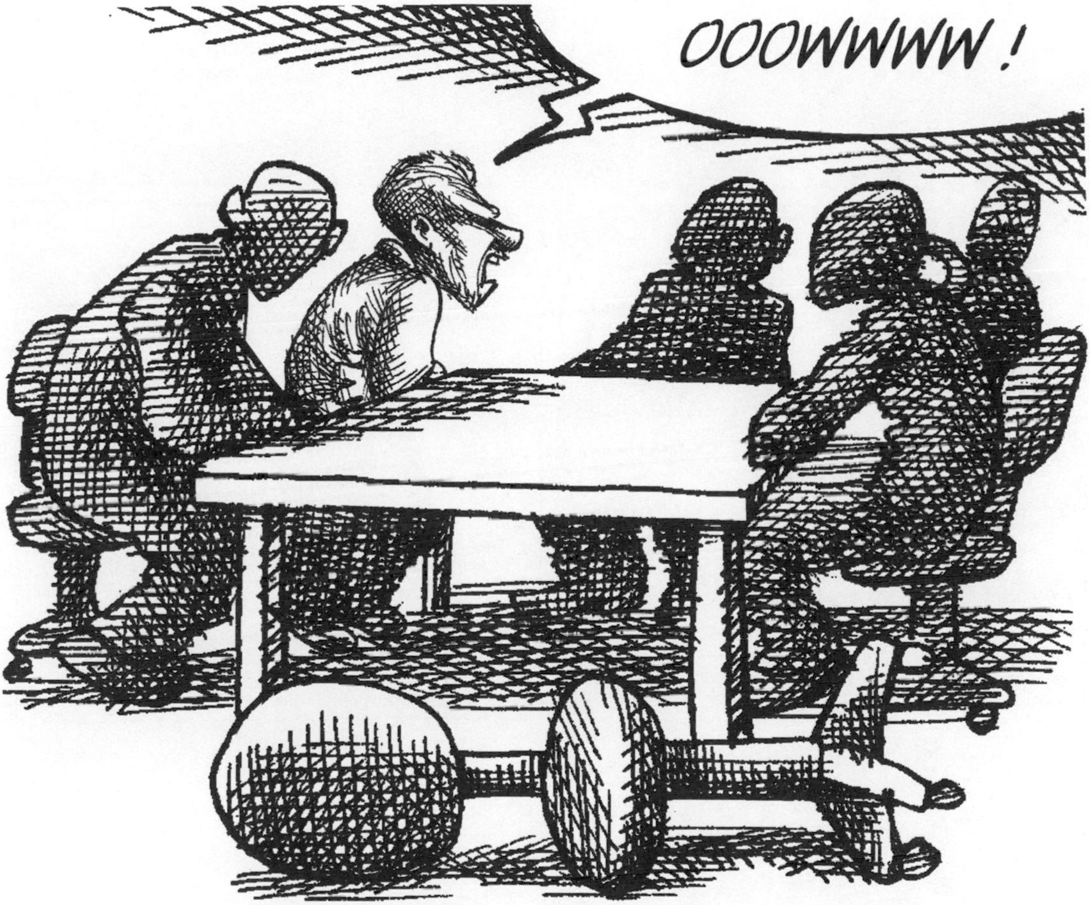
OOOWWWW !

WHAT'S WRONG? MEHRDAD? ARE YOU OK?

OWWW!

MY KIDNEYS ARE GOING TO EXPLODE AND NO ONE WILL OPEN THAT FUCKING DOOR!

MEHRDAD HAD A KIDNEY PROBLEM. HE HAD TO DRINK A LOT OF WATER AND GO TO THE WASHROOM OFTEN. WE HAD TO PUSH A PIECE OF PAPER UNDER THE DOOR...

WHEN A GUARD SAW THE PAPER HE'D TAKE US TO THE WASHROOM BLINDFOLDED.

TRY TO HOLD ON. THE GUARD WILL COME ANY MOMENT.

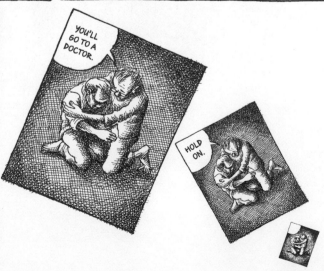

YOU'LL GO TO A DOCTOR.

HOLD ON.

CHAPTER SEVEN:

THE WORKERS' SECTION.

ON THE 51st DAY THE GUARD CAME.

PRISONERS WOULD ONLY BE ASKED TO DO THIS WHEN THEY WERE BEING RELEASED.

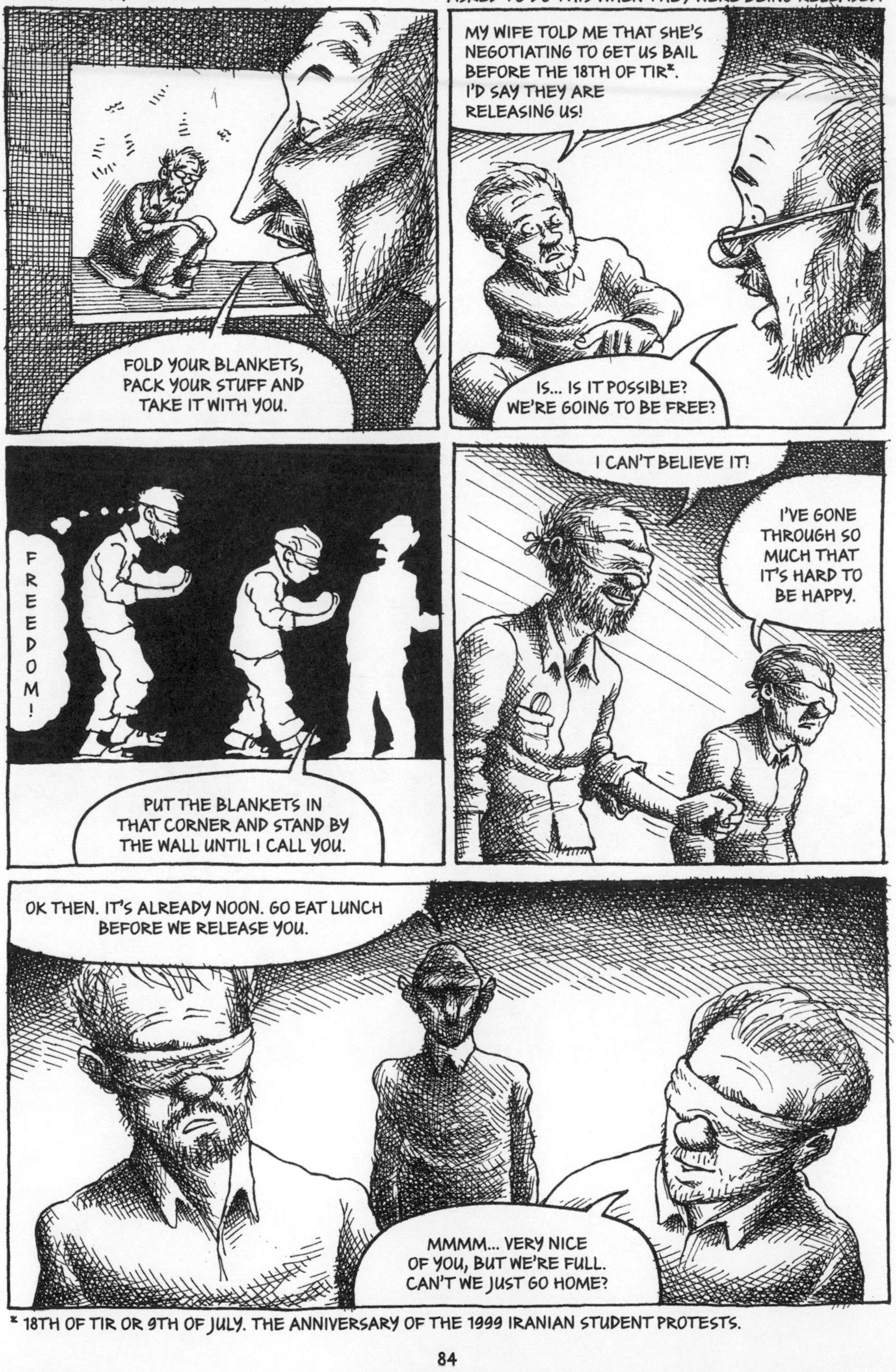
FOLD YOUR BLANKETS, PACK YOUR STUFF AND TAKE IT WITH YOU.
MY WIFE TOLD ME THAT SHE'S NEGOTIATING TO GET US BAIL BEFORE THE 18TH OF TIR*. I'D SAY THEY ARE RELEASING US!
IS... IS IT POSSIBLE? WE'RE GOING TO BE FREE?
FREEDOM!
PUT THE BLANKETS IN THAT CORNER AND STAND BY THE WALL UNTIL I CALL YOU.
I CAN'T BELIEVE IT!
I'VE GONE THROUGH SO MUCH THAT IT'S HARD TO BE HAPPY.
OK THEN. IT'S ALREADY NOON. GO EAT LUNCH BEFORE WE RELEASE YOU.
MMMM... VERY NICE OF YOU, BUT WE'RE FULL. CAN'T WE JUST GO HOME?

* 18TH OF TIR OR 9TH OF JULY. THE ANNIVERSARY OF THE 1999 IRANIAN STUDENT PROTESTS.

WHO SAID YOU'RE GOING HOME? YOUR FAMILIES REQUESTED A TRANSFER TO THE MAIN SECTION AND THE JUDGE AGREED. I THINK YOU'LL REGRET THIS. YOU'LL WANT TO CAME BACK.

GO TO LUNCH!

THEY FIRST TOOK US TO THE WARDEN.

WE'RE MOVING YOU TO SECTION 350; THE WORKERS' SECTION. IT'S GREAT. THE INMATES ARE IN MOSTLY FOR FINANCIAL CRIMES.

DURING THE DAY THEY WORK ALL AROUND EVIN. AT NIGHT THEY GO BACK TO THEIR OWN SECTION. ONE PROBLEM: WE HAVE A FEW PRISONERS WITH TURKISH BACKGROUND THERE.

IF YOU GO IN WITH YOUR REAL IDENTITY IT MIGHT CAUSE TROUBLE. WE THOUGHT IT BEST TO CREATE ALIASES.

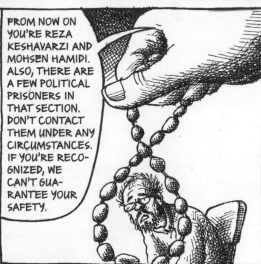

FROM NOW ON YOU'RE REZA KESHAVARZI AND MOHSEN HAMIDI. ALSO, THERE ARE A FEW POLITICAL PRISONERS IN THAT SECTION. DON'T CONTACT THEM UNDER ANY CIRCUMSTANCES. IF YOU'RE RECOGNIZED, WE CAN'T GUARANTEE YOUR SAFETY.

WE WERE TRANSFERRED TO QUARANTINE AND THEY STARTED NEW FILES ON US.

PRESS YOUR HAND ON THE PAD AND THEN PRESS IT ON THE PAPER.

85

MANA NEYESTANI EXISTED NO MORE

I WAS REZA KESHAVARZI; A SWINDLER ARRESTED
FOR WRITING BAD CHECKS.

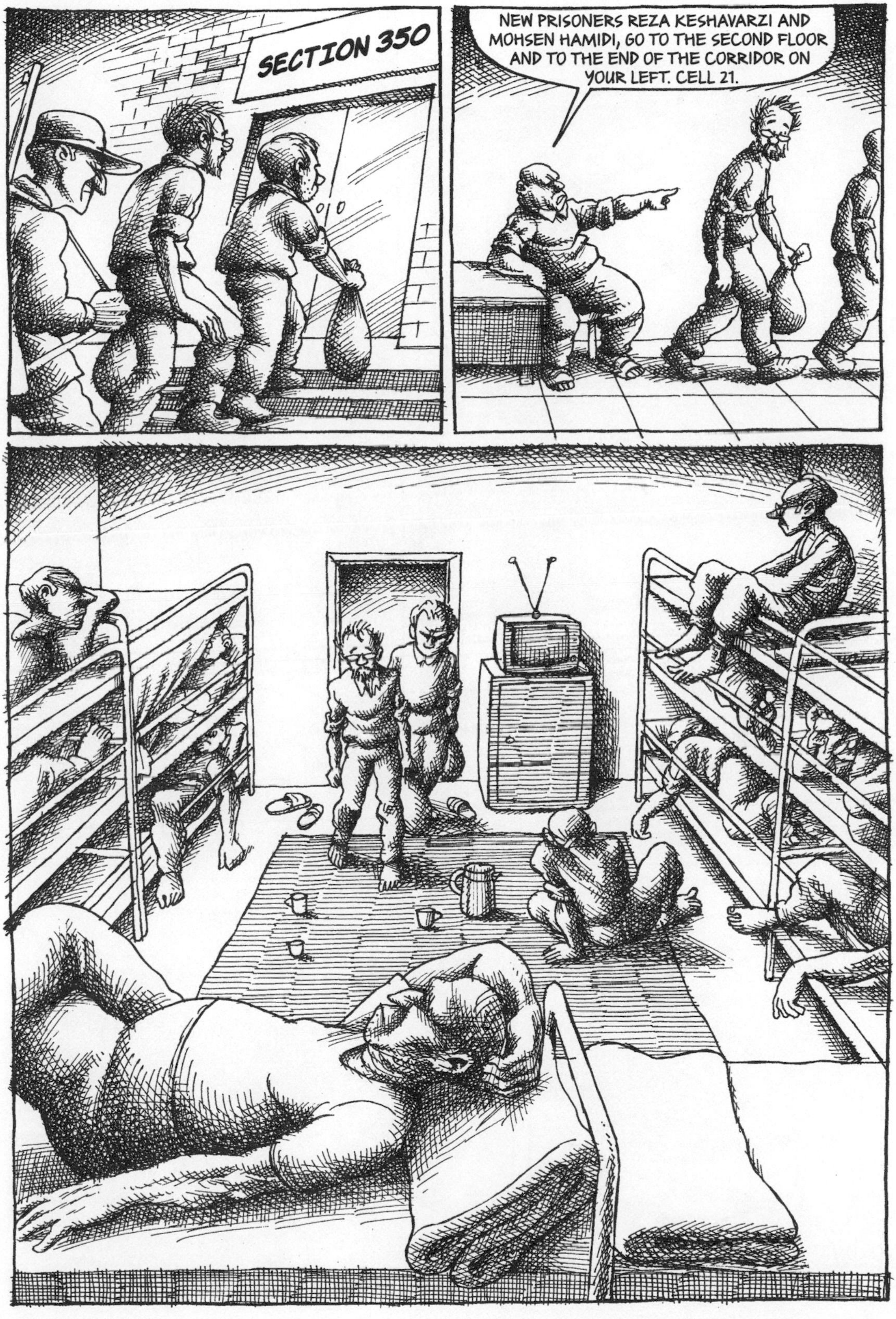
SECTION 350
NEW PRISONERS REZA KESHAVARZI AND MOHSEN HAMIDI, GO TO THE SECOND FLOOR AND TO THE END OF THE CORRIDOR ON YOUR LEFT. CELL 21.

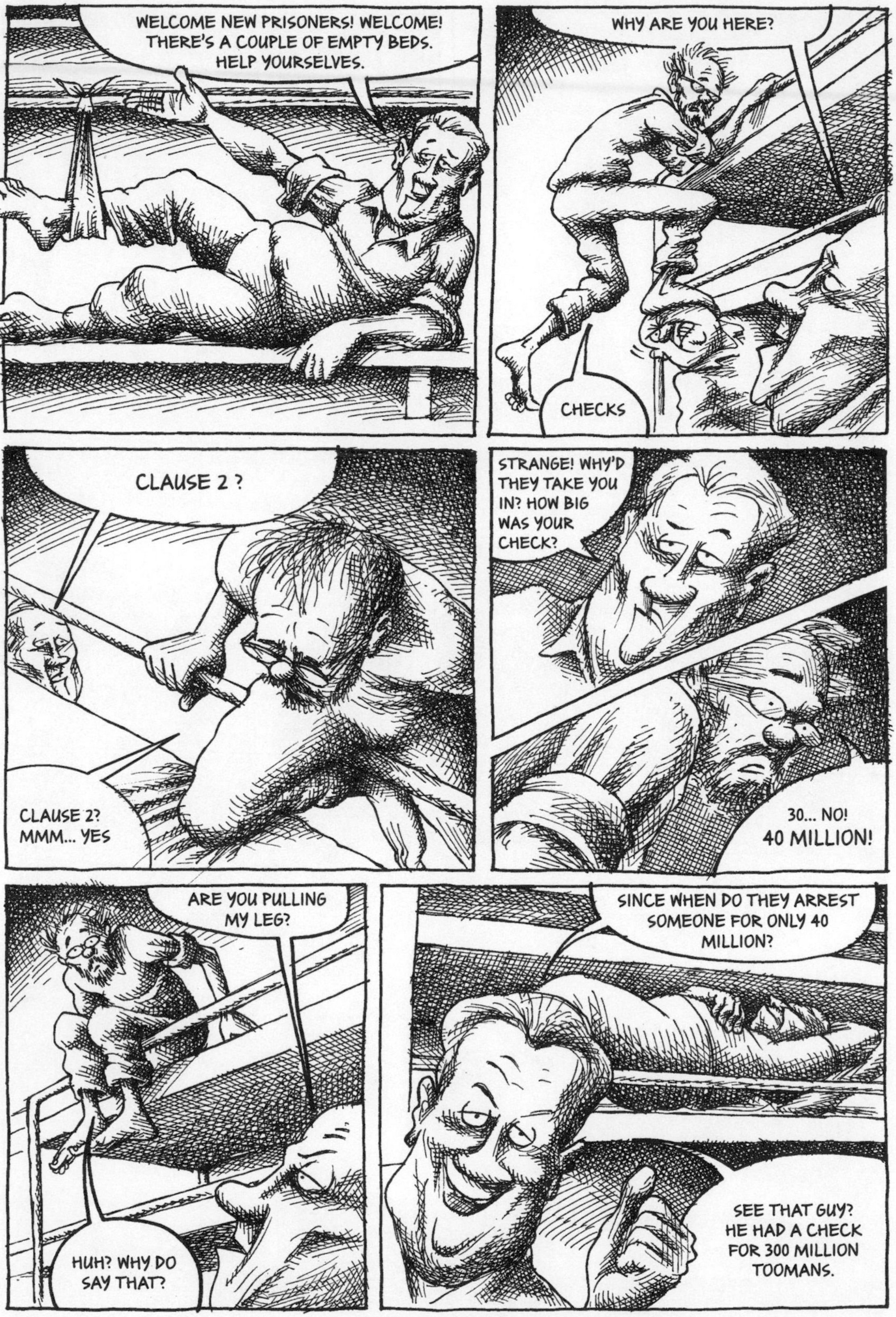
WELCOME NEW PRISONERS! WELCOME! THERE'S A COUPLE OF EMPTY BEDS. HELP YOURSELVES.
WHY ARE YOU HERE?
CHECKS
CLAUSE 2 ?
CLAUSE 2? MMM... YES
STRANGE! WHY'D THEY TAKE YOU IN? HOW BIG WAS YOUR CHECK?
30... NO! 40 MILLION!
ARE YOU PULLING MY LEG?
HUH? WHY DO SAY THAT?
SINCE WHEN DO THEY ARREST SOMEONE FOR ONLY 40 MILLION?
SEE THAT GUY? HE HAD A CHECK FOR 300 MILLION TOOMANS.

THAT GUY'S COMPANY WENT BANKRUPT. HE OWES A BILLIAN TOOMANS.

THAT GUY'S WIFE TOOK HIM TO COURT TO GET HIM TO PAY HER THE 400 MILLION MAHRIEH* HE PROMISED.

FUCKING BITCH!

I LAUNDERED 500 MILLION... IF YOU DON'T WANT TO TELL US WHY YOU ARE HERE, THAT'S FINE. JUST DON'T THINK YOU CAN FOOL US.

IF YOU WEREN'T A POLITICAL PRISONER YOU HAD TO WORK.

SCRUB THAT A/C UNIT! CAN YOU DO ANY-THING? OR JUST STEAL MONEY?

THAT EVENING WAS REST TIME IN THE COURTYARD.

LET'S SIT HERE.

*MAHRIEH IS A FORM OF MANDATORY PAYMENT, PAID BY THE GROOM OR BY THE GROOM'S FATHER, TO THE BRIDE AT THE TIME OF MARRIAGE THAT LEGALLY BECOMES HER PROPERTY.

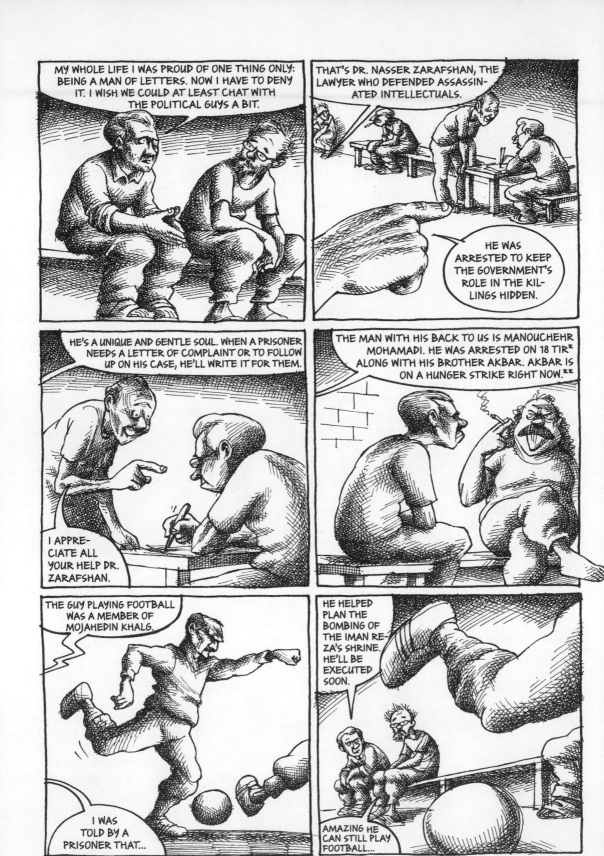

MY WHOLE LIFE I WAS PROUD OF ONE THING ONLY: BEING A MAN OF LETTERS. NOW I HAVE TO DENY IT. I WISH WE COULD AT LEAST CHAT WITH THE POLITICAL GUYS A BIT.

THAT'S DR. NASSER ZARAFSHAN, THE LAWYER WHO DEFENDED ASSASSIN-ATED INTELLECTUALS.

HE WAS ARRESTED TO KEEP THE GOVERNMENT'S ROLE IN THE KIL-LINGS HIDDEN.

HE'S A UNIQUE AND GENTLE SOUL. WHEN A PRISONER NEEDS A LETTER OF COMPLAINT OR TO FOLLOW UP ON HIS CASE, HE'LL WRITE IT FOR THEM.

I APPRE-CIATE ALL YOUR HELP DR. ZARAFSHAN.

THE MAN WITH HIS BACK TO US IS MANOUCHEHR MOHAMADI. HE WAS ARRESTED ON 18 TIR* ALONG WITH HIS BROTHER AKBAR. AKBAR IS ON A HUNGER STRIKE RIGHT NOW.**

THE GUY PLAYING FOOTBALL WAS A MEMBER OF MOJAHEDIN KHALG.

I WAS TOLD BY A PRISONER THAT...

HE HELPED PLAN THE BOMBING OF THE IMAN RE-ZA'S SHRINE. HE'LL BE EXECUTED SOON.

AMAZING HE CAN STILL PLAY FOOTBALL...

* JULY 9TH. ** TEN DAYS LATER AKBAR MOHAMADI DIED IN PRISON.

90

HELLO GENTLEMEN. YOU WEREN'T IN 209, THE INTELLIGENCE SECTION? WERE YOU?

SECTION... SECTION 209... OH NO! YOU MUST HAVE US CONFUSED WITH SOMEONE ELSE. I AM REZA KESHAVARZI, CHARGED WITH CHECK FRAUD.

AND I'M ABBAS, DUDE! YOU SURE YOU WEREN'T IN 209?

EVERYONE! LINE UP IN THE MIDDLE! TIME FOR A HEAD COUNT.

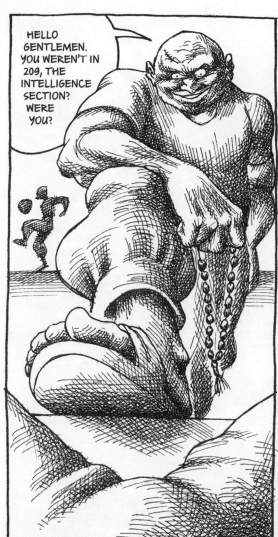

20... 30... 44... AND 3 OF THEM ARE IN THE HOSPITAL SO A TOTAL OF 47...

PSSST, HEY YOU!

WEREN'T YOU IN THE 209 SECTION?

NO. I DON'T KNOW WHAT YOU'RE TALKING ABOUT.

AND TWO ARE IN THE KITCHEN SO 49.

MEHRDAD, HOW DO THEY KNOW US?

I'VE NO IDEA.

GO BACK TO YOUR CELLS.

IT'S INTELLIGENCE; NO DOUBT ABOUT IT. THEY SNITCHED ON US.

REZA KESHA-VARZI!

THEY PROBABLY HAVE A PLAN TO MURDER US AND BLAME IT ON AN ANGRY AZERI PRISONER.

MR. REZA.

HEY! YOUR NAME IS REZA ISN'T IT? OR MAYBE YOU ARE DEAF?

YOU'RE ASSIGNED TO WORK AT THE BAKERY TOMORROW MORNING. BE HERE AT 6 AM. AND YOU LOOK LIKE A BUM.

GO STRAIGHT TO THE BARBER. GET A SHAVE AND A HAIRCUT.

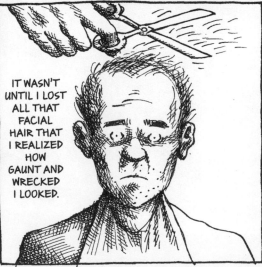

IT WASN'T UNTIL I LOST ALL THAT FACIAL HAIR THAT I REALIZED HOW GAUNT AND WRECKED I LOOKED.

NIGHTTIME

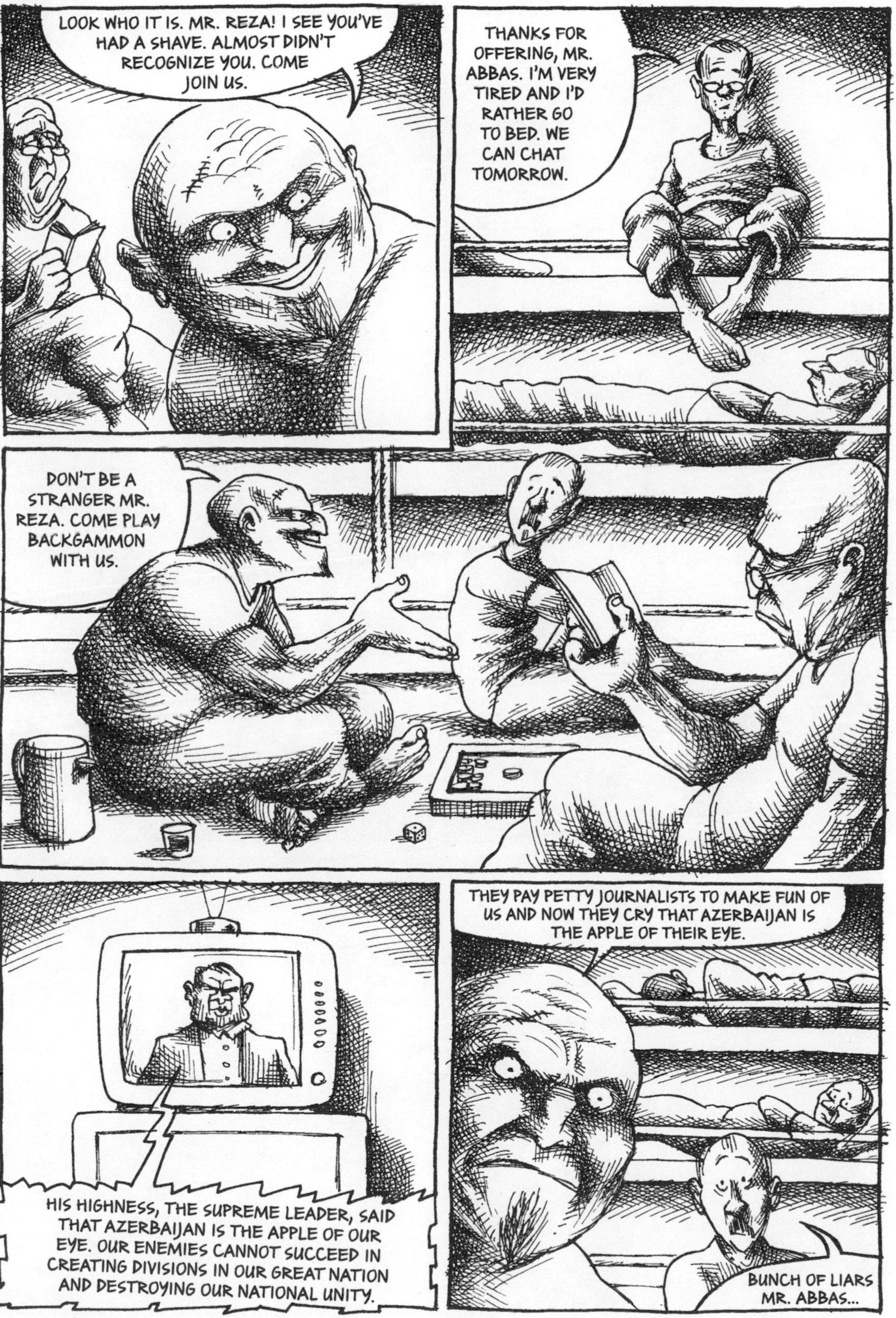
LOOK WHO IT IS. MR. REZA! I SEE YOU'VE HAD A SHAVE. ALMOST DIDN'T RECOGNIZE YOU. COME JOIN US.
THANKS FOR OFFERING, MR. ABBAS. I'M VERY TIRED AND I'D RATHER GO TO BED. WE CAN CHAT TOMORROW.
DON'T BE A STRANGER MR. REZA. COME PLAY BACKGAMMON WITH US.
HIS HIGHNESS, THE SUPREME LEADER, SAID THAT AZERBAIJAN IS THE APPLE OF OUR EYE. OUR ENEMIES CANNOT SUCCEED IN CREATING DIVISIONS IN OUR GREAT NATION AND DESTROYING OUR NATIONAL UNITY.
THEY PAY PETTY JOURNALISTS TO MAKE FUN OF US AND NOW THEY CRY THAT AZERBAIJAN IS THE APPLE OF THEIR EYE.
BUNCH OF LIARS MR. ABBAS...

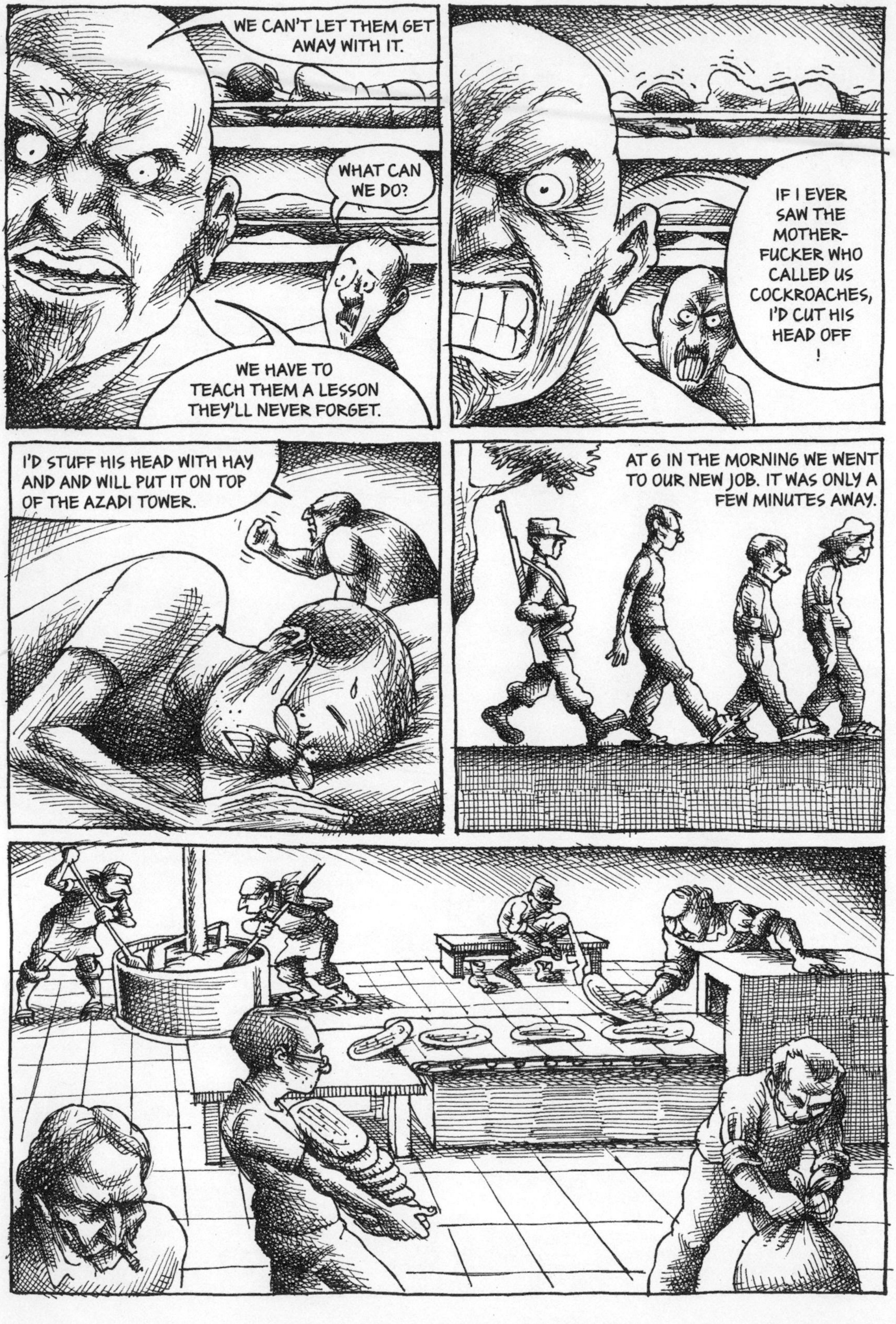

WE CAN'T LET THEM GET AWAY WITH IT.
WHAT CAN WE DO?
WE HAVE TO TEACH THEM A LESSON THEY'LL NEVER FORGET.
IF I EVER SAW THE MOTHER-FUCKER WHO CALLED US COCKROACHES, I'D CUT HIS HEAD OFF !
I'D STUFF HIS HEAD WITH HAY AND AND WILL PUT IT ON TOP OF THE AZADI TOWER.
AT 6 IN THE MORNING WE WENT TO OUR NEW JOB. IT WAS ONLY A FEW MINUTES AWAY.

REZA! YOU DON'T EVEN KNOW HOW TO PACK THE BREAD. ALL THE LOAVES ARE FUCKED...
I'M SORRY ...
AT NOON I WENT TO REST A BIT.
HELLO, EYEPATCH, STARVING CAT ...
STARVING EYEPATCHED CAT ...
HAVEN'T WE MET BEFORE ?
HUH?
CAN YOU SEE THE THRESHOLD? KEEP GOING.
I REALIZED THE BAKERY WAS DIRECTLY IN FRONT OF SECTION 209. TO PASS TIME THE WORKERS WATCHED THE INTELLIGENCE AGENCY PRISONERS. THAT'S HOW THEY KNEW US. NOT BECAUSE OF SOME CONSPIRACY, BUT SIMPLE STUPIDITY.

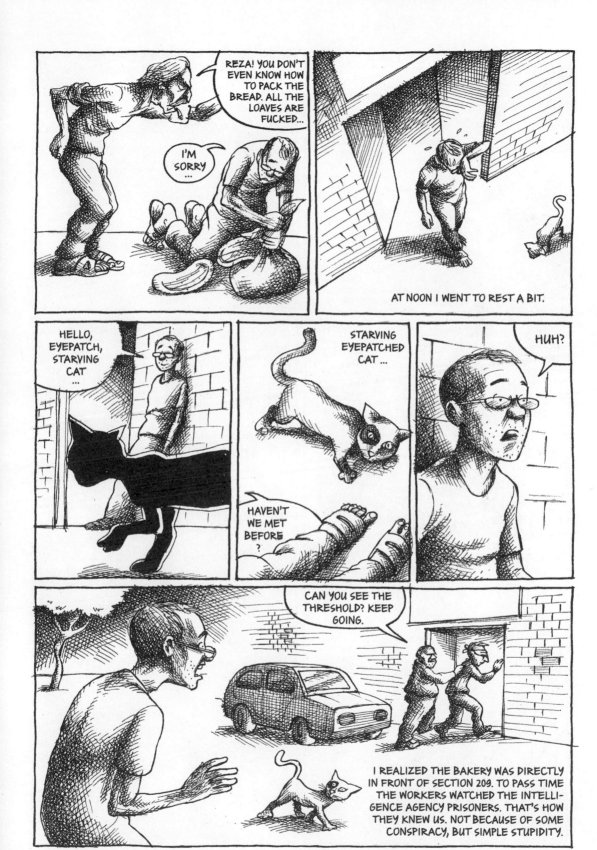

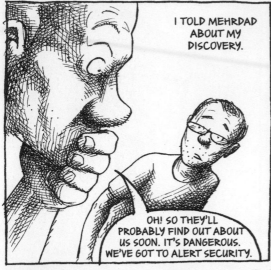

I TOLD MEHRDAD ABOUT MY DISCOVERY.

OH! SO THEY'LL PROBABLY FIND OUT ABOUT US SOON. IT'S DANGEROUS. WE'VE GOT TO ALERT SECURITY.

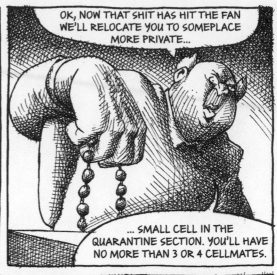

OK, NOW THAT SHIT HAS HIT THE FAN WE'LL RELOCATE YOU TO SOMEPLACE MORE PRIVATE...

... SMALL CELL IN THE QUARANTINE SECTION. YOU'LL HAVE NO MORE THAN 3 OR 4 CELLMATES.

THE QUARANTINE WAS THE FIRST SECTION OF EVIN PRISON; A KIND OF WAITING AREA.

GET IN THERE AND FUCK OFF!

PRISONERS WERE KEPT IN CELLS ON BOTH SIDES OF A LONG CORRIDOR FOR 24 HOURS. WHEN THEIR CASES FINISHED THEY'D BE MOVED TO OTHER SECTIONS OR OTHER PRISONS.

MOVE YOUR ASSES, IDIOTS.

THERE WERE FOUR MAIN ROOMS.

ONE WAS DEDICATED FOR EMBEZZLERS, CORRUPT LAWYERS, BRIBERS, BANKRUPT AND DEADBEAT MERCHANTS.

ANOTHER CELL KEPT NOVICE CRIMINALS, PETTY THEIVES, PICKPOCKETS AND OTHER GREENHORNS.

ONE CELL WAS FOR CRIMINAL VETERANS AND THOSE CHARGED WITH SERIOUS OFFENSES.

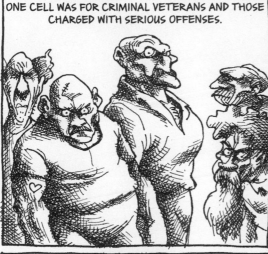

THE LAST ROOM WAS FOR AFGHANS ARRESTED FOR GOOD OR NO GOOD REASONS, BUT MAINLY FOR NOT HAVING THEIR DOCUMENTS WITH THEM.

THE "MAINTENANCE ROOM," FOR LONG-TERM PRISONERS WAS THE FIRST CELL IN THE CORRIDOR.

CHAPTER EIGHT:

THE POSSESSED

HELLO... I'M MOSHEN AND THIS IS REZA.

WE'RE IN FOR CHECK FRUAD.

HELLO. I'M AMIR BUT PEOPLE CALL ME THE ENGINEER. THIS IS ALI, MAJID AND ASQAR.

AND YOU'RE MEHRDAD AND MANA AND YOU'RE HERE FOR THE COCKROACH CASE. I TOOK YOUR FINGER-PRINTS THE OTHER DAY, REMEMBER?

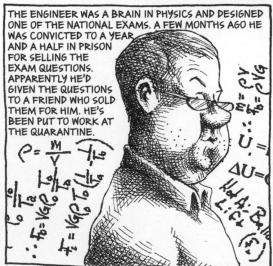

THE ENGINEER WAS A BRAIN IN PHYSICS AND DESIGNED ONE OF THE NATIONAL EXAMS. A FEW MONTHS AGO HE WAS CONVICTED TO A YEAR AND A HALF IN PRISON FOR SELLING THE EXAM QUESTIONS. APPARENTLY HE'D GIVEN THE QUESTIONS TO A FRIEND WHO SOLD THEM FOR HIM. HE'S BEEN PUT TO WORK AT THE QUARANTINE.

ALI WAS IN FOR NOT PAYING THE MAHRIEH HE PROMISED. THE FIRST TIME I SAW ALI, HE WAS TRYING TO DISCIPLINE OTHER PRISONERS AND I THOUGHT HE WAS ONE OF THE GUARDS. HE WAS HUGE AND INTIMIDATING.

HE HAD A SPLIT PERSONALITY. HE MERCILESSLY PUNISHED UNCOOPERATIVE PRISONERS. THIS COULD CAUSE HIM A HELL OF A LOT OF TROUBLE.

BUT WHILE WATCHING CARTOONS HE'D LAUGH LIKE A SEVEN YEAR OLD.

SHUT THE FUCK UP, YOU ASS! GET BACK TO YOUR CELL!

HA, HA, HA, HA, HA, HA!

MAHJID TAJERI WAS A DEADBEAT WHO'D GET DEEPLY DEPRESSED WITHOUT HIS PILLS. ALSO, HE SWORE PATHOLOGICALLY.

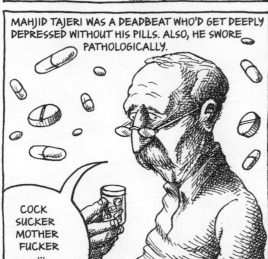

COCK SUCKER MOTHER FUCKER ...

ASQAR WAS A PROFESSIONAL FRAUD WITH A DECEPTIVE APPEARANCE. HE WAS HANDSOME AND GOOD AT CONVERSATION. HE TAUGHT HIMSELF A LOT ABOUT HEART DISEASES BY DOING EXTENSIVE RESEARCH.

HIS TRICK WAS TO GET HIRED AS A DOCTOR IN A HOSPITAL WITH FAKE QUALIFICATIONS.

SOON AFTER, HE'D INVITE A CURRENCY EXCHANGER TO THE HOSPITAL...

... PRETENDING HE HAD A LOT OF CURRENCY TO EXCHANGE. THEN HE'D GRAB THE DOLLARS...

AND LEAVE THE ROOM ON THE PRETEXT OF FETCHING HIS TOOMANS. INSTEAD HE'D FLEE.

BUT HE WASN'T VERY CREATIVE AND THE POLICE WERE EASILY ABLE TO TRAP AND ARREST HIM. HE WAS SERVING HIS 6TH YEAR.

WHEN WE MET HIM HE WAS PROMOTED TO HEAD OF THE CLEANERS. HE HAD A GOOD SENSE OF HUMOR.

MR. NEYESTANI, DON'T YOU AGREE THAT THIS IS NOT THE BEST USE OF A HEART SPECIALIST TO MAKE HIM RESPONSIBLE OVER FOUR MEASLY CLEANERS?

HEART SPECIALIST! HA HA HA HA!

THE CLEANERS WERE CHOSEN FROM THE AFGHAN DETAINEES. THEY WORKED FOR THE RIGHT TO MAKE A PHONE CALL.

NORMALLY THEY DIDN'T HAVE ANYONE TO RUN THEIR CASE FOR THEM. THEY WERE IN PRISON FOR MONTHS WITHOUT KNOWING WHAT'S GOING ON. THEY WERE TOTALLY OPPRESSED AND SUBMISSIVE.

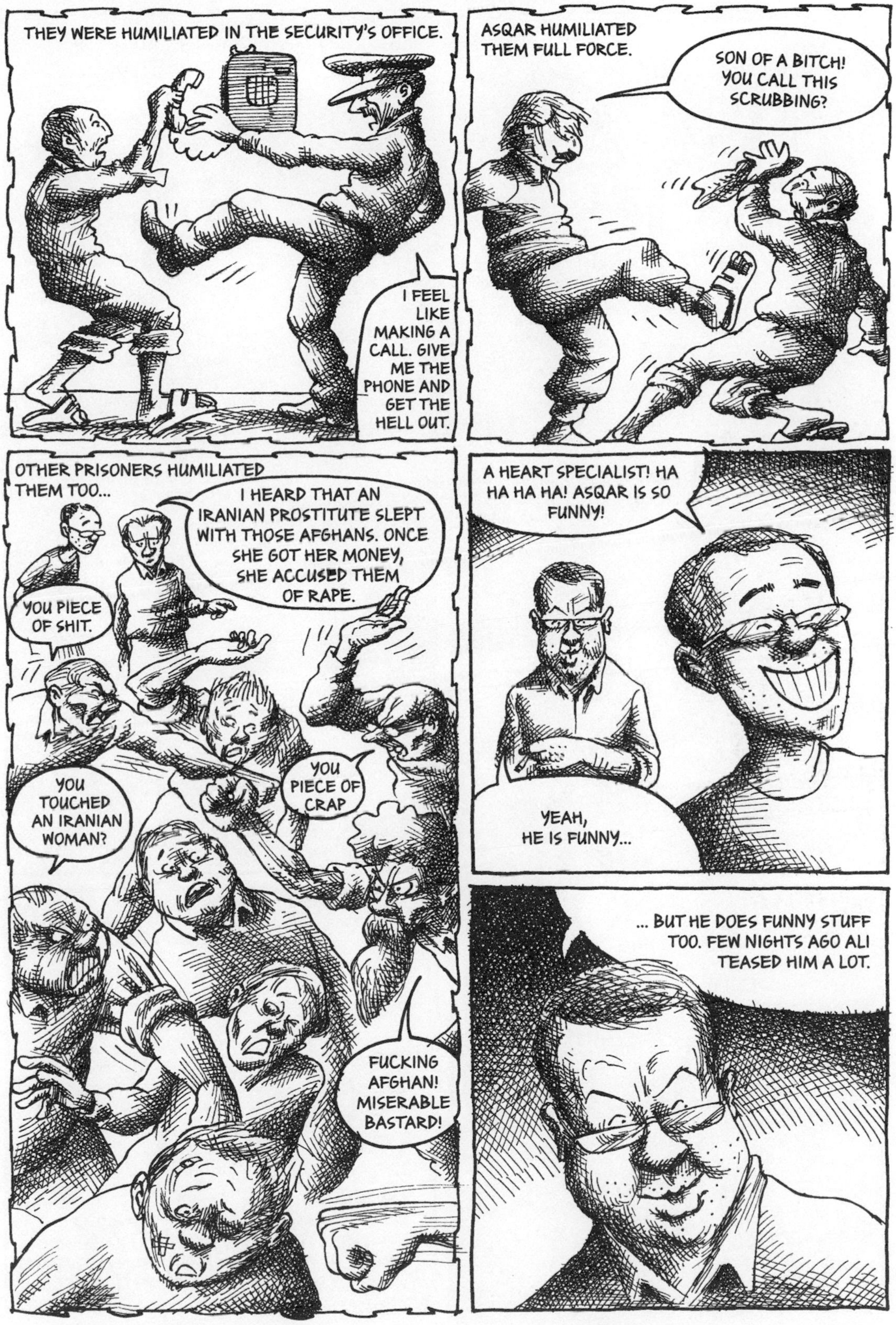
THEY WERE HUMILIATED IN THE SECURITY'S OFFICE.
I FEEL LIKE MAKING A CALL. GIVE ME THE PHONE AND GET THE HELL OUT.
ASQAR HUMILIATED THEM FULL FORCE.
SON OF A BITCH! YOU CALL THIS SCRUBBING?
OTHER PRISONERS HUMILIATED THEM TOO...
I HEARD THAT AN IRANIAN PROSTITUTE SLEPT WITH THOSE AFGHANS. ONCE SHE GOT HER MONEY, SHE ACCUSED THEM OF RAPE.
YOU PIECE OF SHIT.
YOU TOUCHED AN IRANIAN WOMAN?
YOU PIECE OF CRAP
FUCKING AFGHAN! MISERABLE BASTARD!
A HEART SPECIALIST! HA HA HA HA! ASQAR IS SO FUNNY!
YEAH, HE IS FUNNY...
... BUT HE DOES FUNNY STUFF TOO. FEW NIGHTS AGO ALI TEASED HIM A LOT.

AT MIDNIGHT ALI HEARD HARD BREATHING SOUNDS COMING FROM THE BATHROOM. WHEN HE OPENED THE DOOR HE SAW ASQAR SCREWING ANOTHER PRISONER. RIGHT WHEN HE WAS ABOUT TO COME, ALI SHRIEKED.

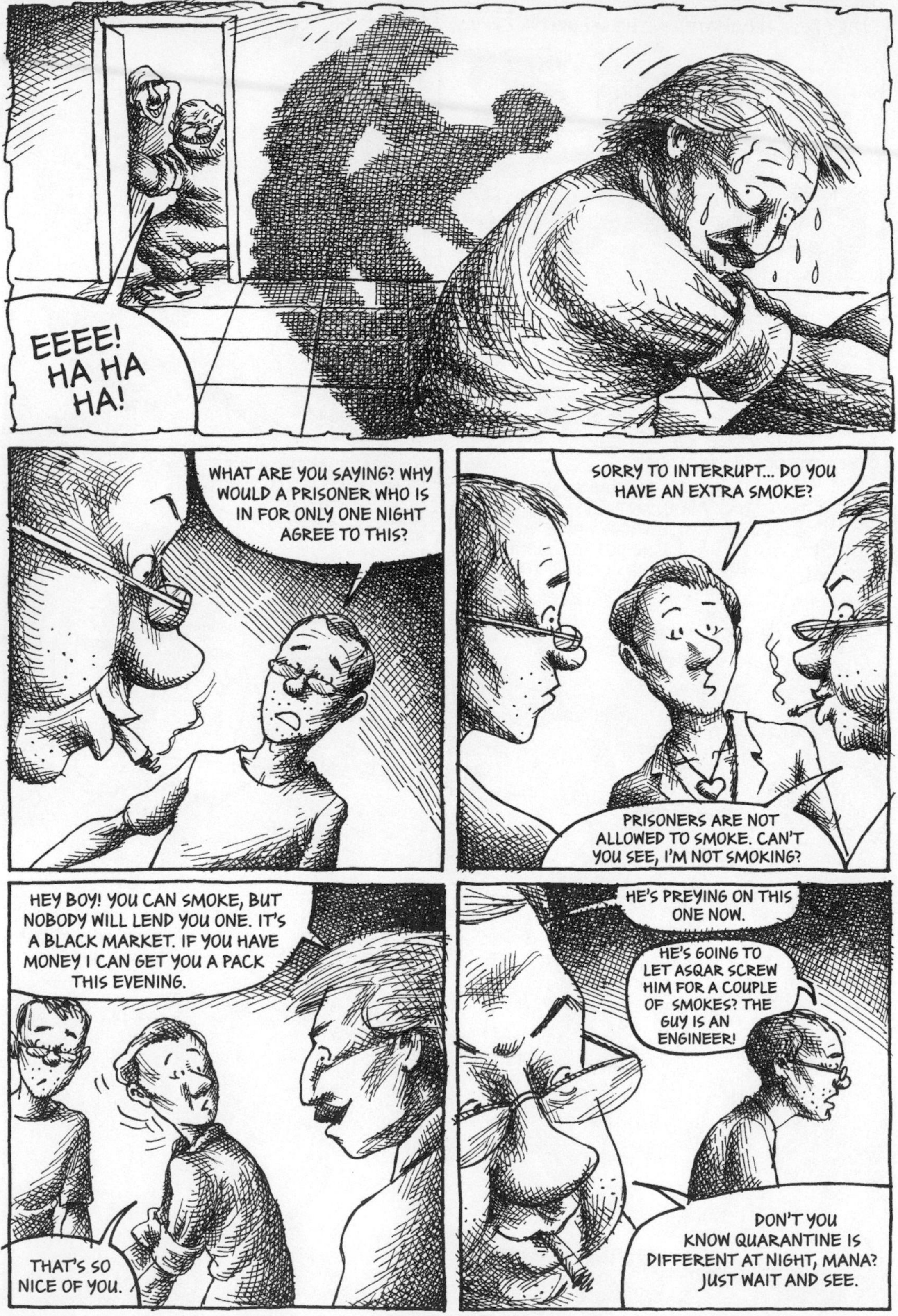
EEEE! HA HA HA!
WHAT ARE YOU SAYING? WHY WOULD A PRISONER WHO IS IN FOR ONLY ONE NIGHT AGREE TO THIS?
SORRY TO INTERRUPT... DO YOU HAVE AN EXTRA SMOKE?
PRISONERS ARE NOT ALLOWED TO SMOKE. CAN'T YOU SEE, I'M NOT SMOKING?
HEY BOY! YOU CAN SMOKE, BUT NOBODY WILL LEND YOU ONE. IT'S A BLACK MARKET. IF YOU HAVE MONEY I CAN GET YOU A PACK THIS EVENING.
THAT'S SO NICE OF YOU.
HE'S PREYING ON THIS ONE NOW.
HE'S GOING TO LET ASQAR SCREW HIM FOR A COUPLE OF SMOKES? THE GUY IS AN ENGINEER!
DON'T YOU KNOW QUARANTINE IS DIFFERENT AT NIGHT, MANA? JUST WAIT AND SEE.

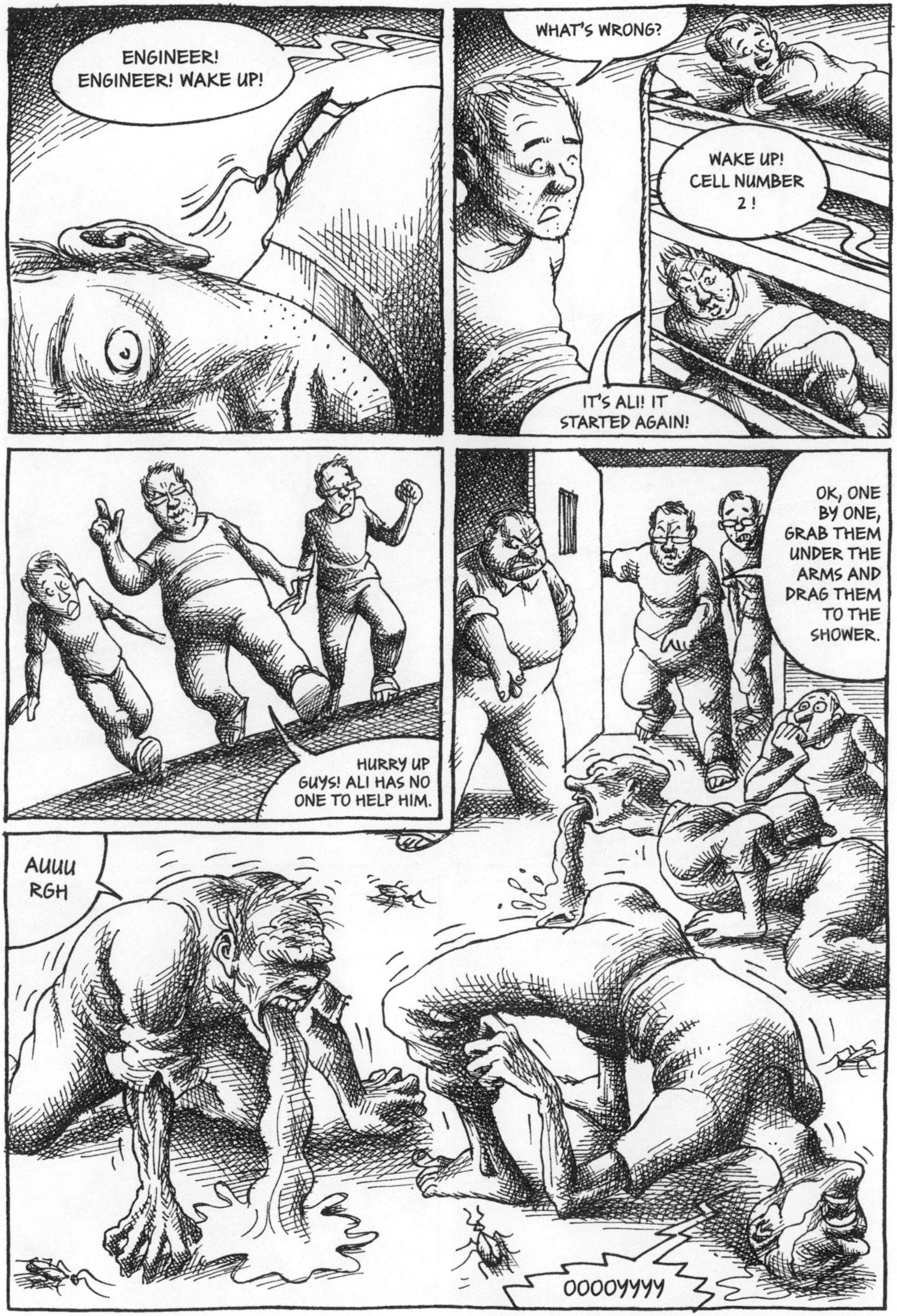
ENGINEER! ENGINEER! WAKE UP!
WHAT'S WRONG?
WAKE UP! CELL NUMBER 2 !
IT'S ALI! IT STARTED AGAIN!
HURRY UP GUYS! ALI HAS NO ONE TO HELP HIM.
OK, ONE BY ONE, GRAB THEM UNDER THE ARMS AND DRAG THEM TO THE SHOWER.
AUUU RGH
OOOOYYYY

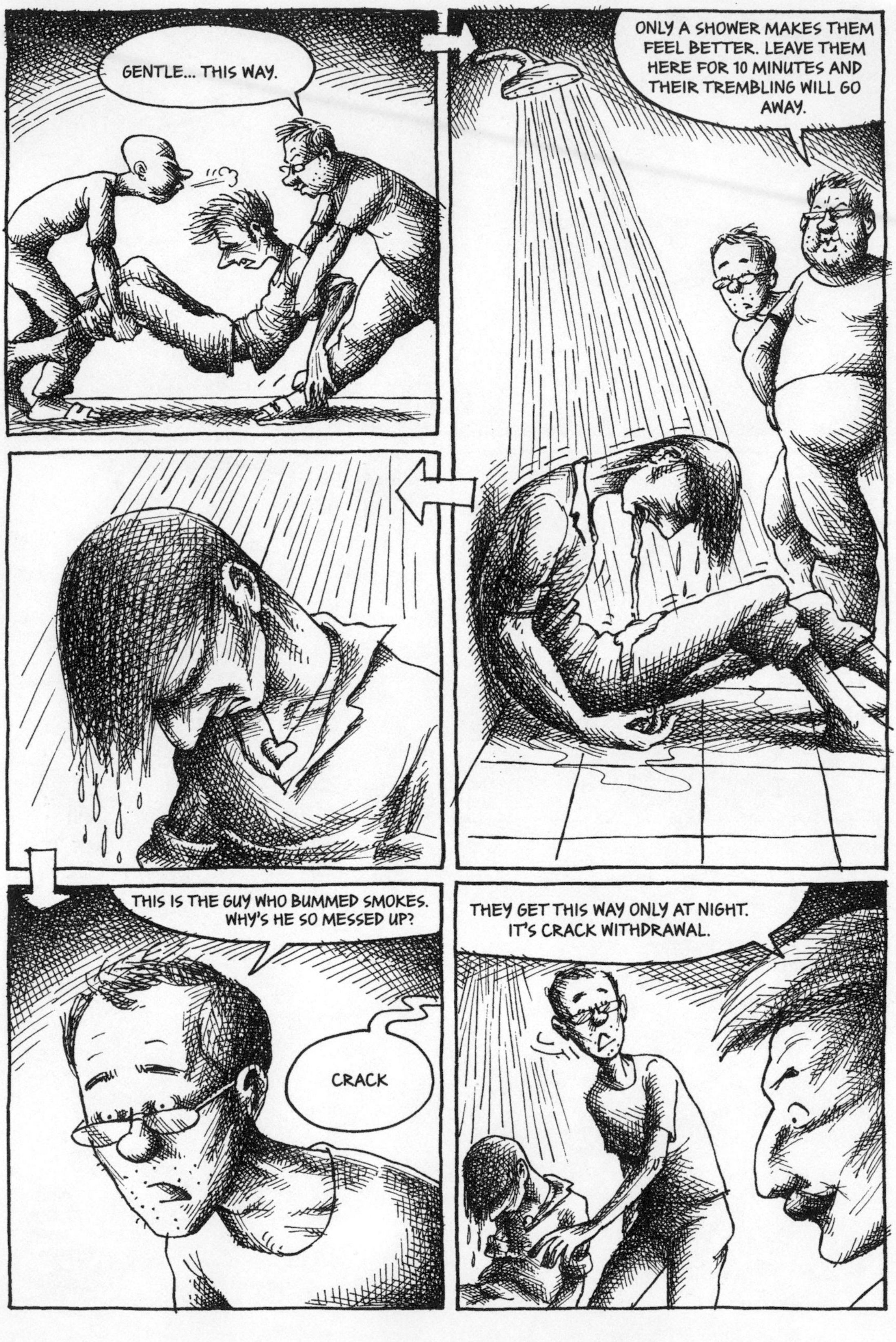
GENTLE... THIS WAY.
ONLY A SHOWER MAKES THEM FEEL BETTER. LEAVE THEM HERE FOR 10 MINUTES AND THEIR TREMBLING WILL GO AWAY.
THIS IS THE GUY WHO BUMMED SMOKES. WHY'S HE SO MESSED UP?
CRACK
THEY GET THIS WAY ONLY AT NIGHT. IT'S CRACK WITHDRAWAL.

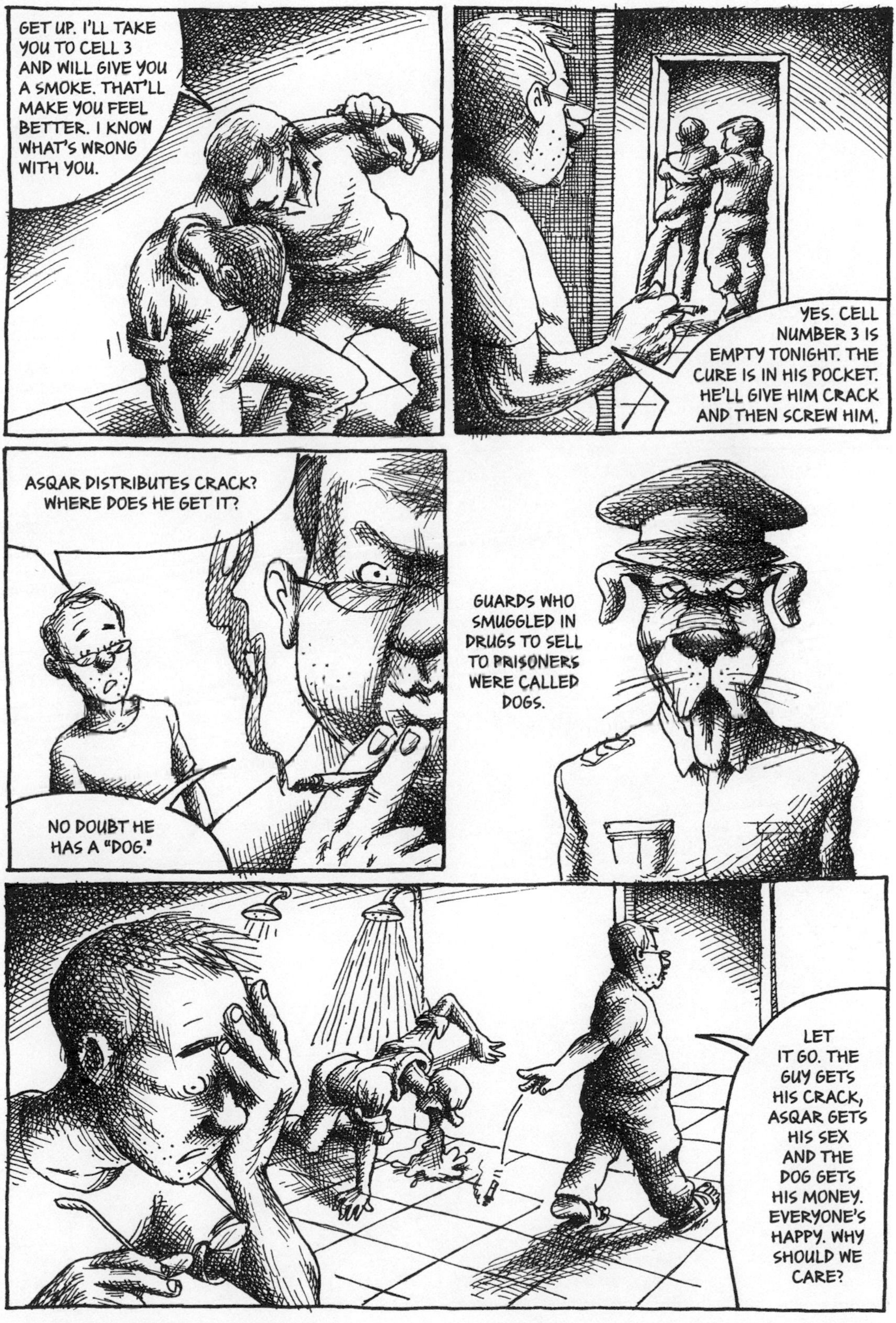
GET UP. I'LL TAKE YOU TO CELL 3 AND WILL GIVE YOU A SMOKE. THAT'LL MAKE YOU FEEL BETTER. I KNOW WHAT'S WRONG WITH YOU.
YES. CELL NUMBER 3 IS EMPTY TONIGHT. THE CURE IS IN HIS POCKET. HE'LL GIVE HIM CRACK AND THEN SCREW HIM.
ASQAR DISTRIBUTES CRACK? WHERE DOES HE GET IT?
NO DOUBT HE HAS A "DOG."
GUARDS WHO SMUGGLED IN DRUGS TO SELL TO PRISONERS WERE CALLED DOGS.
LET IT GO. THE GUY GETS HIS CRACK, ASQAR GETS HIS SEX AND THE DOG GETS HIS MONEY. EVERYONE'S HAPPY. WHY SHOULD WE CARE?

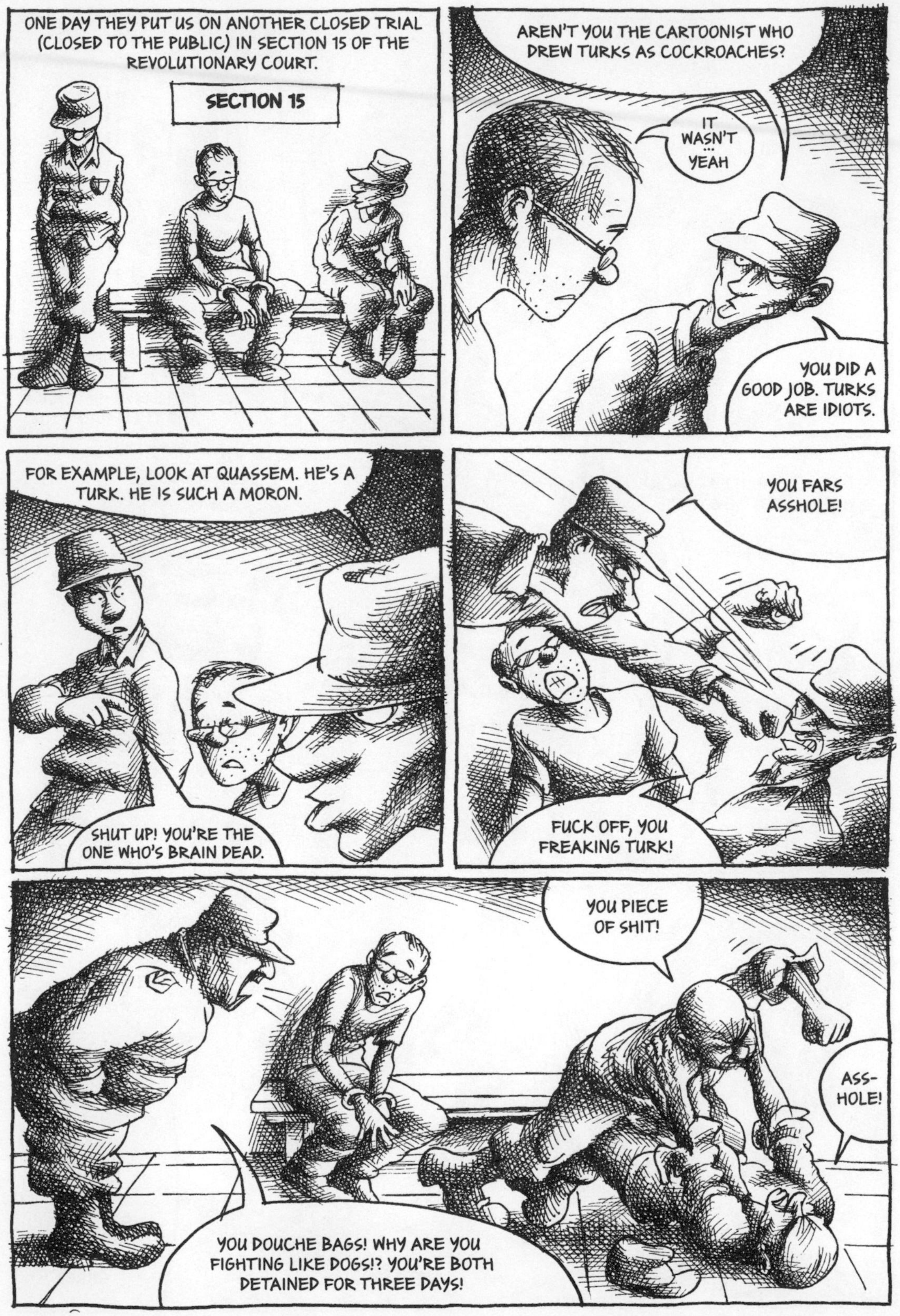
ONE DAY THEY PUT US ON ANOTHER CLOSED TRIAL (CLOSED TO THE PUBLIC) IN SECTION 15 OF THE REVOLUTIONARY COURT.
SECTION 15
AREN'T YOU THE CARTOONIST WHO DREW TURKS AS COCKROACHES?
IT WASN'T ... YEAH
YOU DID A GOOD JOB. TURKS ARE IDIOTS.
FOR EXAMPLE, LOOK AT QUASSEM. HE'S A TURK. HE IS SUCH A MORON.
SHUT UP! YOU'RE THE ONE WHO'S BRAIN DEAD.
YOU FARS ASSHOLE!
FUCK OFF, YOU FREAKING TURK!
YOU PIECE OF SHIT!
ASS-HOLE!
YOU DOUCHE BAGS! WHY ARE YOU FIGHTING LIKE DOGS!? YOU'RE BOTH DETAINED FOR THREE DAYS!

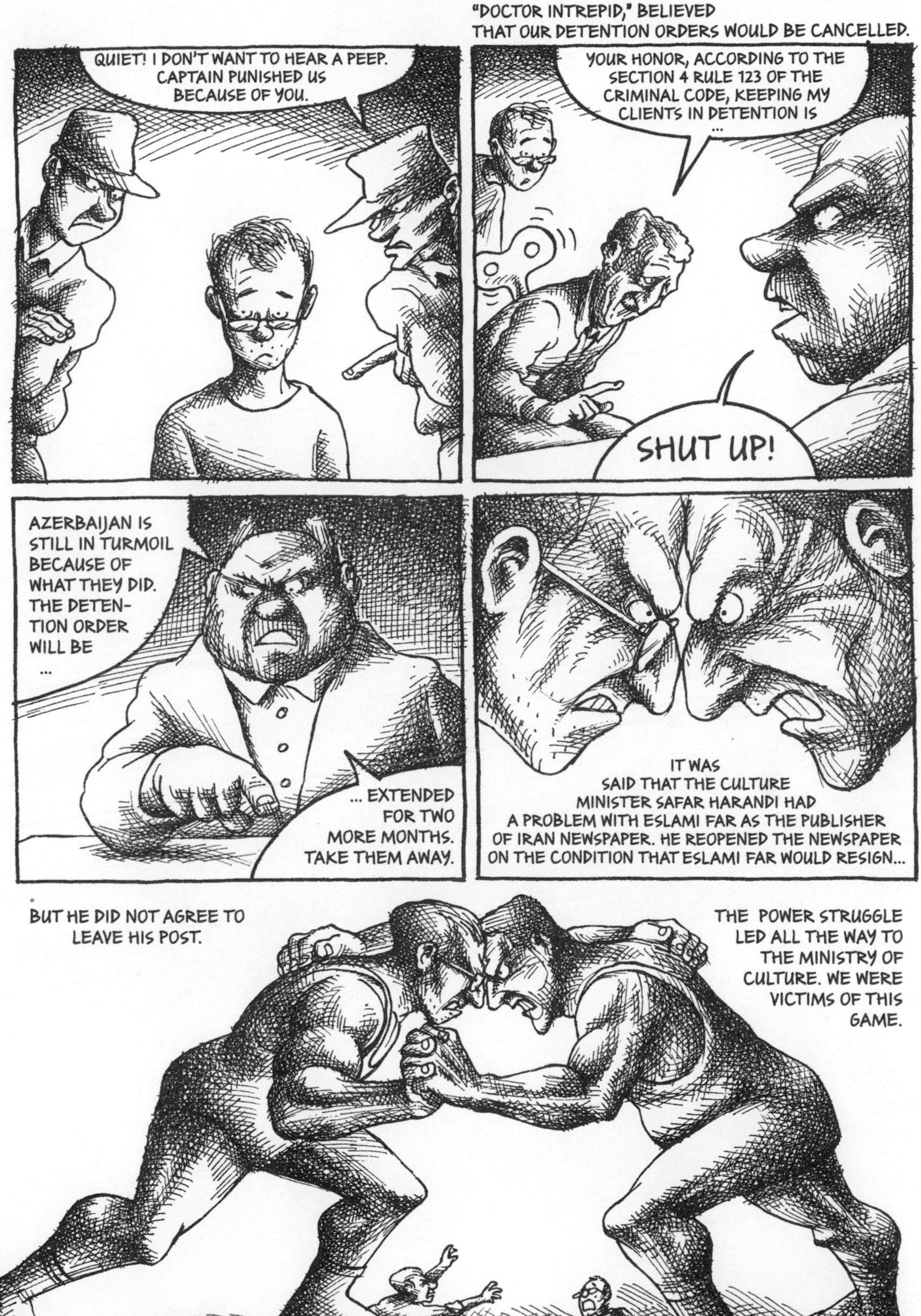
"DOCTOR INTREPID," BELIEVED THAT OUR DETENTION ORDERS WOULD BE CANCELLED.
QUIET! I DON'T WANT TO HEAR A PEEP. CAPTAIN PUNISHED US BECAUSE OF YOU.
YOUR HONOR, ACCORDING TO THE SECTION 4 RULE 123 OF THE CRIMINAL CODE, KEEPING MY CLIENTS IN DETENTION IS ...
SHUT UP!
AZERBAIJAN IS STILL IN TURMOIL BECAUSE OF WHAT THEY DID. THE DETENTION ORDER WILL BE ...
... EXTENDED FOR TWO MORE MONTHS. TAKE THEM AWAY.
IT WAS SAID THAT THE CULTURE MINISTER SAFAR HARANDI HAD A PROBLEM WITH ESLAMI FAR AS THE PUBLISHER OF IRAN NEWSPAPER. HE REOPENED THE NEWSPAPER ON THE CONDITION THAT ESLAMI FAR WOULD RESIGN...
BUT HE DID NOT AGREE TO LEAVE HIS POST.
THE POWER STRUGGLE LED ALL THE WAY TO THE MINISTRY OF CULTURE. WE WERE VICTIMS OF THIS GAME.

CHAPTER NINE:

THE NUT WHO NEVER PARTED WITH HIS BAG

I DIDN'T KNOW WHEN I WOULD BE WITH MANSOUREH AGAIN.

I HAD A PICTURE OF HER WITH ME.
IT HELPED ME FEEL HER PRESENCE BESIDE ME.

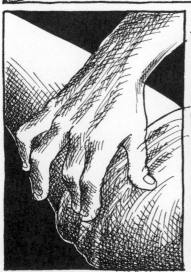

112

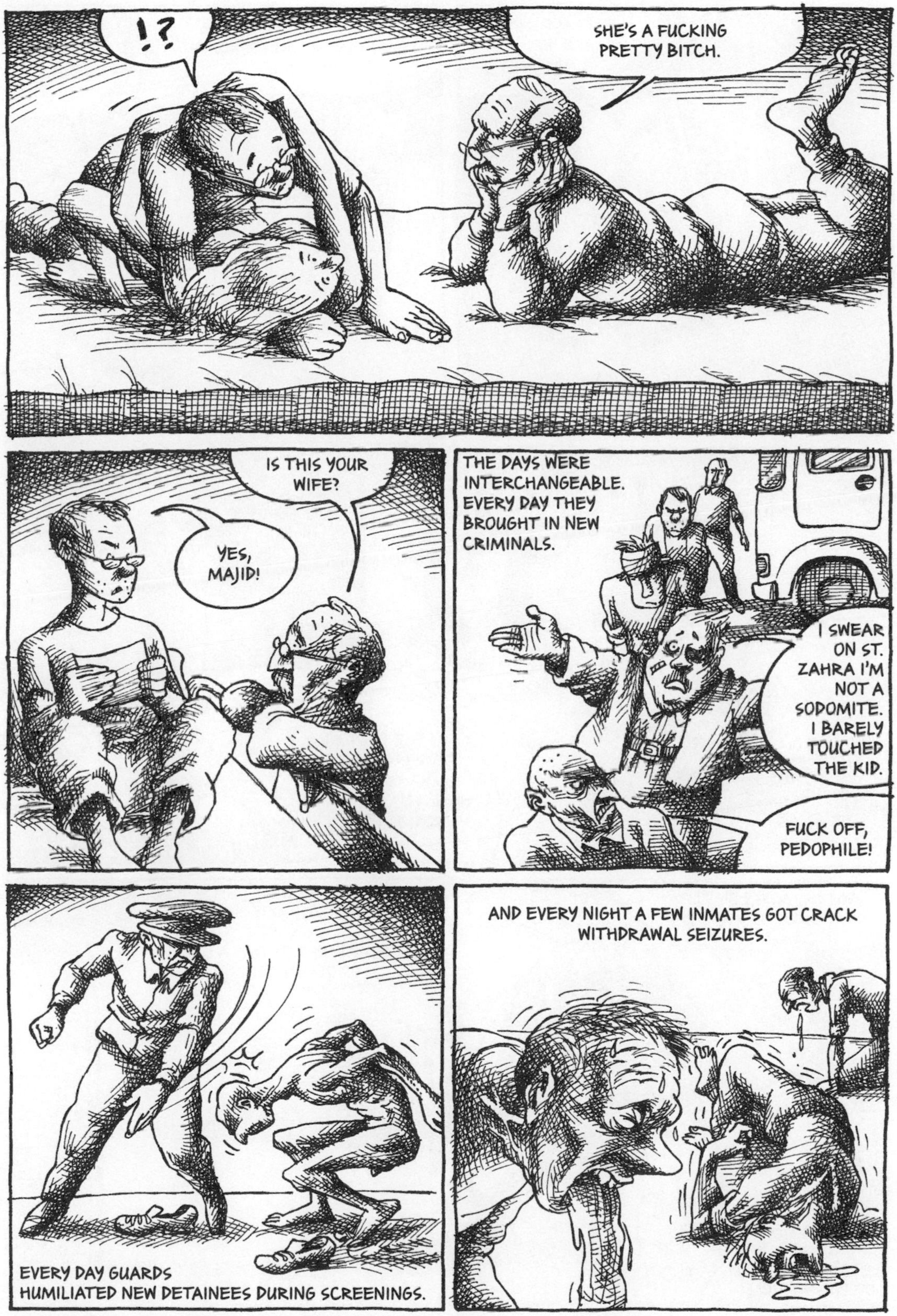
!?
SHE'S A FUCKING PRETTY BITCH.
IS THIS YOUR WIFE?
YES, MAJID!
THE DAYS WERE INTERCHANGEABLE. EVERY DAY THEY BROUGHT IN NEW CRIMINALS.
I SWEAR ON ST. ZAHRA I'M NOT A SODOMITE. I BARELY TOUCHED THE KID.
FUCK OFF, PEDOPHILE!
EVERY DAY GUARDS HUMILIATED NEW DETAINEES DURING SCREENINGS.
AND EVERY NIGHT A FEW INMATES GOT CRACK WITHDRAWAL SEIZURES.

MIDNIGHT.

GUAAARD! WHERE ARE YOU, YOU BASTARD!

SHUT UP! THIS BETTER BE IMPORTANT AT THIS TIME OF THE NIGHT!

S...SORRY... BUT...

YOU BETTER SEE FOR YOURSELF.

THE IDIOT WHO ALWAYS HOLDS ON TO HIS BAG SHIT BY THE WALL. WE CAN'T SLEEP FROM THE SMELL!

WHAT'S GOING ON ALI? WHAT'S WRONG WITH HIM?

HE CRAPPED BY THE WALL AND NOW HE WON'T LET ME TAKE HIM TO THE BATHROOM. FOR SUCH A SCRAWNY GUY HE HAS A LOT OF STRENGTH!

STRENGTH! LET ME TAKE CARE OF THIS ASSHOLE.

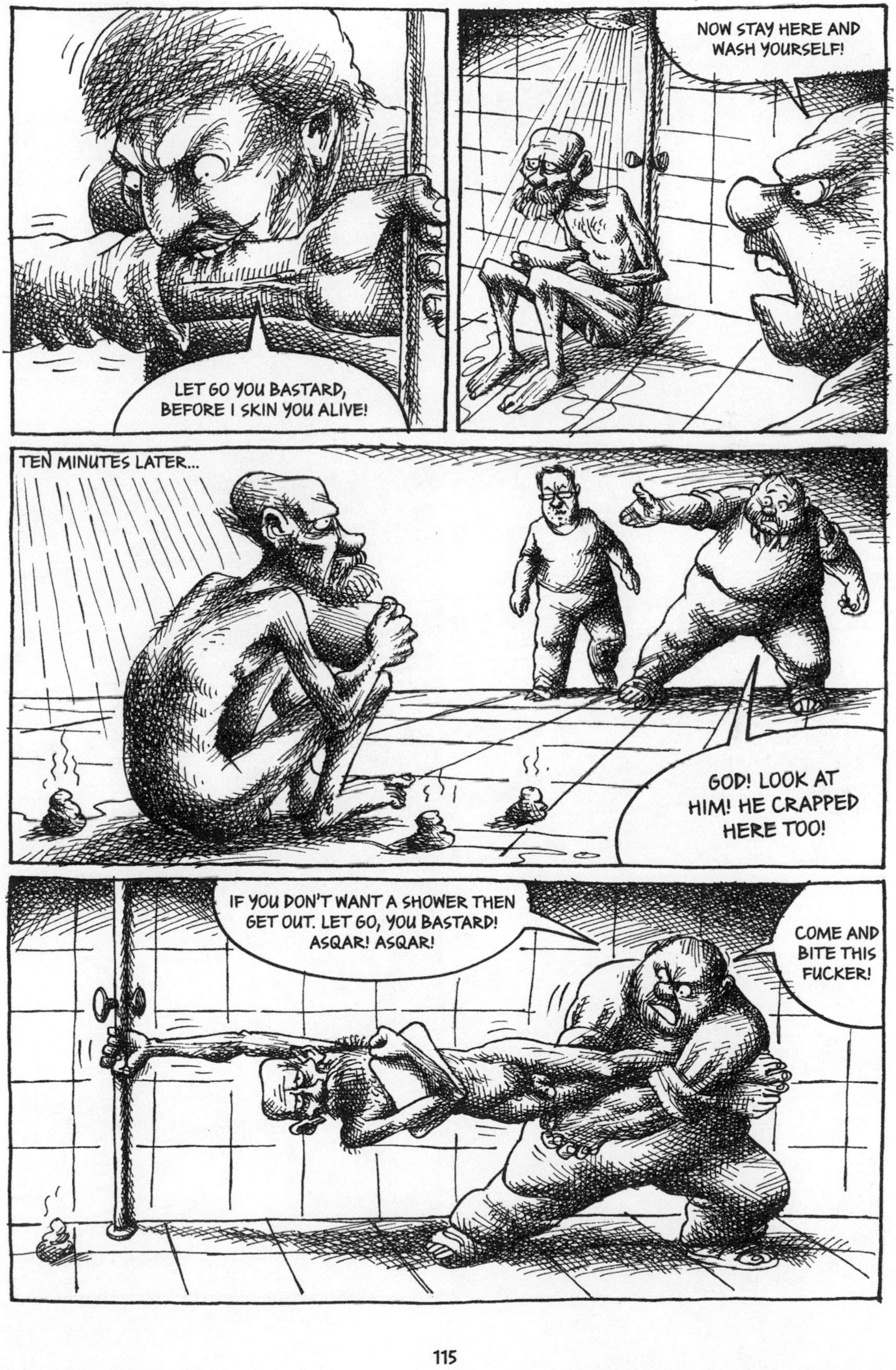
LET GO YOU BASTARD, BEFORE I SKIN YOU ALIVE!
NOW STAY HERE AND WASH YOURSELF!
TEN MINUTES LATER...
GOD! LOOK AT HIM! HE CRAPPED HERE TOO!
IF YOU DON'T WANT A SHOWER THEN GET OUT. LET GO, YOU BASTARD! ASQAR! ASQAR!
COME AND BITE THIS FUCKER!

AS A PUNISHMENT HE WAS LEFT NAKED IN THE COURTYARD

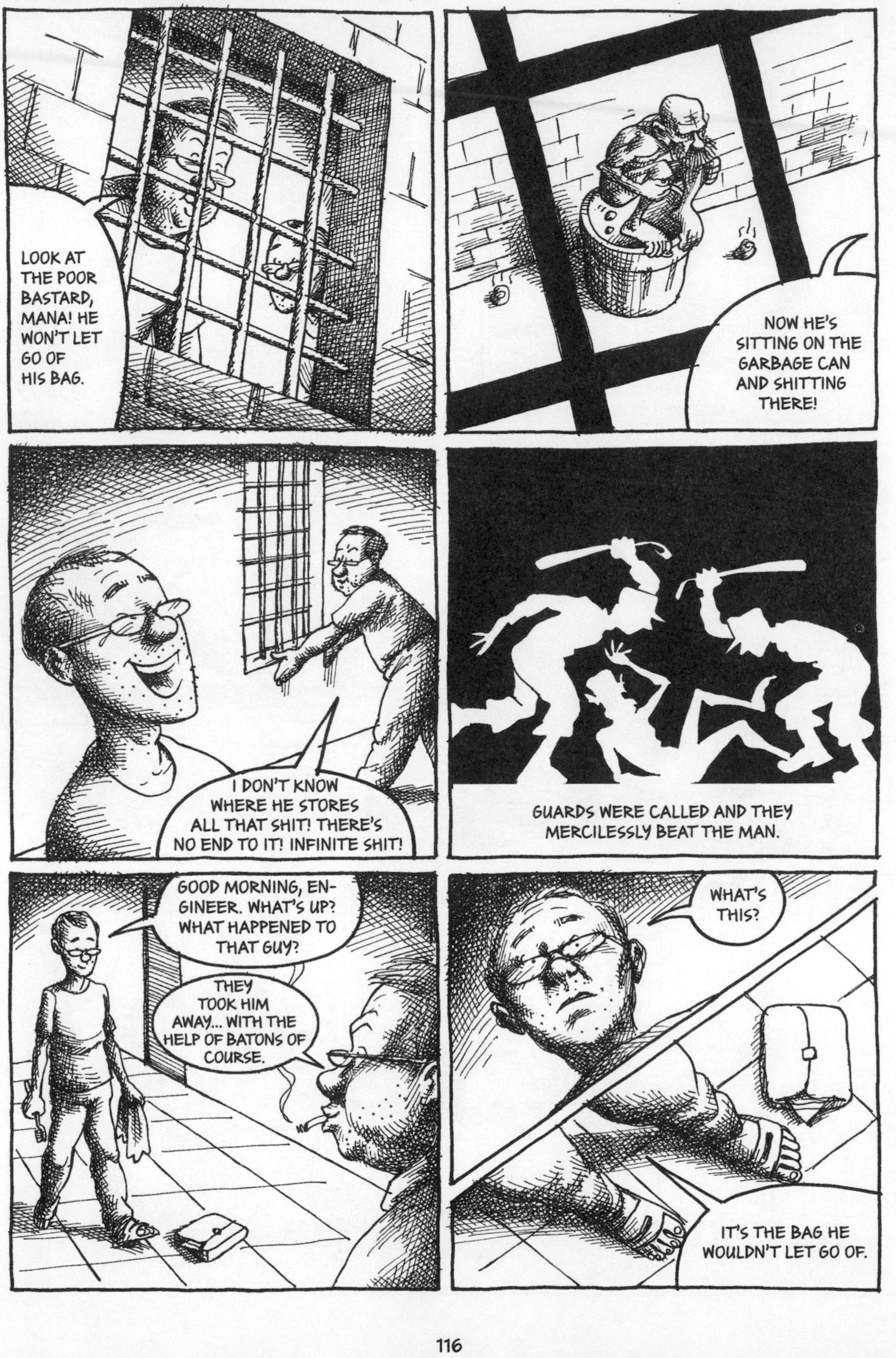
LOOK AT THE POOR BASTARD, MANA! HE WON'T LET GO OF HIS BAG.
NOW HE'S SITTING ON THE GARBAGE CAN AND SHITTING THERE!
I DON'T KNOW WHERE HE STORES ALL THAT SHIT! THERE'S NO END TO IT! INFINITE SHIT!
GUARDS WERE CALLED AND THEY MERCILESSLY BEAT THE MAN.
GOOD MORNING, ENGINEER. WHAT'S UP? WHAT HAPPENED TO THAT GUY?
THEY TOOK HIM AWAY... WITH THE HELP OF BATONS OF COURSE.
WHAT'S THIS?
IT'S THE BAG HE WOULDN'T LET GO OF.

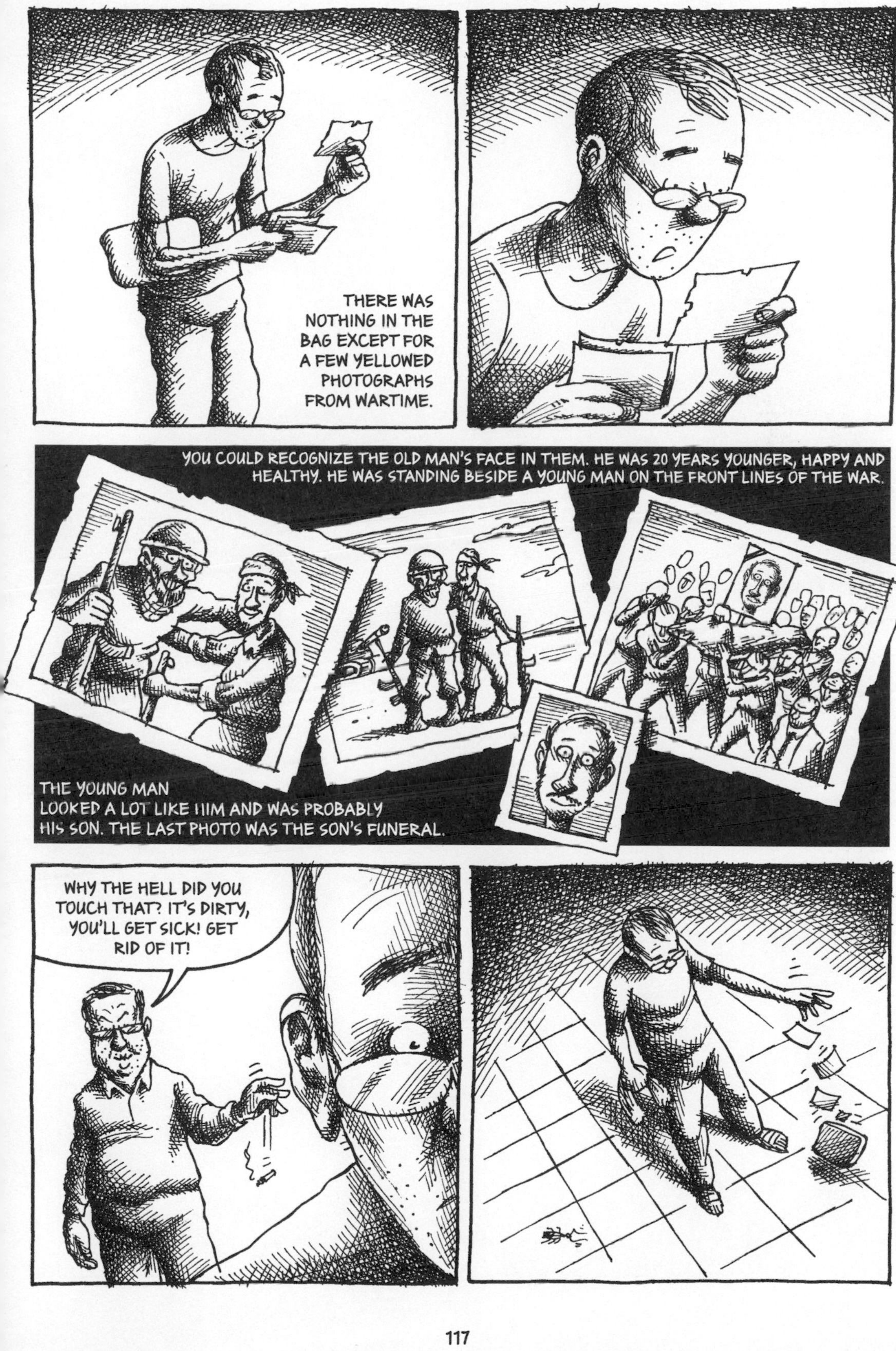

THERE WAS NOTHING IN THE BAG EXCEPT FOR A FEW YELLOWED PHOTOGRAPHS FROM WARTIME.
YOU COULD RECOGNIZE THE OLD MAN'S FACE IN THEM. HE WAS 20 YEARS YOUNGER, HAPPY AND HEALTHY. HE WAS STANDING BESIDE A YOUNG MAN ON THE FRONT LINES OF THE WAR.
THE YOUNG MAN LOOKED A LOT LIKE HIM AND WAS PROBABLY HIS SON. THE LAST PHOTO WAS THE SON'S FUNERAL.
WHY THE HELL DID YOU TOUCH THAT? IT'S DIRTY, YOU'LL GET SICK! GET RID OF IT!

CHAPTER TEN:

FREEDOM MEANS...

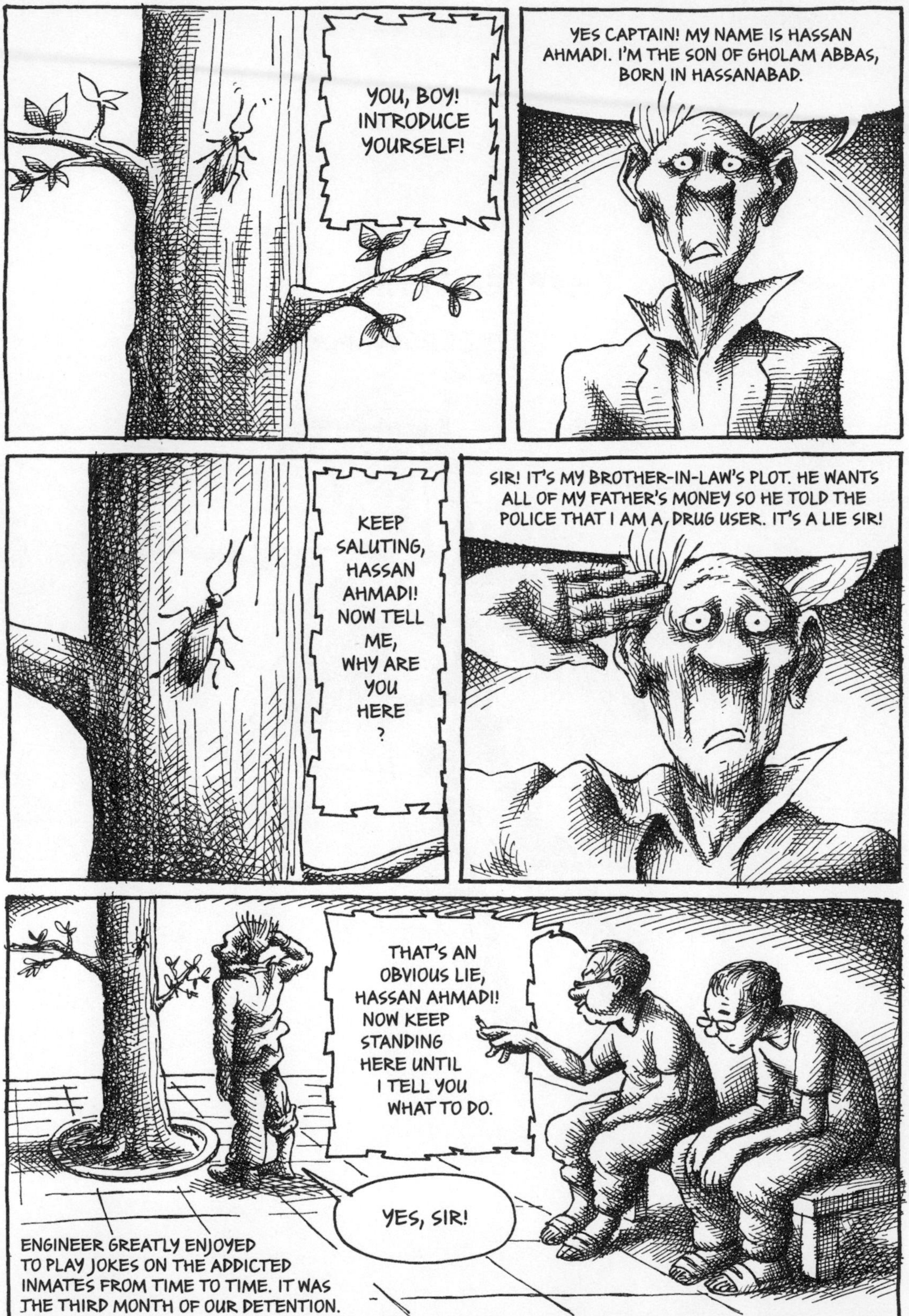
YOU, BOY! INTRODUCE YOURSELF!
YES CAPTAIN! MY NAME IS HASSAN AHMADI. I'M THE SON OF GHOLAM ABBAS, BORN IN HASSANABAD.
KEEP SALUTING, HASSAN AHMADI! NOW TELL ME, WHY ARE YOU HERE ?
SIR! IT'S MY BROTHER-IN-LAW'S PLOT. HE WANTS ALL OF MY FATHER'S MONEY SO HE TOLD THE POLICE THAT I AM A DRUG USER. IT'S A LIE SIR!
THAT'S AN OBVIOUS LIE, HASSAN AHMADI! NOW KEEP STANDING HERE UNTIL I TELL YOU WHAT TO DO.
YES, SIR!
ENGINEER GREATLY ENJOYED TO PLAY JOKES ON THE ADDICTED INMATES FROM TIME TO TIME. IT WAS THE THIRD MONTH OF OUR DETENTION.

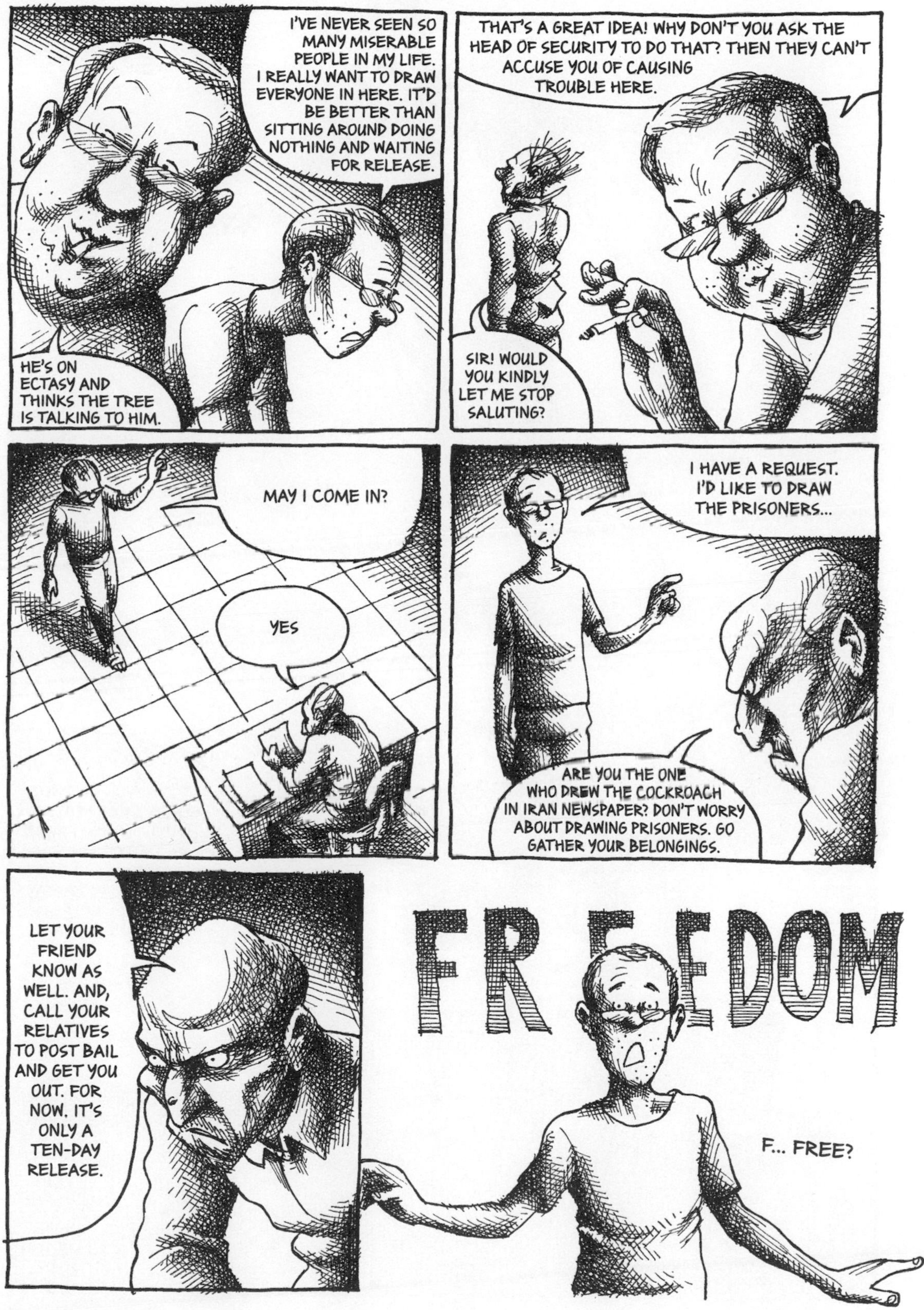
I'VE NEVER SEEN SO MANY MISERABLE PEOPLE IN MY LIFE. I REALLY WANT TO DRAW EVERYONE IN HERE. IT'D BE BETTER THAN SITTING AROUND DOING NOTHING AND WAITING FOR RELEASE.
HE'S ON ECTASY AND THINKS THE TREE IS TALKING TO HIM.
THAT'S A GREAT IDEA! WHY DON'T YOU ASK THE HEAD OF SECURITY TO DO THAT? THEN THEY CAN'T ACCUSE YOU OF CAUSING TROUBLE HERE.
SIR! WOULD YOU KINDLY LET ME STOP SALUTING?
MAY I COME IN?
YES
I HAVE A REQUEST. I'D LIKE TO DRAW THE PRISONERS...
ARE YOU THE ONE WHO DREW THE COCKROACH IN IRAN NEWSPAPER? DON'T WORRY ABOUT DRAWING PRISONERS. GO GATHER YOUR BELONGINGS.
LET YOUR FRIEND KNOW AS WELL. AND, CALL YOUR RELATIVES TO POST BAIL AND GET YOU OUT. FOR NOW, IT'S ONLY A TEN-DAY RELEASE.
FREEDOM
F... FREE?

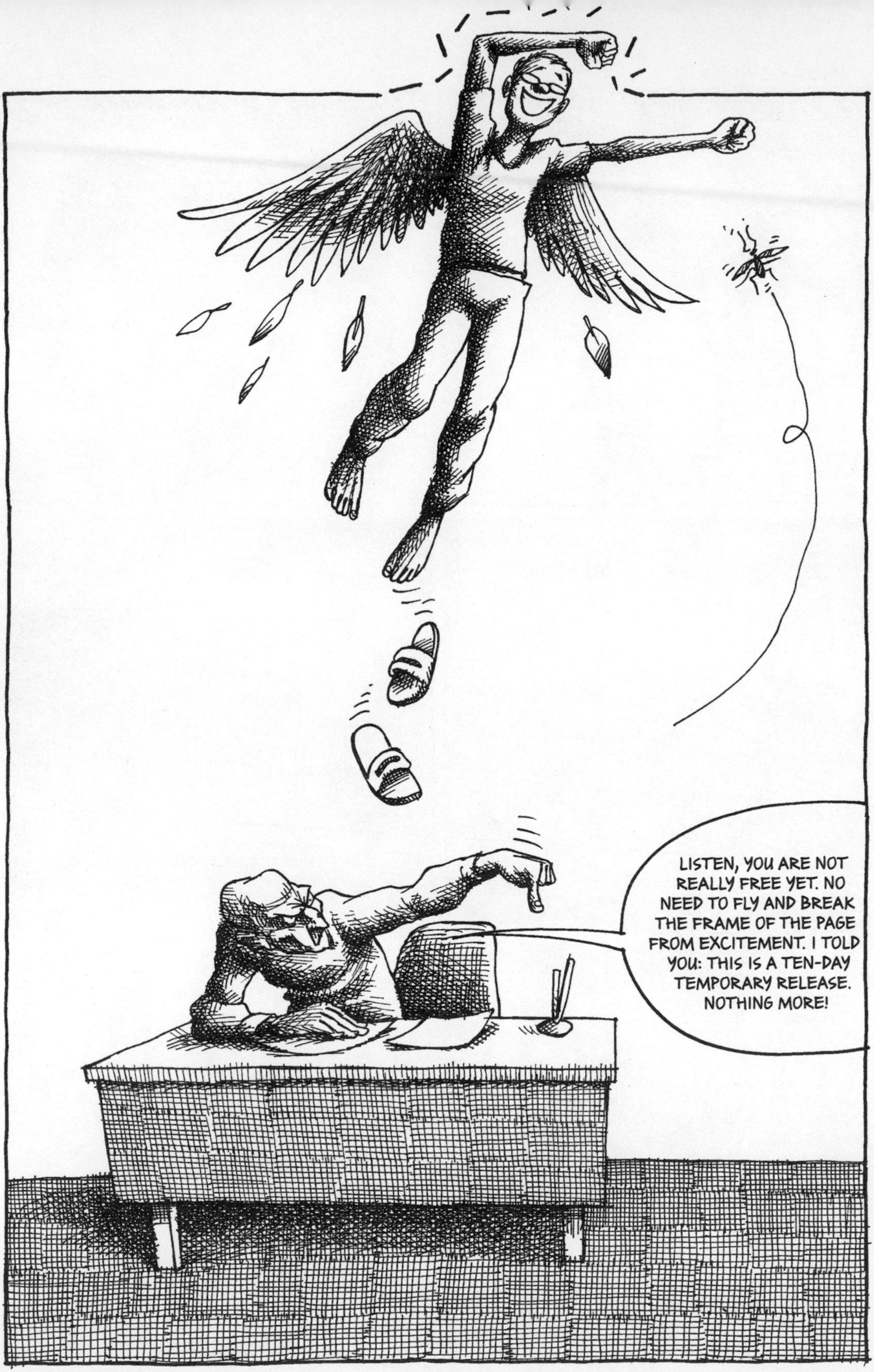
LISTEN, YOU ARE NOT REALLY FREE YET. NO NEED TO FLY AND BREAK THE FRAME OF THE PAGE FROM EXCITEMENT. I TOLD YOU: THIS IS A TEN-DAY TEMPORARY RELEASE. NOTHING MORE!

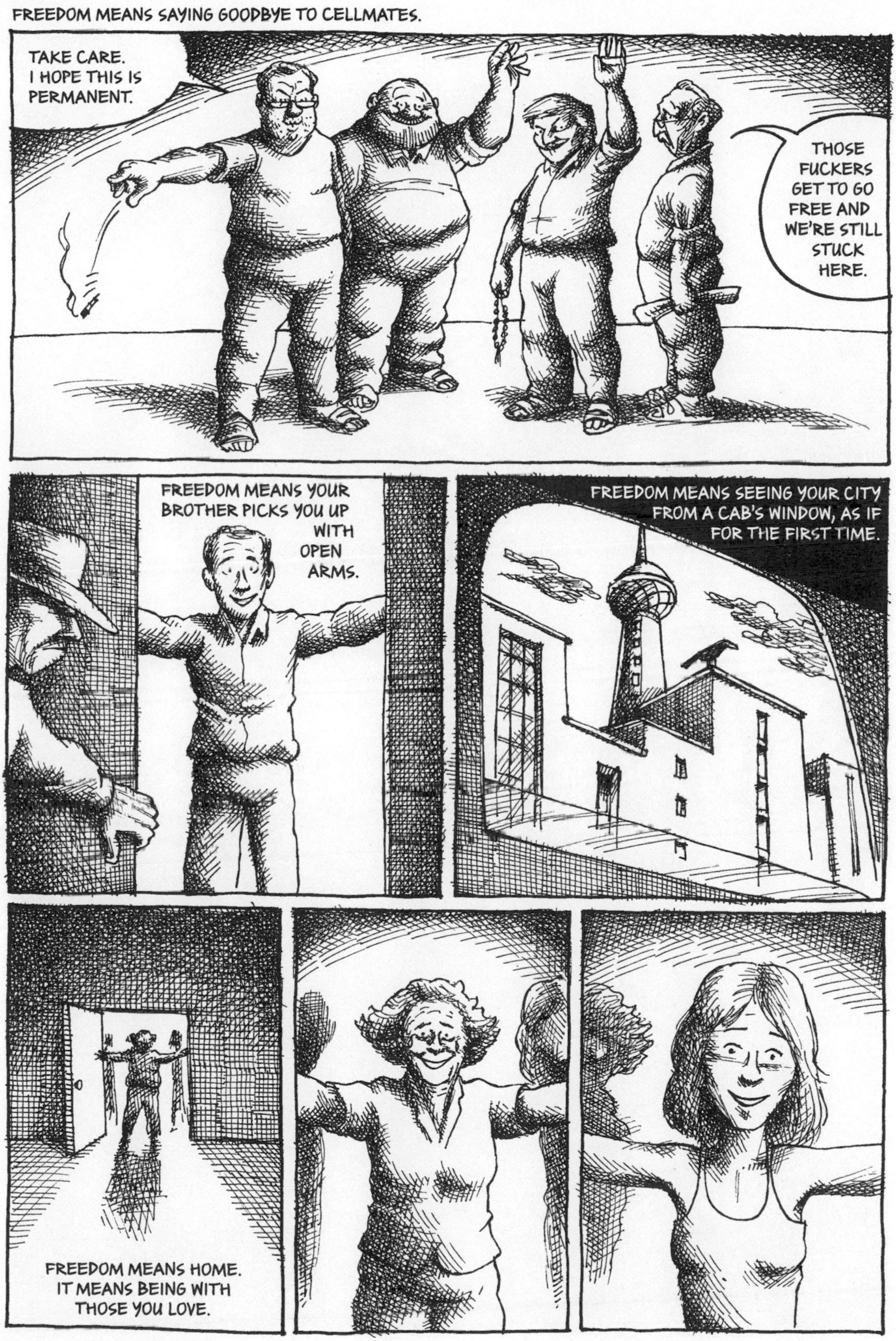
FREEDOM MEANS SAYING GOODBYE TO CELLMATES.
TAKE CARE. I HOPE THIS IS PERMANENT.
THOSE FUCKERS GET TO GO FREE AND WE'RE STILL STUCK HERE.
FREEDOM MEANS YOUR BROTHER PICKS YOU UP WITH OPEN ARMS.
FREEDOM MEANS SEEING YOUR CITY FROM A CAB'S WINDOW, AS IF FOR THE FIRST TIME.
FREEDOM MEANS HOME. IT MEANS BEING WITH THOSE YOU LOVE.

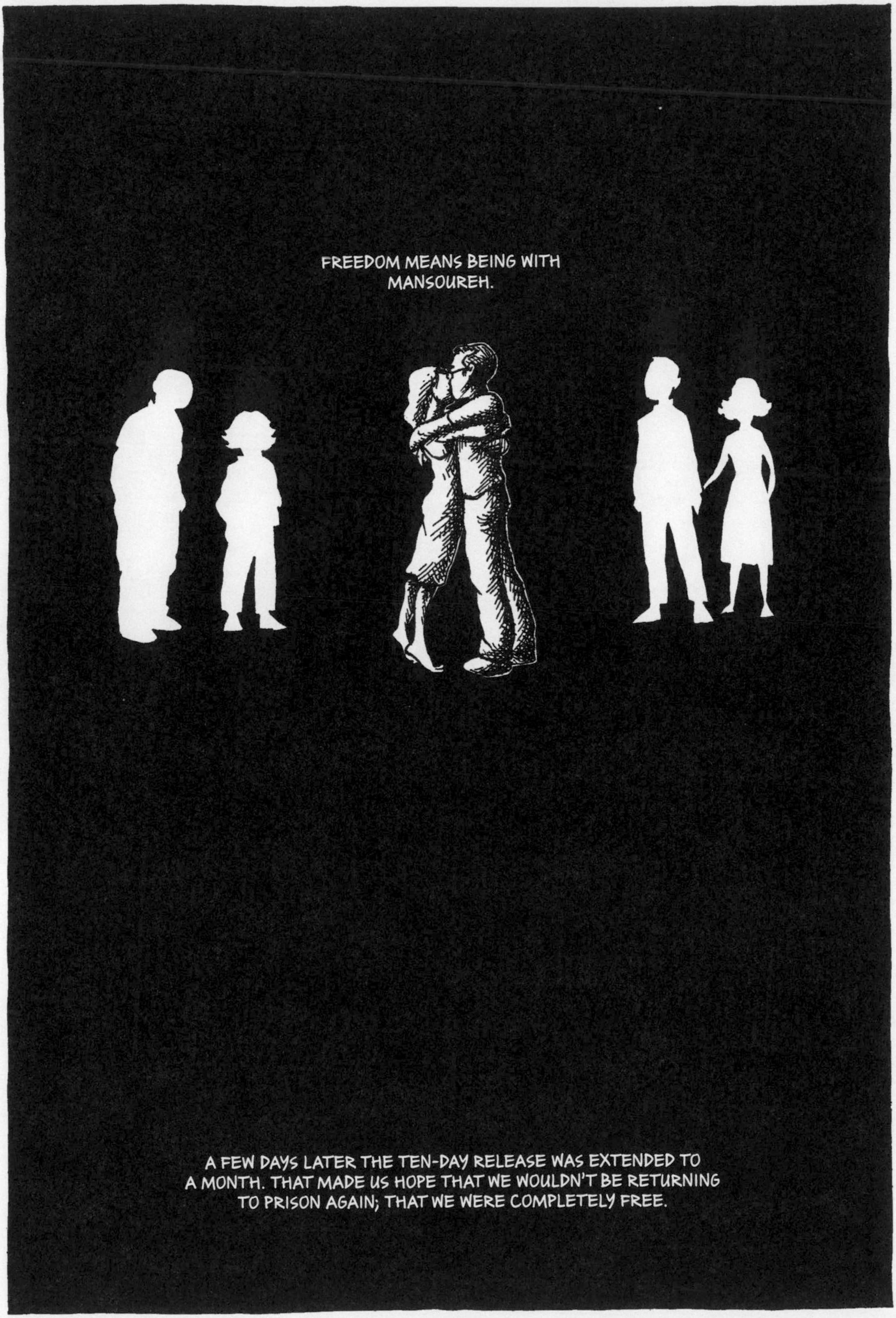
FREEDOM MEANS BEING WITH MANSOUREH.
A FEW DAYS LATER THE TEN-DAY RELEASE WAS EXTENDED TO A MONTH. THAT MADE US HOPE THAT WE WOULDN'T BE RETURNING TO PRISON AGAIN; THAT WE WERE COMPLETELY FREE.

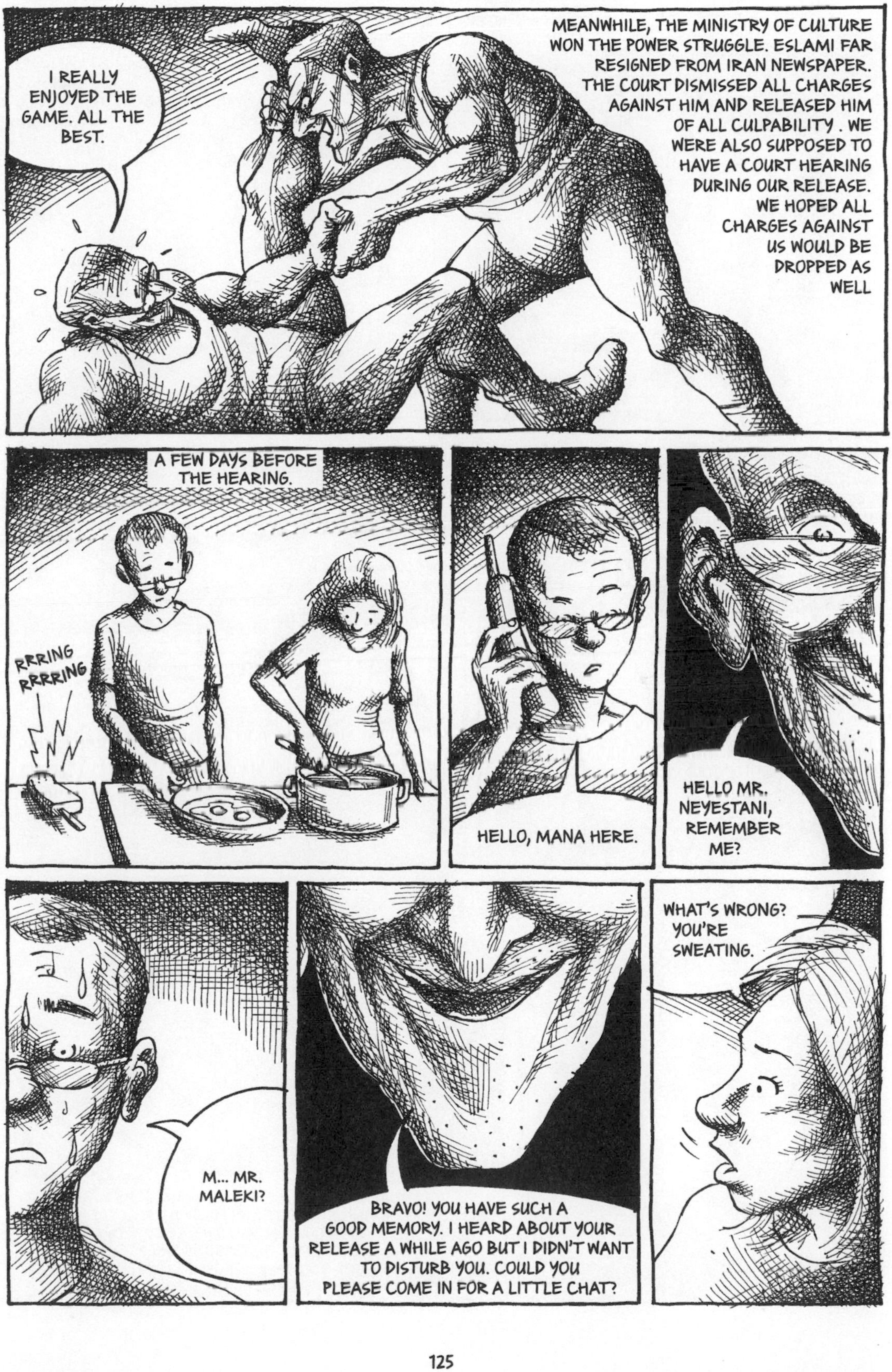
MEANWHILE, THE MINISTRY OF CULTURE WON THE POWER STRUGGLE. ESLAMI FAR RESIGNED FROM IRAN NEWSPAPER. THE COURT DISMISSED ALL CHARGES AGAINST HIM AND RELEASED HIM OF ALL CULPABILITY . WE WERE ALSO SUPPOSED TO HAVE A COURT HEARING DURING OUR RELEASE. WE HOPED ALL CHARGES AGAINST US WOULD BE DROPPED AS WELL
I REALLY ENJOYED THE GAME. ALL THE BEST.
A FEW DAYS BEFORE THE HEARING.
RRRING RRRRING
HELLO, MANA HERE.
HELLO MR. NEYESTANI, REMEMBER ME?
M... MR. MALEKI?
BRAVO! YOU HAVE SUCH A GOOD MEMORY. I HEARD ABOUT YOUR RELEASE A WHILE AGO BUT I DIDN'T WANT TO DISTURB YOU. COULD YOU PLEASE COME IN FOR A LITTLE CHAT?
WHAT'S WRONG? YOU'RE SWEATING.

THAT WAS MY INTER-ROGATOR. HE WANTS TO SEE ME.

DON'T WORRY. MAYBE HE WANTS TO ADVISE YOU ON WHAT TO SAY IN COURT?

ON THE FOLLOWING DAY WE MET IN A MINISTRY INTELLIGENCE OFFICE.

MR. NEYESTANI, I'D LIKE TO EXPRESS MY REGRETS ABOUT THE WHOLE SITUATION.

WE BELIEVE THAT ALL THIS WAS UNINTEN-TIONAL. BUT, SOME-TIMES THERE MUST BE CONSEQUENCES.

FORTUNA-TELY THE HIGHER-UPS ARE FINALLY TAKING THE CHAOS IN AZERBAI-JAN MORE SERIOUSLY.

HERE'S ANOTHER SLOPPY CARTOON-IST. HE DREW THE PRESIDENT AS A DONKEY ON A CHESSBOARD. IN A COUPLE OF DAYS THE PAPER WILL CLOSE BECAUSE OF THIS.

DO YOU KNOW THIS CAR-TOONIST? WHAT CAN YOU TELL US ABOUT HIM?

شرق

I DON'T KNOW HIM. HONESTLY, I'M A BIT OF A RECLUSE. AND THIS CARTOONIST IS NOT WELL KNOWN... AT LEAST NOT TO ME.

MY DEAR MR. NEYESTANI, OUR MINISTRY HAS A NEGATIVE OPINION ABOUT MANY OF YOUR COLLEAGUES. OUR CONCERN IS TO MAINTAIN THE SECURITY OF OUR COUNTRY. SOME OF YOUR COLLEAGUES HELP US WILLINGLY; AS A DUTY. WE NEED YOU TO KEEP THE COUNTRY IN ORDER. WE'LL TALK MORE ABOUT THIS IN THE FUTURE.

FREEDOM MEANS SITTING WITH FRIENDS IN YOUR FAVORITE CAFÉ.

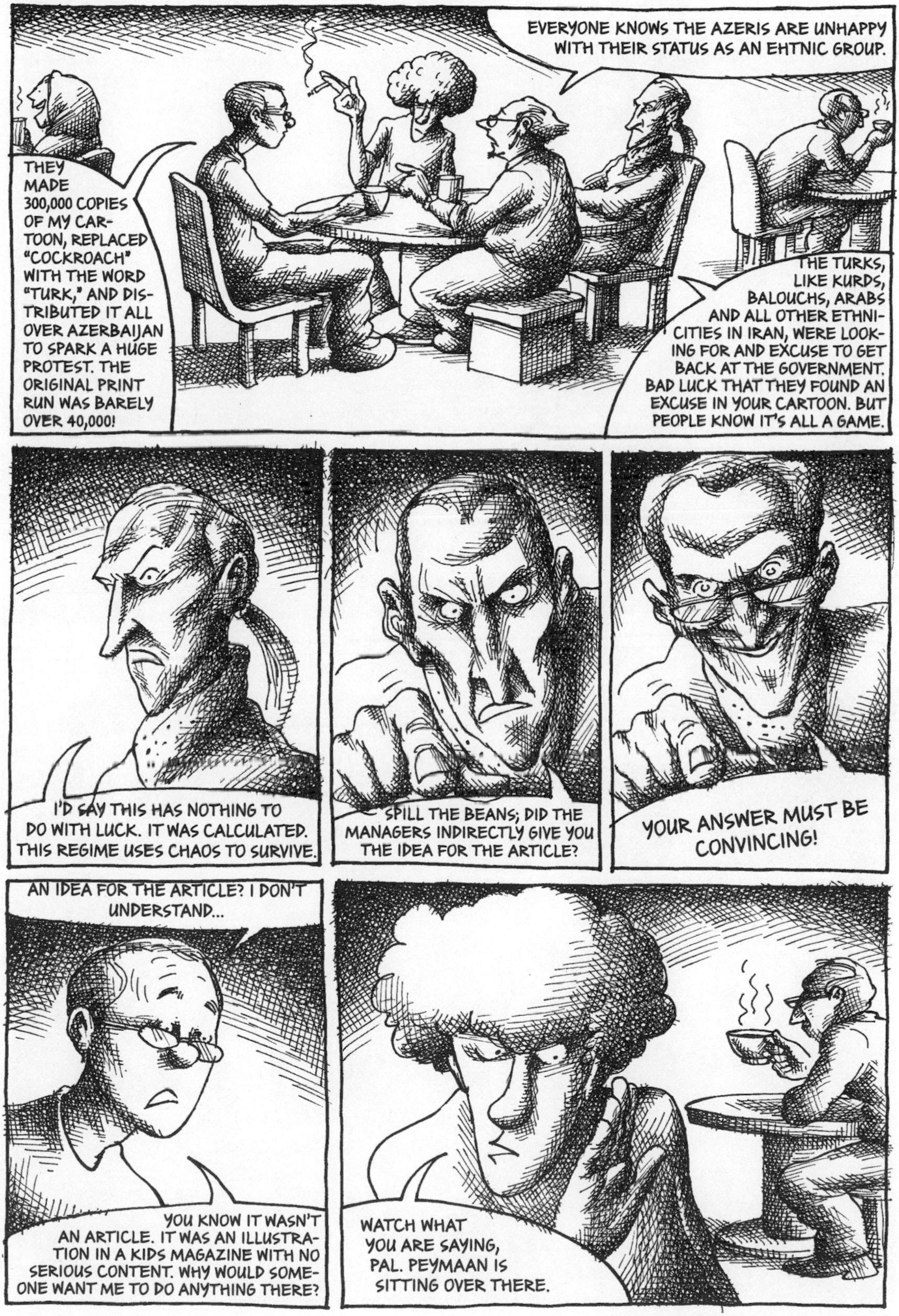
EVERYONE KNOWS THE AZERIS ARE UNHAPPY WITH THEIR STATUS AS AN EHTNIC GROUP.
THEY MADE 300,000 COPIES OF MY CARTOON, REPLACED "COCKROACH" WITH THE WORD "TURK," AND DISTRIBUTED IT ALL OVER AZERBAIJAN TO SPARK A HUGE PROTEST. THE ORIGINAL PRINT RUN WAS BARELY OVER 40,000!
THE TURKS, LIKE KURDS, BALOUCHS, ARABS AND ALL OTHER ETHNICITIES IN IRAN, WERE LOOKING FOR AND EXCUSE TO GET BACK AT THE GOVERNMENT. BAD LUCK THAT THEY FOUND AN EXCUSE IN YOUR CARTOON. BUT PEOPLE KNOW IT'S ALL A GAME.
I'D SAY THIS HAS NOTHING TO DO WITH LUCK. IT WAS CALCULATED. THIS REGIME USES CHAOS TO SURVIVE.
SPILL THE BEANS; DID THE MANAGERS INDIRECTLY GIVE YOU THE IDEA FOR THE ARTICLE?
YOUR ANSWER MUST BE CONVINCING!
AN IDEA FOR THE ARTICLE? I DON'T UNDERSTAND...
YOU KNOW IT WASN'T AN ARTICLE. IT WAS AN ILLUSTRATION IN A KIDS MAGAZINE WITH NO SERIOUS CONTENT. WHY WOULD SOMEONE WANT ME TO DO ANYTHING THERE?
WATCH WHAT YOU ARE SAYING, PAL. PEYMAAN IS SITTING OVER THERE.

PEYMAAN WAS A YOUNG JOURNALIST WHO WAS ONCE ARRESTED FOR CULTURAL ACTIVITIES AGAINST THE REGIME. FOR A COUPLE OF MONTHS HE WAS KEPT IN AN UNKNOWN DETENTION CENTER WHERE HE WAS INTERROGATED AND TORTURED.

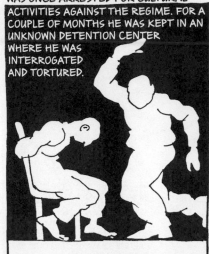

HE TOLD ME TO KEEP AWAY BECAUSE HE'D HAVE TO REPORT EVERYTHING TO THE MINISTRY OF INTELLIGENCE. HE WAS FORCED TO SPY FOR THEM.

FREEDOM MEANS FEELING SAFE AMONG YOUR OWN PEOPLE.

CHAPTER ELEVEN:

ESCAPE

WHEN I GOT HOME MANSOUREH WAS A MESS.

WHAT'S WRONG?

SOMEBODY CALLED AND CALLED US NAMES.

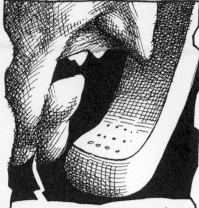

TELL YOUR HUSBAND WE'LL SOON TEACH YOU A LESSON, YOU FARS BITCH!

DON'T WORRY DARLING. LET IT GO. OUR COURT SESSION WILL GO WELL TOMORROW AND EVERYTHING WILL GRADUALLY DIE DOWN.

THE NEXT DAY DR. INTREPID WAS OPTIMISTIC AS ALWAYS.

ACCORDING TO ARTICLE 16 OF LAW 27, IF THE PUBLISHER IS AQUITTED THE JUDGE MUST FREE YOU TOO.

WHO LET THESE TROUBLEMAKERS OUT!? I'LL ORDER YOU RIGHT BACK TO EVIN THIS INSTANT!

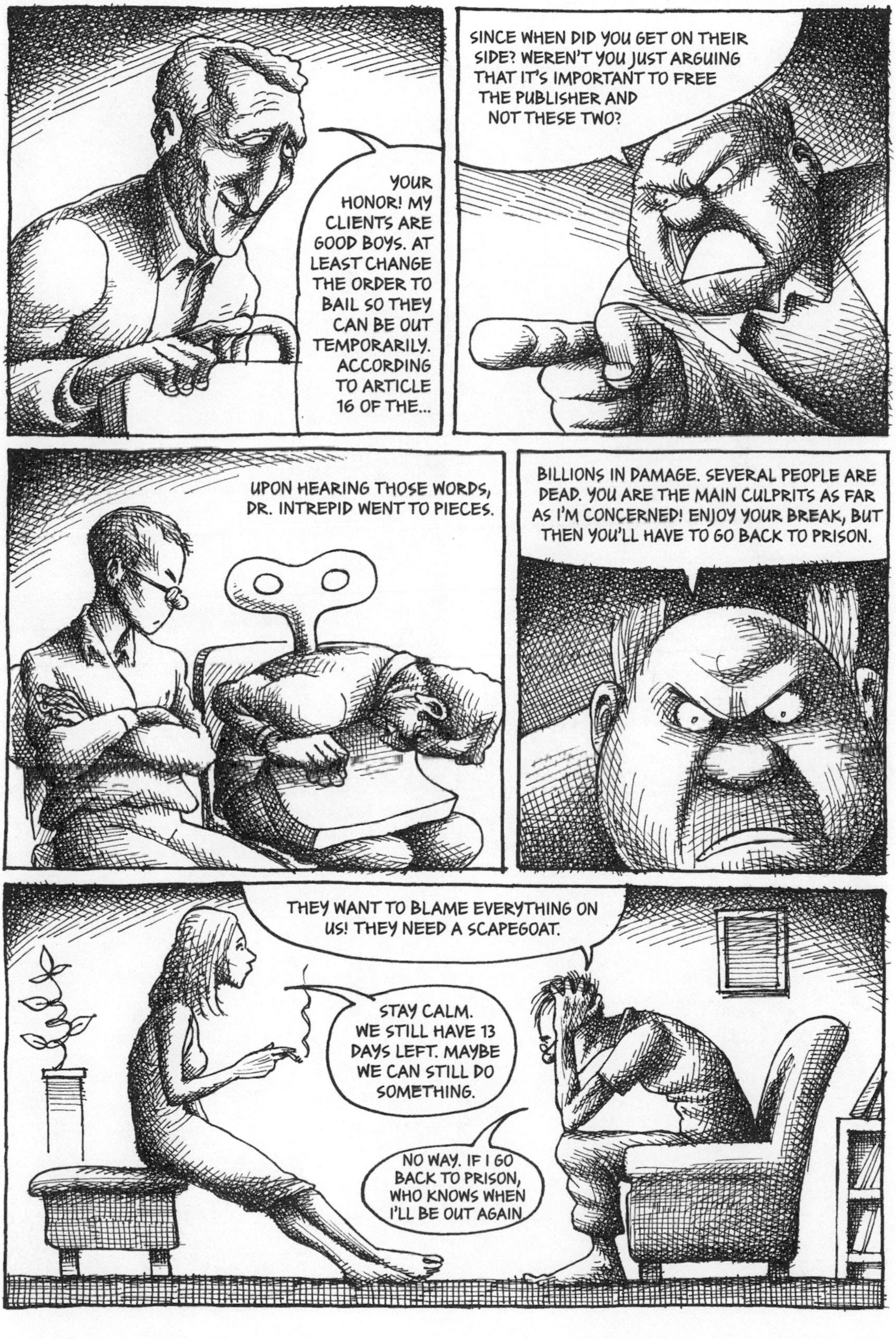
YOUR HONOR! MY CLIENTS ARE GOOD BOYS. AT LEAST CHANGE THE ORDER TO BAIL SO THEY CAN BE OUT TEMPORARILY. ACCORDING TO ARTICLE 16 OF THE...
SINCE WHEN DID YOU GET ON THEIR SIDE? WEREN'T YOU JUST ARGUING THAT IT'S IMPORTANT TO FREE THE PUBLISHER AND NOT THESE TWO?
UPON HEARING THOSE WORDS, DR. INTREPID WENT TO PIECES.
BILLIONS IN DAMAGE. SEVERAL PEOPLE ARE DEAD. YOU ARE THE MAIN CULPRITS AS FAR AS I'M CONCERNED! ENJOY YOUR BREAK, BUT THEN YOU'LL HAVE TO GO BACK TO PRISON.
THEY WANT TO BLAME EVERYTHING ON US! THEY NEED A SCAPEGOAT.
STAY CALM. WE STILL HAVE 13 DAYS LEFT. MAYBE WE CAN STILL DO SOMETHING.
NO WAY. IF I GO BACK TO PRISON, WHO KNOWS WHEN I'LL BE OUT AGAIN

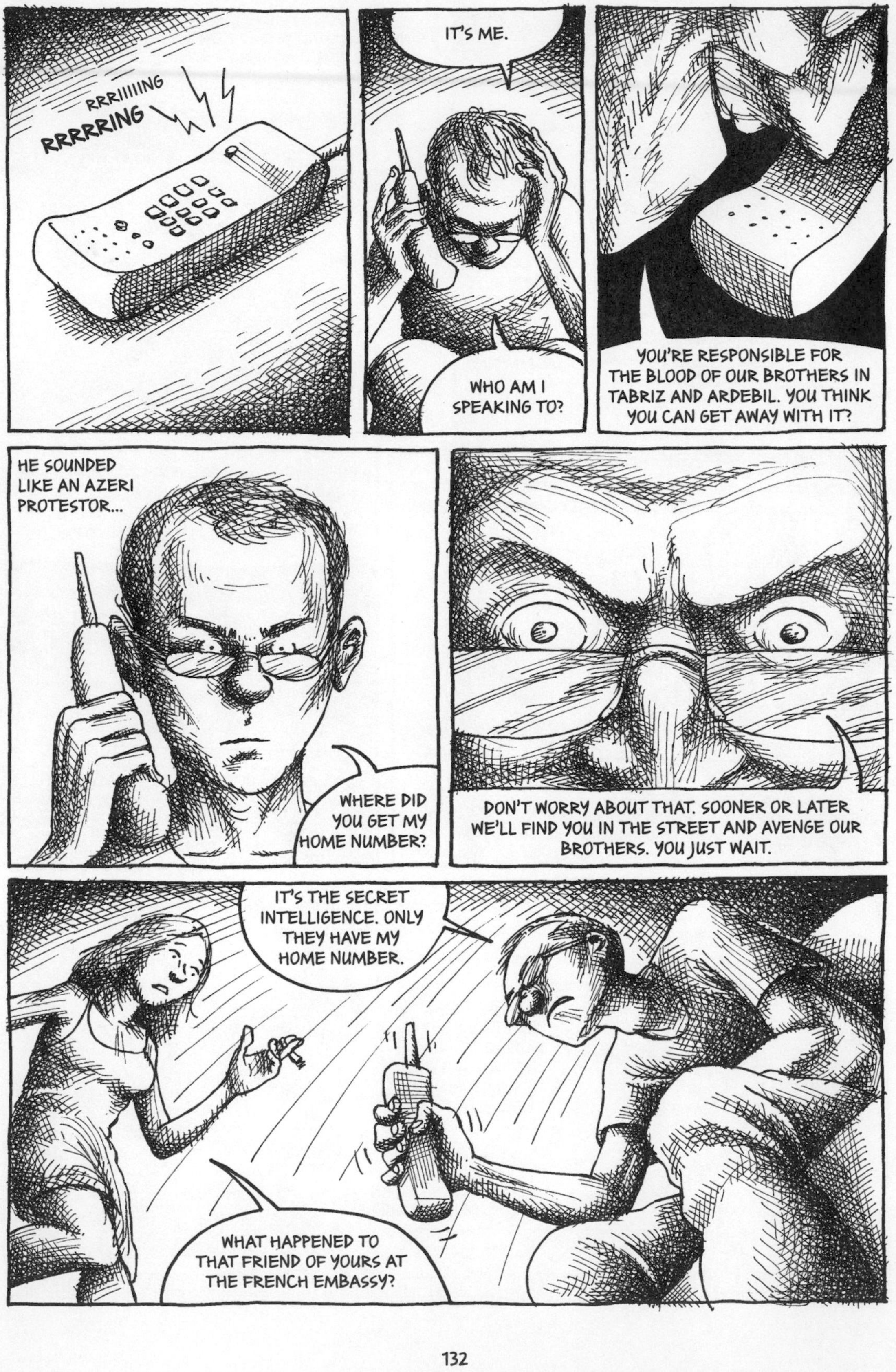
RRRIIIIING
RRRRRING
IT'S ME.
WHO AM I SPEAKING TO?
YOU'RE RESPONSIBLE FOR THE BLOOD OF OUR BROTHERS IN TABRIZ AND ARDEBIL. YOU THINK YOU CAN GET AWAY WITH IT?
HE SOUNDED LIKE AN AZERI PROTESTOR...
WHERE DID YOU GET MY HOME NUMBER?
DON'T WORRY ABOUT THAT. SOONER OR LATER WE'LL FIND YOU IN THE STREET AND AVENGE OUR BROTHERS. YOU JUST WAIT.
IT'S THE SECRET INTELLIGENCE. ONLY THEY HAVE MY HOME NUMBER.
WHAT HAPPENED TO THAT FRIEND OF YOURS AT THE FRENCH EMBASSY?

FEARFUL OF BEING WATCHED, WE WENT TO THE FRENCH EMBASSY.

FRENCH EMBASSY

...THAT'S THE STORY. IF I DON'T GET OUT OF THE COUNTRY IN 12 DAYS...

I'LL HAVE TO RETURN TO EVIN. I DON'T KNOW HOW LONG THEY'D KEEP ME THERE.

MONSIEUR JEAN IS SYMPATHETIC TO YOUR PLIGHT. HE SAYS HE'LL ISSUE AN EMERGENCY VISA FOR YOU.

OUI !

MY JEAN-JACQUES ROSSEAU!

NEXT DAY, I WAS SUPPOSED TO MAKE A FOLLOW-UP CALL TO THE EMBASSY.

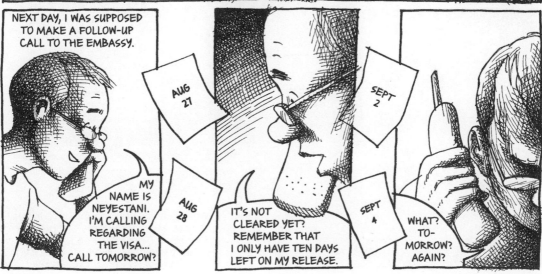

AUG 27

SEPT 2

MY NAME IS NEYESTANI. I'M CALLING REGARDING THE VISA... CALL TOMORROW?

AUG 28

IT'S NOT CLEARED YET? REMEMBER THAT I ONLY HAVE TEN DAYS LEFT ON MY RELEASE.

SEPT 4

WHAT? TO-MORROW? AGAIN?

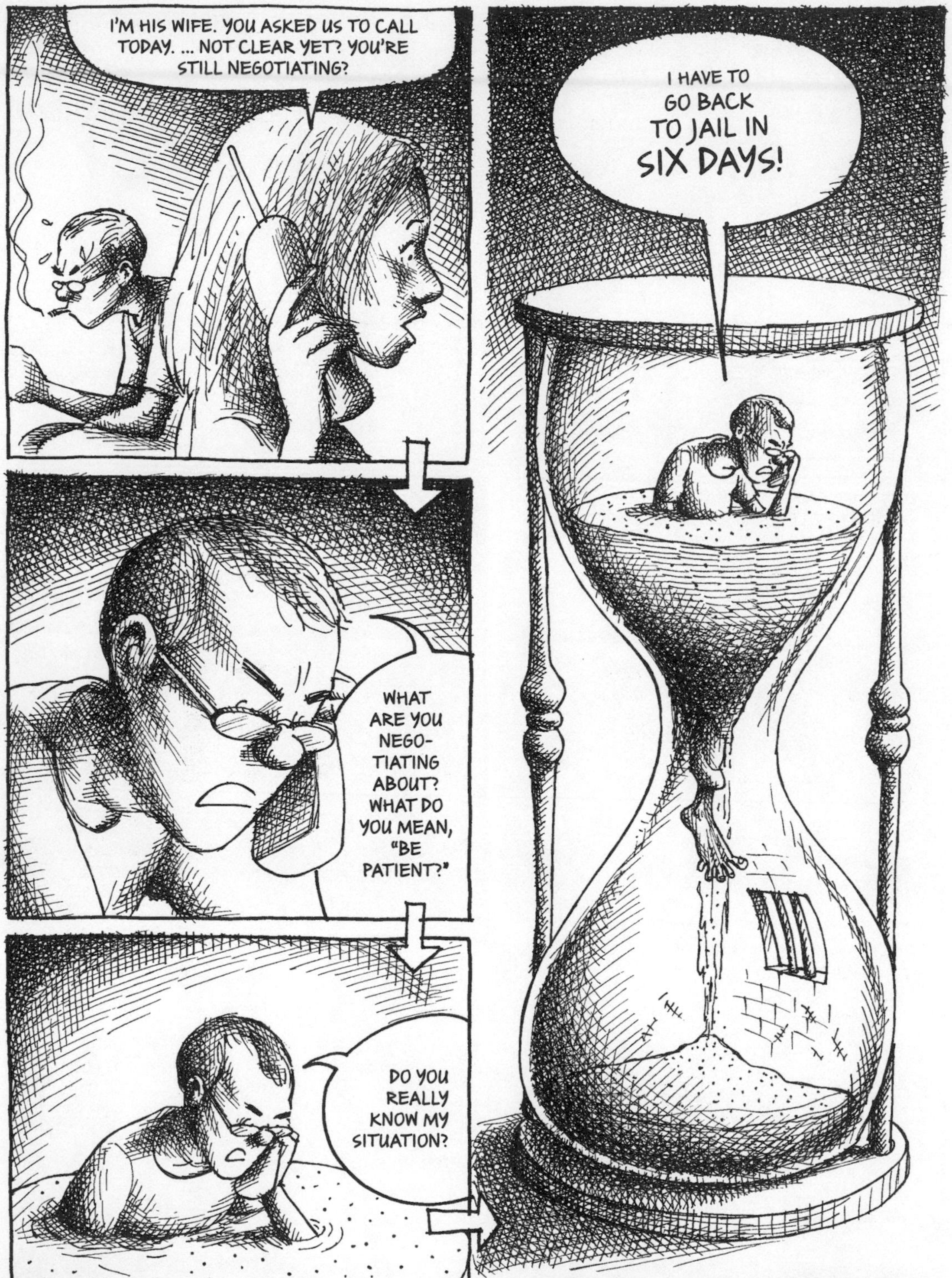
I'M HIS WIFE. YOU ASKED US TO CALL TODAY. ... NOT CLEAR YET? YOU'RE STILL NEGOTIATING?
WHAT ARE YOU NEGO-TIATING ABOUT? WHAT DO YOU MEAN, "BE PATIENT?"
DO YOU REALLY KNOW MY SITUATION?
I HAVE TO GO BACK TO JAIL IN SIX DAYS!

I LOST FAITH IN THE FRENCH. I DECIDED TO APPLY SOMEWHERE ELSE BEFORE RUNNING OUT OF TIME. I CONSULTED NIK, A JOURNALIST FRIEND OF MINE LIVING IN CANADA WHO WAS WORKING WITH AN NGO THAT SUPPORTS CARTOONISTS' RIGHTS.

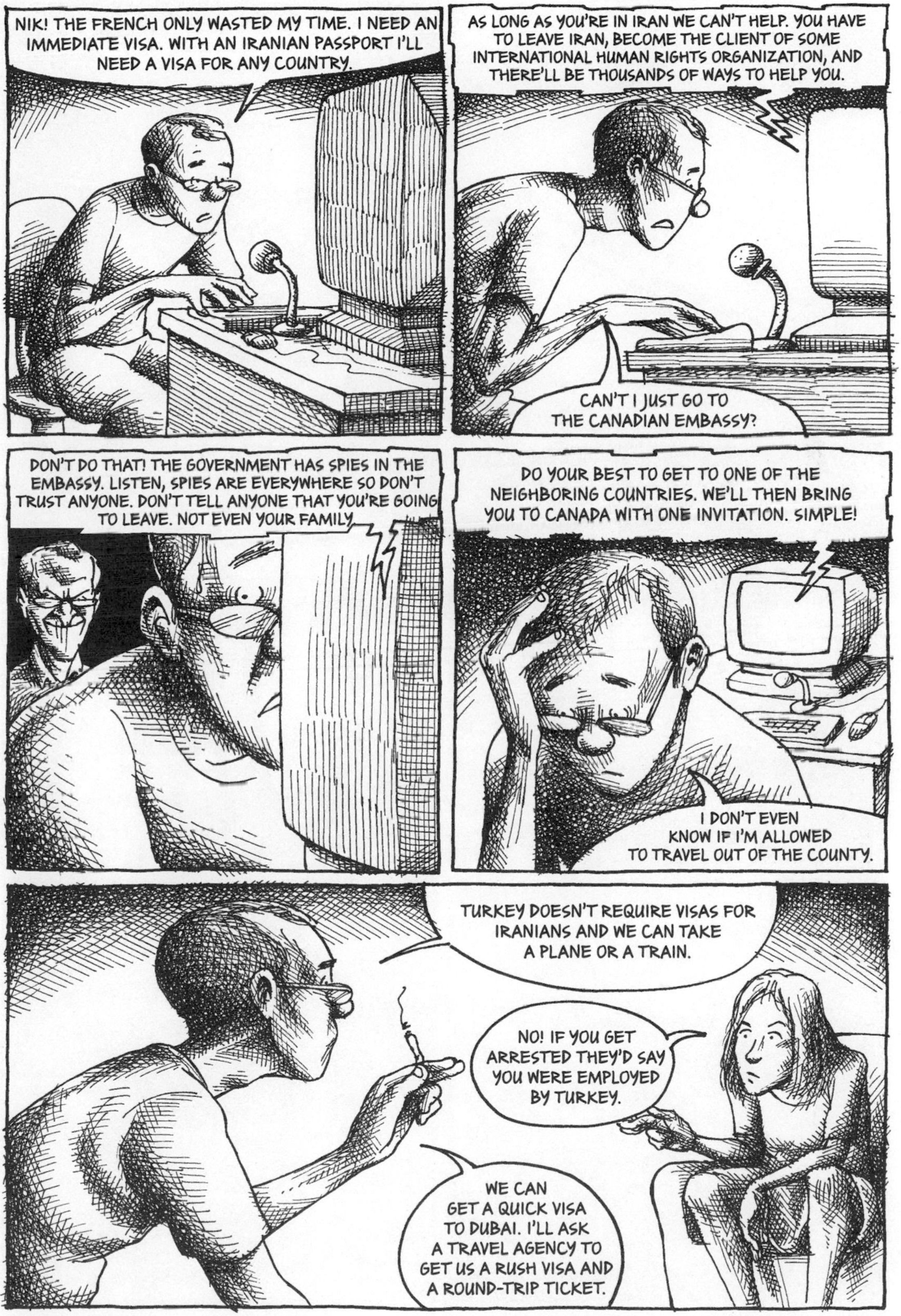

NIK! THE FRENCH ONLY WASTED MY TIME. I NEED AN IMMEDIATE VISA. WITH AN IRANIAN PASSPORT I'LL NEED A VISA FOR ANY COUNTRY.
AS LONG AS YOU'RE IN IRAN WE CAN'T HELP. YOU HAVE TO LEAVE IRAN, BECOME THE CLIENT OF SOME INTERNATIONAL HUMAN RIGHTS ORGANIZATION, AND THERE'LL BE THOUSANDS OF WAYS TO HELP YOU.
CAN'T I JUST GO TO THE CANADIAN EMBASSY?
DON'T DO THAT! THE GOVERNMENT HAS SPIES IN THE EMBASSY. LISTEN, SPIES ARE EVERYWHERE SO DON'T TRUST ANYONE. DON'T TELL ANYONE THAT YOU'RE GOING TO LEAVE. NOT EVEN YOUR FAMILY.
DO YOUR BEST TO GET TO ONE OF THE NEIGHBORING COUNTRIES. WE'LL THEN BRING YOU TO CANADA WITH ONE INVITATION. SIMPLE!
I DON'T EVEN KNOW IF I'M ALLOWED TO TRAVEL OUT OF THE COUNTY.
TURKEY DOESN'T REQUIRE VISAS FOR IRANIANS AND WE CAN TAKE A PLANE OR A TRAIN.
NO! IF YOU GET ARRESTED THEY'D SAY YOU WERE EMPLOYED BY TURKEY.
WE CAN GET A QUICK VISA TO DUBAI. I'LL ASK A TRAVEL AGENCY TO GET US A RUSH VISA AND A ROUND-TRIP TICKET.

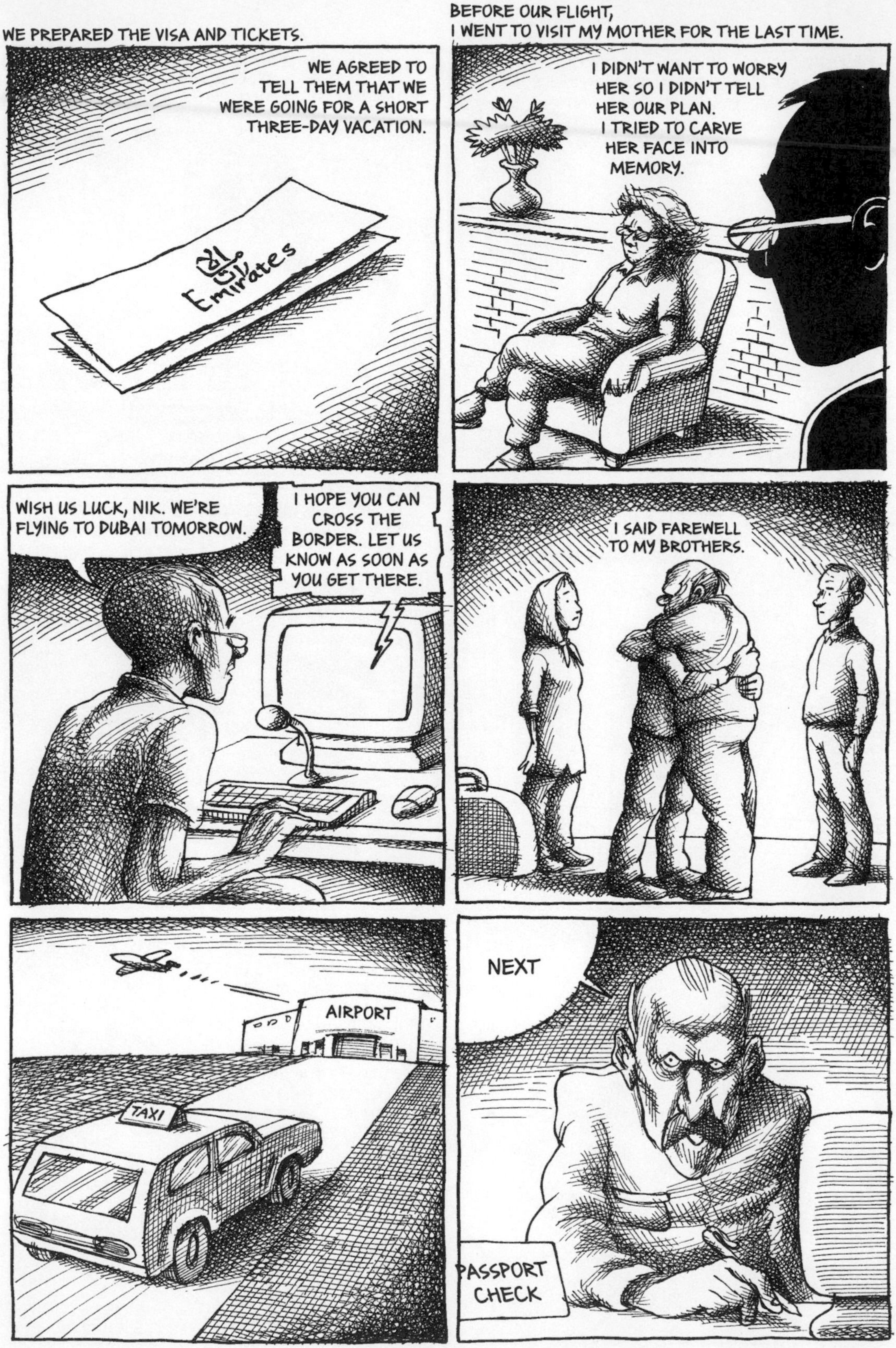
WE PREPARED THE VISA AND TICKETS.
WE AGREED TO TELL THEM THAT WE WERE GOING FOR A SHORT THREE-DAY VACATION.
Emirates
BEFORE OUR FLIGHT, I WENT TO VISIT MY MOTHER FOR THE LAST TIME.
I DIDN'T WANT TO WORRY HER SO I DIDN'T TELL HER OUR PLAN. I TRIED TO CARVE HER FACE INTO MEMORY.
WISH US LUCK, NIK. WE'RE FLYING TO DUBAI TOMORROW.
I HOPE YOU CAN CROSS THE BORDER. LET US KNOW AS SOON AS YOU GET THERE.
I SAID FAREWELL TO MY BROTHERS.
AIRPORT
TAXI
NEXT
PASSPORT CHECK

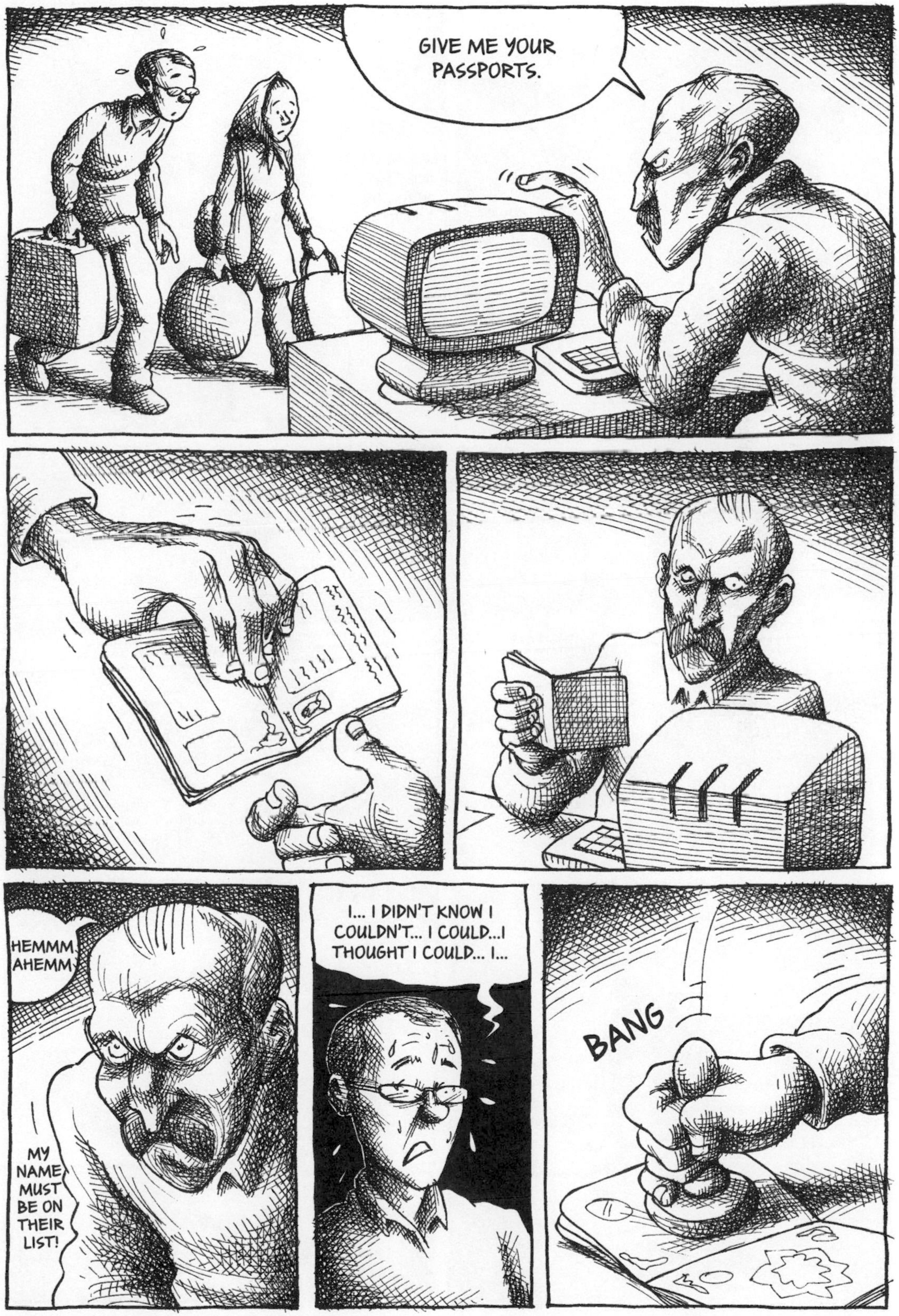
GIVE ME YOUR PASSPORTS.
HEMMM. AHEMM.
MY NAME MUST BE ON THEIR LIST!
I... I DIDN'T KNOW I COULDN'T... I COULD...I THOUGHT I COULD... I...
BANG

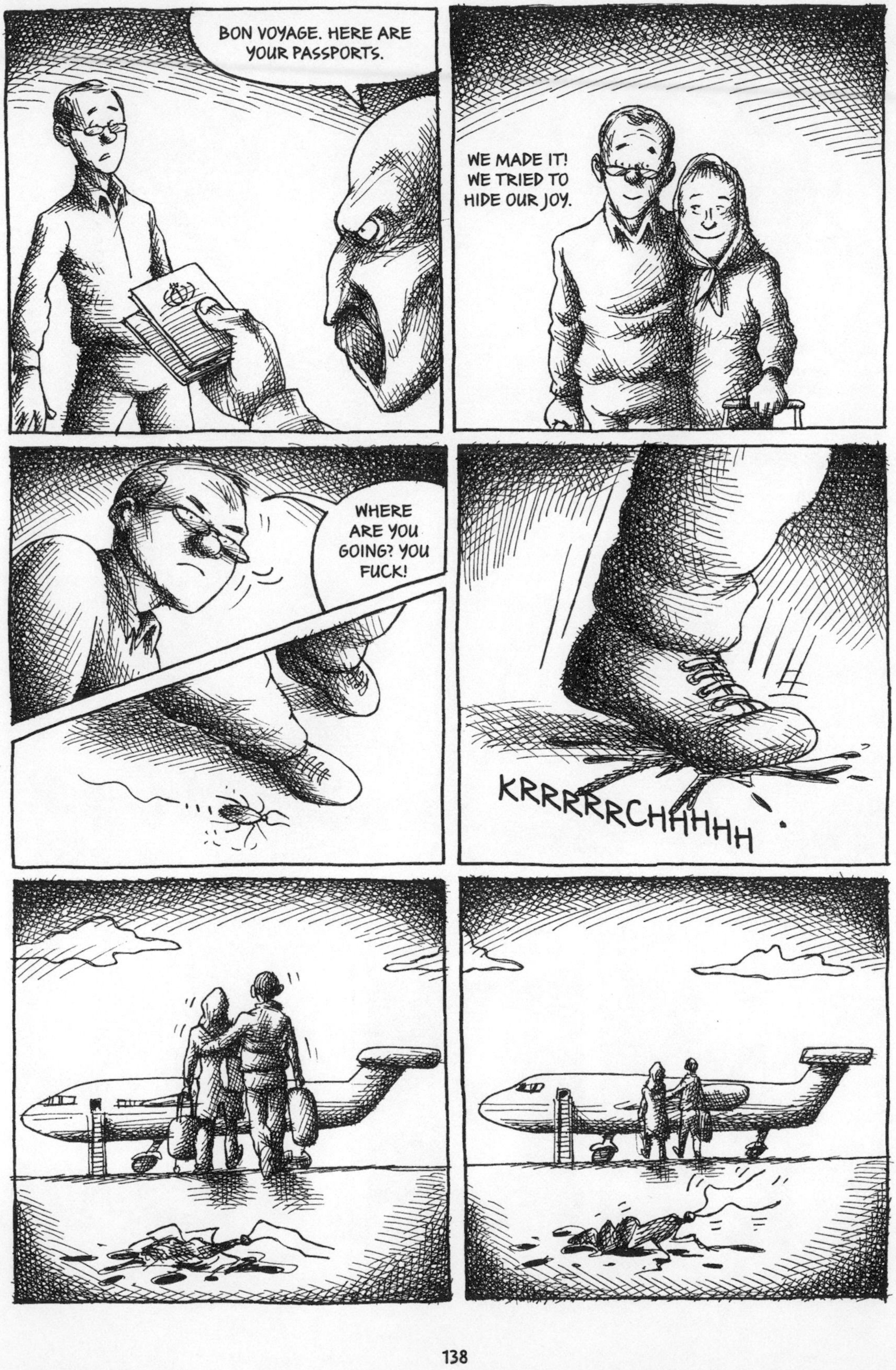
BON VOYAGE. HERE ARE YOUR PASSPORTS.
WE MADE IT! WE TRIED TO HIDE OUR JOY.
WHERE ARE YOU GOING? YOU FUCK!
KRRRRRCHHHHH

CHAPTER TWELVE

EMERGENCY IN DUBAI

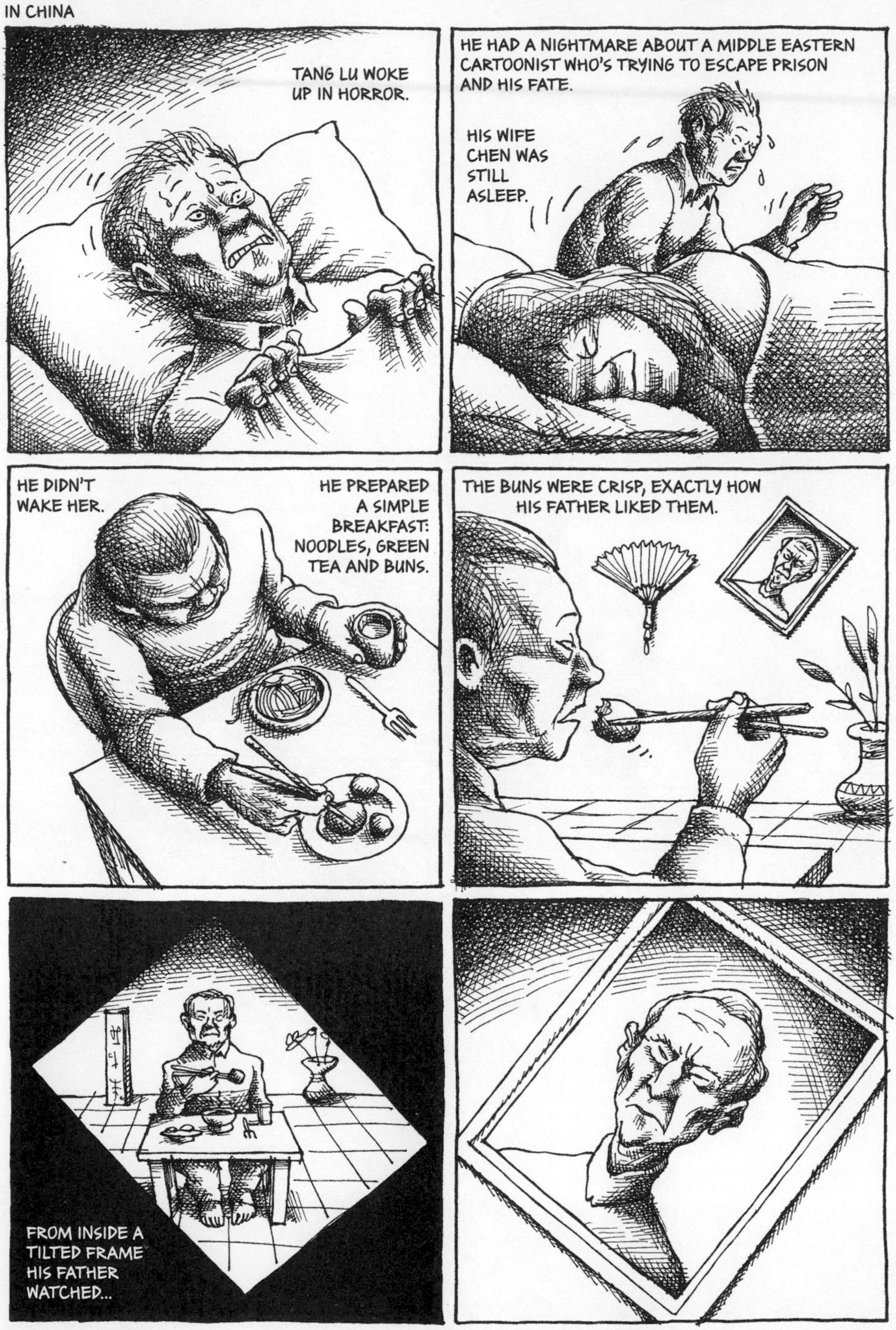

IN CHINA
TANG LU WOKE UP IN HORROR.
HE HAD A NIGHTMARE ABOUT A MIDDLE EASTERN CARTOONIST WHO'S TRYING TO ESCAPE PRISON AND HIS FATE.
HIS WIFE CHEN WAS STILL ASLEEP.
HE DIDN'T WAKE HER.
HE PREPARED A SIMPLE BREAKFAST: NOODLES, GREEN TEA AND BUNS.
THE BUNS WERE CRISP, EXACTLY HOW HIS FATHER LIKED THEM.
FROM INSIDE A TILTED FRAME HIS FATHER WATCHED...

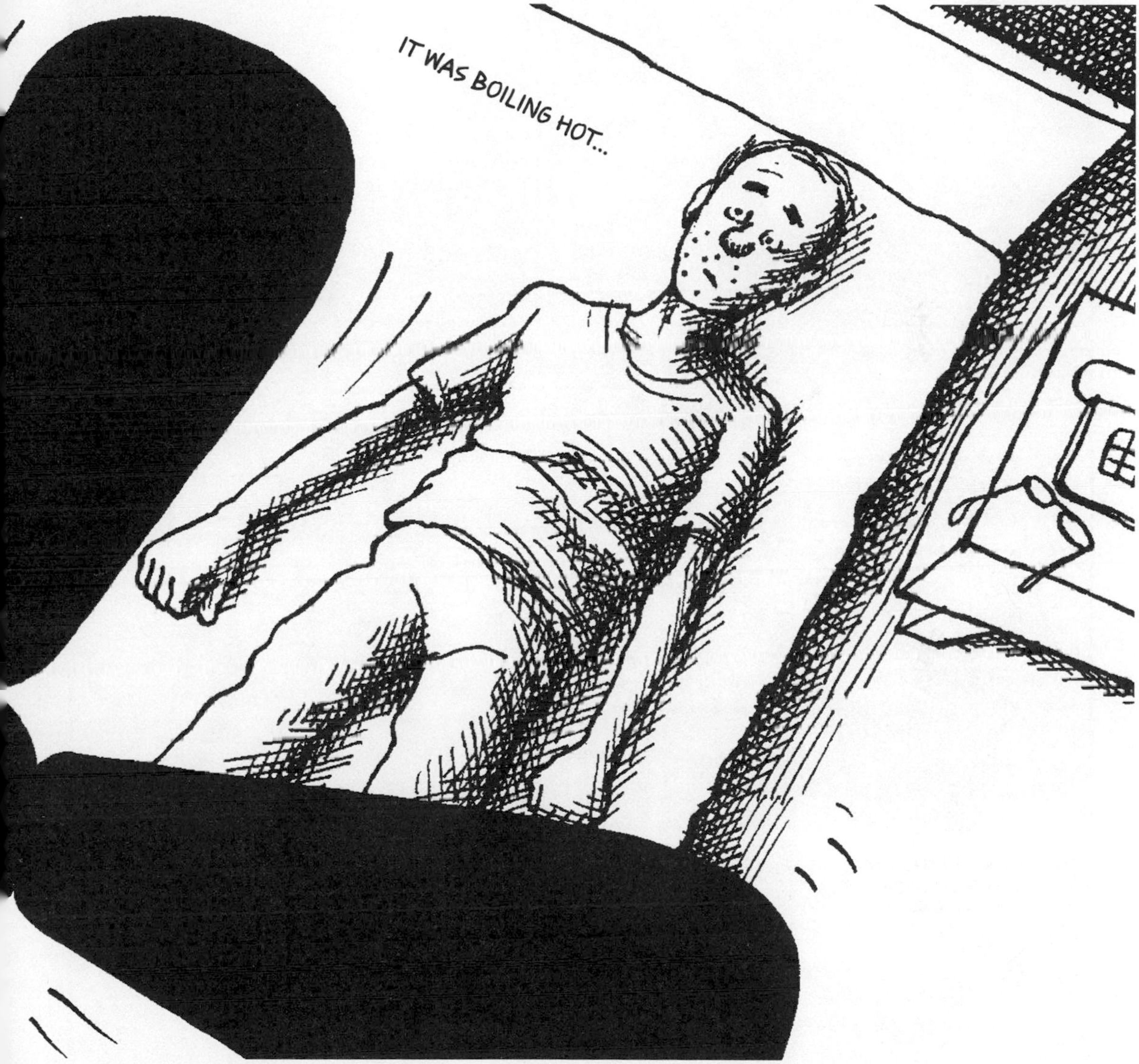
IT WAS BOILING HOT...

45 DAYS PASSED SINCE WE ARRIVED IN DUBAI.

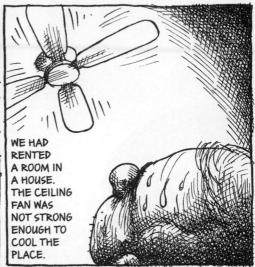

WE HAD RENTED A ROOM IN A HOUSE. THE CEILING FAN WAS NOT STRONG ENOUGH TO COOL THE PLACE.

WE WERE WAITING FOR THE PHONE TO RING AND GIVE US GOOD NEWS.

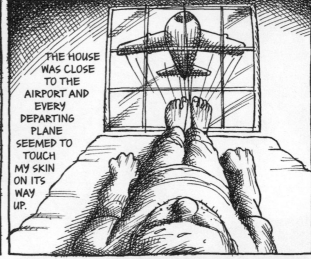

THE HOUSE WAS CLOSE TO THE AIRPORT AND EVERY DEPARTING PLANE SEEMED TO TOUCH MY SKIN ON ITS WAY UP.

THE SOUND OF AIRPLANES REMINDED ME OF OUR FIRST HOUR IN DUBAI.

HEY! WE'RE AT THE DUBAI AIRPORT. WE MADE IT! WHAT'S THE PLAN?

EXCELLENT! I SENT YOU AN INVITATION FROM OUR ORGANIZATION. IT'S FOR AN ART EXHIBITION AND A TALK IN CANADA. SHOW IT TO THE CANADIAN EMBASSY AND ASK FOR VISA. MAKE SURE YOU DON'T TELL THEM YOU HAVE A POLITICAL PROBLEM.

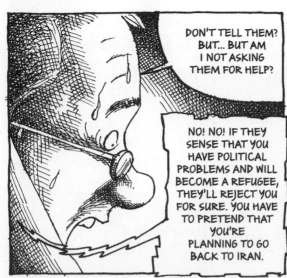

DON'T TELL THEM? BUT... BUT AM I NOT ASKING THEM FOR HELP?

NO! NO! IF THEY SENSE THAT YOU HAVE POLITICAL PROBLEMS AND WILL BECOME A REFUGEE, THEY'LL REJECT YOU FOR SURE. YOU HAVE TO PRETEND THAT YOU'RE PLANNING TO GO BACK TO IRAN.

WE WENT TO THE CANADIAN EMBASSY WITH THE INVITATION.

AN INVITATION FOR A TALK AND EXHIBITION IN TORONTO ... WHY DIDN'T YOU APPLY FROM TEHRAN?

MY HUSBAND IS A JOURNALIST AND, AS YOU KNOW, IRAN'S GOVERNMENT DOES NOT LOOK KINDLY ON JOURNALISTS WITH TIES TO FOREIGN EMBASSIES.

I UNDERSTAND, BUT IT'S NOT OUR PROBLEM, MISS.

YOU'RE HERE ON A TOURIST VISA. YOU CAN'T APPLY FOR ANOTHER TOURIST VISA. YOU HAVE TO GO BACK TO IRAN AND APPLY THERE.

SORRY

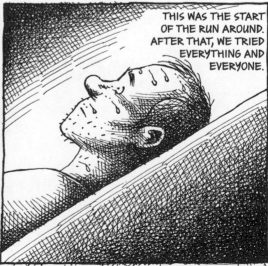

THIS WAS THE START OF THE RUN AROUND. AFTER THAT, WE TRIED EVERYTHING AND EVERYONE.

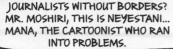
JOURNALISTS WITHOUT BORDERS? MR. MOSHIRI, THIS IS NEYESTANI... MANA, THE CARTOONIST WHO RAN INTO PROBLEMS.

THE "NAMANA" PROBLEM? HA HA HA, SUCH A FUNNY STORY, MR. NEYESTANI!

HELLO? MR. FARSHID? UNFORTUNATELY I'M STUCK IN DUBAI... ON A TWO MONTH VISA.

IF THE HUMAN RIGHTS WATCH WOULD HELP ME IT'D MEAN THE WORLD TO ME!

YES, I TALKED TO AKBAR GANJI AND MANY OTHERS. EVERYBODY BUT THE HEAD OF UNITED NATIONS. ALL IN VAIN.

THANK YOU HOSSEIN. I HOPE SO. YOU'LL CONTACT THE FRENCH AMBASSADOR TOMORROW, RIGHT?

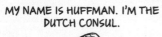
YES, HELLO. I HEARD MRS. JOLIE AND MR. PITT ADOPT KIDS FROM THE MIDDLE EAST.

JUST WANTED TO KNOW IF ANY AGE LIMITS APPLY.

ALL THE CALLS WERE FUTILE. NO ONE WOULD SAY, "I CAN'T," BUT STILL, NOTHING WOULD HAPPEN. FINALLY, NIK CALLED ONE DAY TO SAY THE DUTCH EMBASSY WAS GOING TO ISSUE A VISA FOR US.

MY NAME IS HUFFMAN. I'M THE DUTCH CONSUL.

UNFORTUNATELY NO ONE NOTIFIED US ABOUT YOU.

WE WERE TOLD THAT YOU'D BEEN INFORMED... MY HUSBAND IS A FAMOUS IRANIAN CARTOONIST. HE WAS IN PRISON BECAUSE OF HIS WORK... IRAN AND DUBAI HAVE AN EXTRADITION TREATY. WE DON'T HAVE MUCH TIME LEFT ON OUR VISA.

EGG-ZAKT-LI!

I DON'T FOLLOW INTERNAL IRANIAN ISSUES BUT I DON'T THINK THEY HAVE SUCH A LAW.

IN ANY CASE, YOU DON'T SEEM TO BE IN TOO MUCH TROUBLE BECAUSE YOU'VE CROSSED THE BORDER WITH YOUR OWN PASSPORTS.

HE HAD A SUSPICIOUS LOOK IN HIS EYES. HOW DID HE SEE US?

EGGZAKTLY... I HAVE PRAABLEEM... PAALITI- KAAL PRAABLEEM

BUT... BELIEVE ME, IF WE GO BACK, THEY'LL PUT MY HUSBAND IN PRISON. CAN YOU PLEASE HELP US?

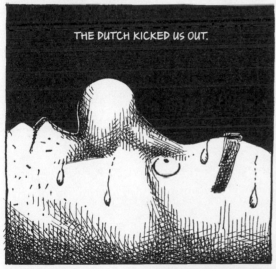

THE DUTCH KICKED US OUT.

HELLO MY DEAR MOSHIRI. I'M WONDE- RING IF THERE ARE ANY NEW DEVELOP- MENTS? MY DUBAI VISA IS EXPIRING. PLEASE HURRY. THANK YOU. I'LL AWAIT YOUR CALL.

WAITING... WAITING...

FINALLY A SPARK OF HOPE.

HELLO HOSSEIN? ...ARE YOU SURE? THE FRENCH AMBASSADOR AGREED? THEY'LL GIVE US A FRENCH VISA? WHEN? MRS. LAFOUNTE? THANK YOU! I APPRECIATE YOUR HELP!

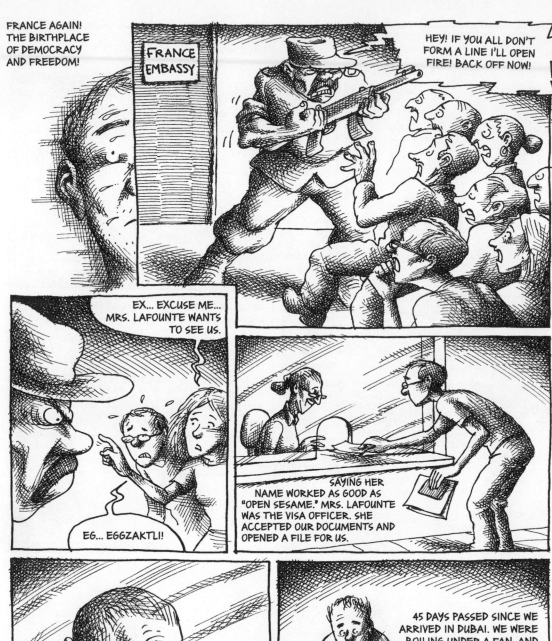

FRANCE AGAIN! THE BIRTHPLACE OF DEMOCRACY AND FREEDOM!

FRANCE EMBASSY

HEY! IF YOU ALL DON'T FORM A LINE I'LL OPEN FIRE! BACK OFF NOW!

EX... EXCUSE ME... MRS. LAFOUNTE WANTS TO SEE US.

EG... EGGZAKTLI!

SAYING HER NAME WORKED AS GOOD AS "OPEN SESAME." MRS. LAFOUNTE WAS THE VISA OFFICER. SHE ACCEPTED OUR DOCUMENTS AND OPENED A FILE FOR US.

ISSUING AN EU VISA WILL TAKE 21 DAYS. WE'LL CALL YOU AS SOON AS IT'S READY.

45 DAYS PASSED SINCE WE ARRIVED IN DUBAI. WE WERE BOILING UNDER A FAN, AND WAITING FOR THE GOOD NEWS FROM THE EMBASSY.

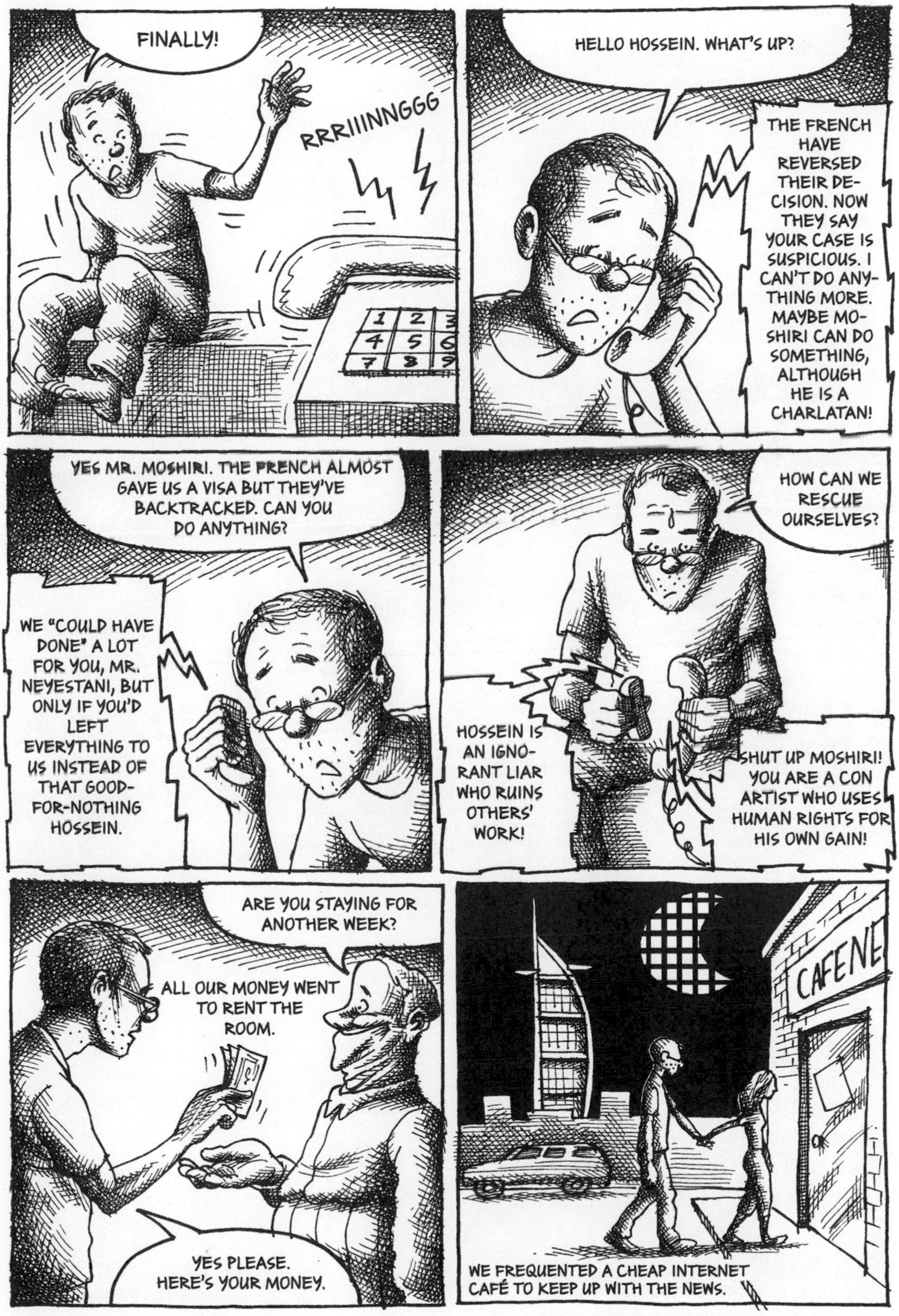
FINALLY!
RRRIIINNGGG
HELLO HOSSEIN. WHAT'S UP?
THE FRENCH HAVE REVERSED THEIR DE-CISION. NOW THEY SAY YOUR CASE IS SUSPICIOUS. I CAN'T DO ANY-THING MORE. MAYBE MO-SHIRI CAN DO SOMETHING, ALTHOUGH HE IS A CHARLATAN!
YES MR. MOSHIRI. THE FRENCH ALMOST GAVE US A VISA BUT THEY'VE BACKTRACKED. CAN YOU DO ANYTHING?
WE "COULD HAVE DONE" A LOT FOR YOU, MR. NEYESTANI, BUT ONLY IF YOU'D LEFT EVERYTHING TO US INSTEAD OF THAT GOOD-FOR-NOTHING HOSSEIN.
HOW CAN WE RESCUE OURSELVES?
HOSSEIN IS AN IGNO-RANT LIAR WHO RUINS OTHERS' WORK!
SHUT UP MOSHIRI! YOU ARE A CON ARTIST WHO USES HUMAN RIGHTS FOR HIS OWN GAIN!
ARE YOU STAYING FOR ANOTHER WEEK?
ALL OUR MONEY WENT TO RENT THE ROOM.
YES PLEASE. HERE'S YOUR MONEY.
CAFE NE
WE FREQUENTED A CHEAP INTERNET CAFÉ TO KEEP UP WITH THE NEWS.

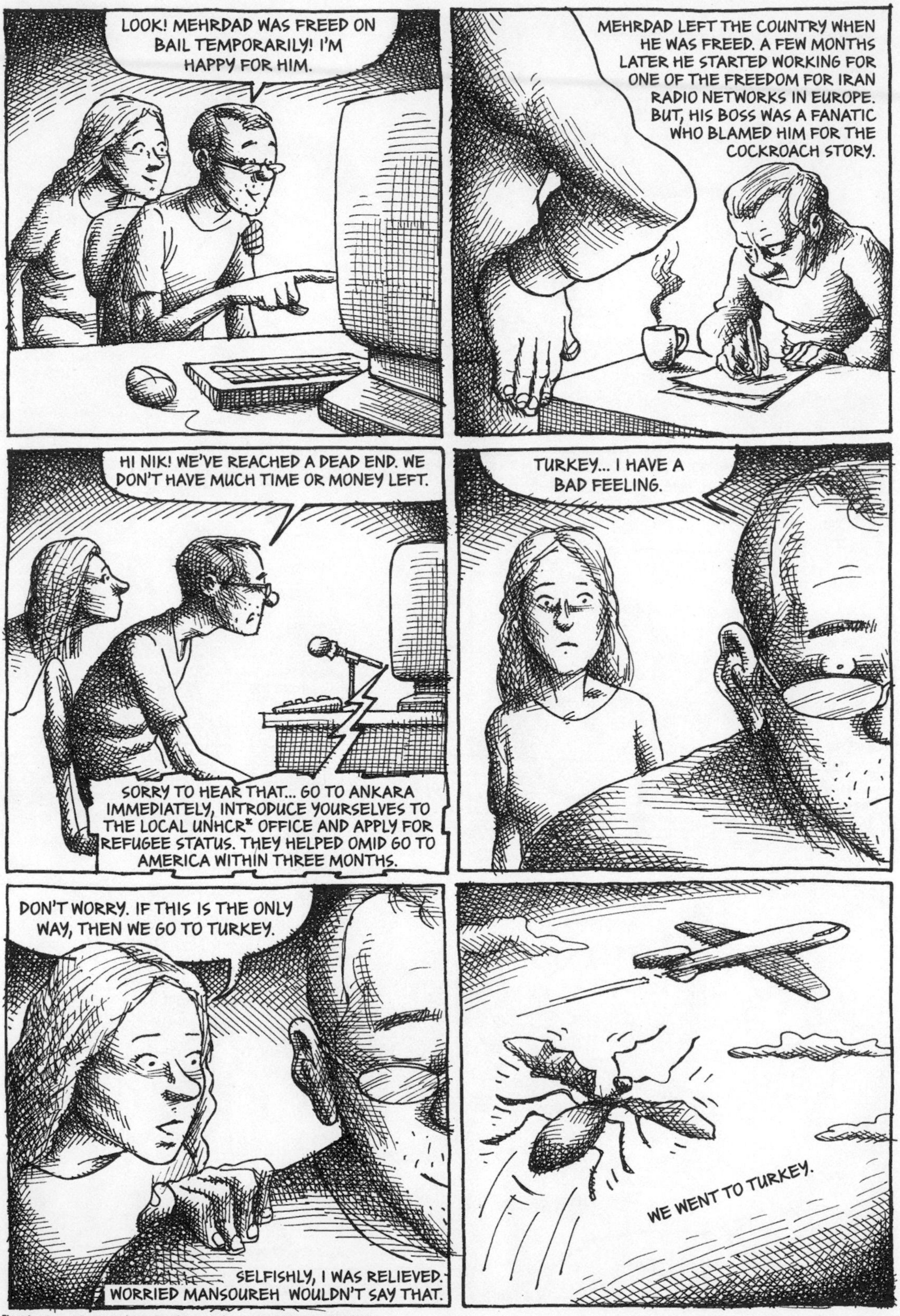

LOOK! MEHRDAD WAS FREED ON BAIL TEMPORARILY! I'M HAPPY FOR HIM.
MEHRDAD LEFT THE COUNTRY WHEN HE WAS FREED. A FEW MONTHS LATER HE STARTED WORKING FOR ONE OF THE FREEDOM FOR IRAN RADIO NETWORKS IN EUROPE. BUT, HIS BOSS WAS A FANATIC WHO BLAMED HIM FOR THE COCKROACH STORY.
HI NIK! WE'VE REACHED A DEAD END. WE DON'T HAVE MUCH TIME OR MONEY LEFT.
SORRY TO HEAR THAT... GO TO ANKARA IMMEDIATELY, INTRODUCE YOURSELVES TO THE LOCAL UNHCR* OFFICE AND APPLY FOR REFUGEE STATUS. THEY HELPED OMID GO TO AMERICA WITHIN THREE MONTHS.
TURKEY... I HAVE A BAD FEELING.
DON'T WORRY. IF THIS IS THE ONLY WAY, THEN WE GO TO TURKEY.
SELFISHLY, I WAS RELIEVED. WORRIED MANSOUREH WOULDN'T SAY THAT.
WE WENT TO TURKEY.

*UNHCR: THE UNITED NATIONS REFUGEE AGENCY

CHAPTER THIRTEEN

REFUGEES

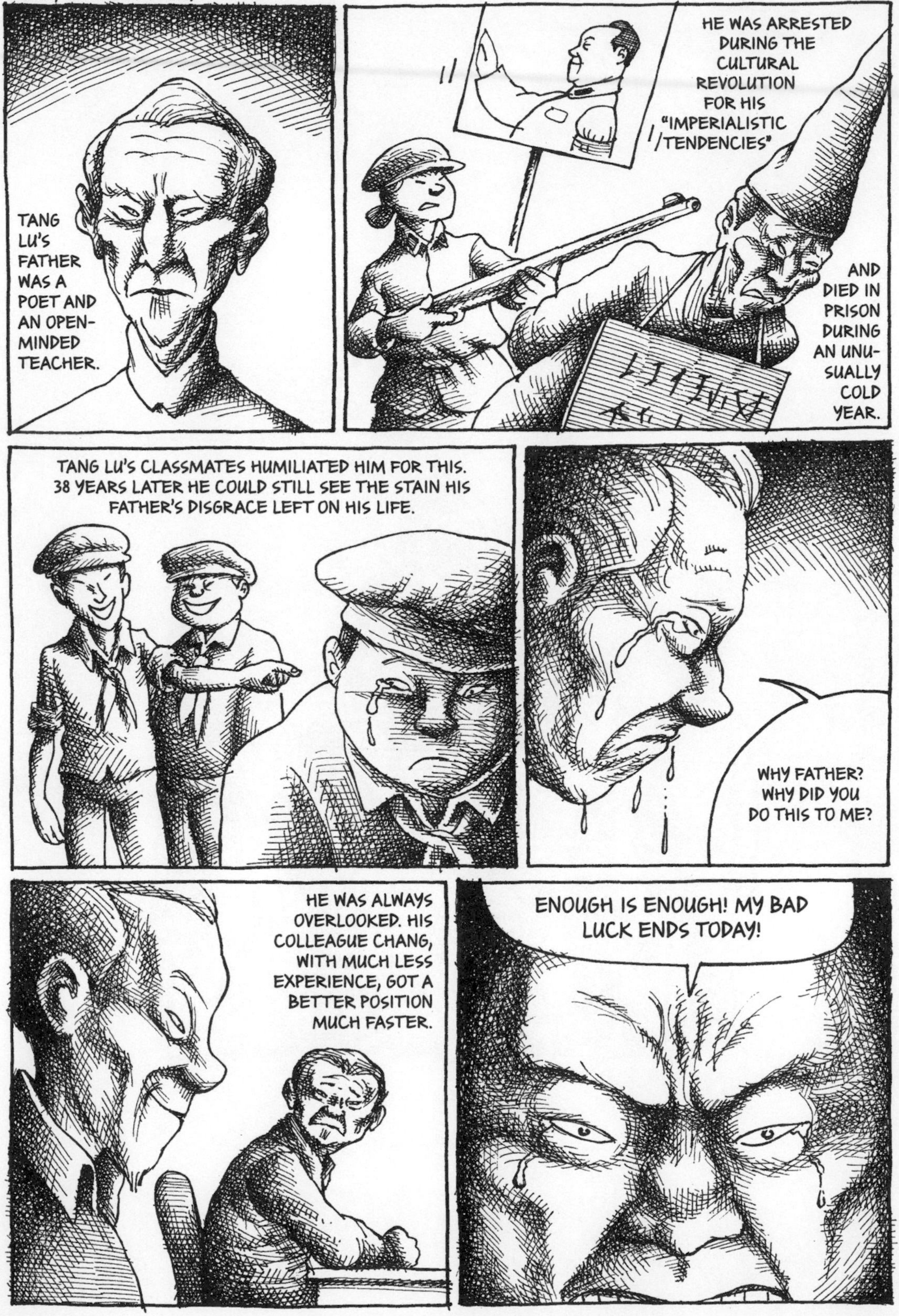
TANG LU'S FATHER WAS A POET AND AN OPEN-MINDED TEACHER.
HE WAS ARRESTED DURING THE CULTURAL REVOLUTION FOR HIS "IMPERIALISTIC TENDENCIES"
AND DIED IN PRISON DURING AN UNUSUALLY COLD YEAR.
TANG LU'S CLASSMATES HUMILIATED HIM FOR THIS. 38 YEARS LATER HE COULD STILL SEE THE STAIN HIS FATHER'S DISGRACE LEFT ON HIS LIFE.
WHY FATHER? WHY DID YOU DO THIS TO ME?
HE WAS ALWAYS OVERLOOKED. HIS COLLEAGUE CHANG, WITH MUCH LESS EXPERIENCE, GOT A BETTER POSITION MUCH FASTER.
ENOUGH IS ENOUGH! MY BAD LUCK ENDS TODAY!

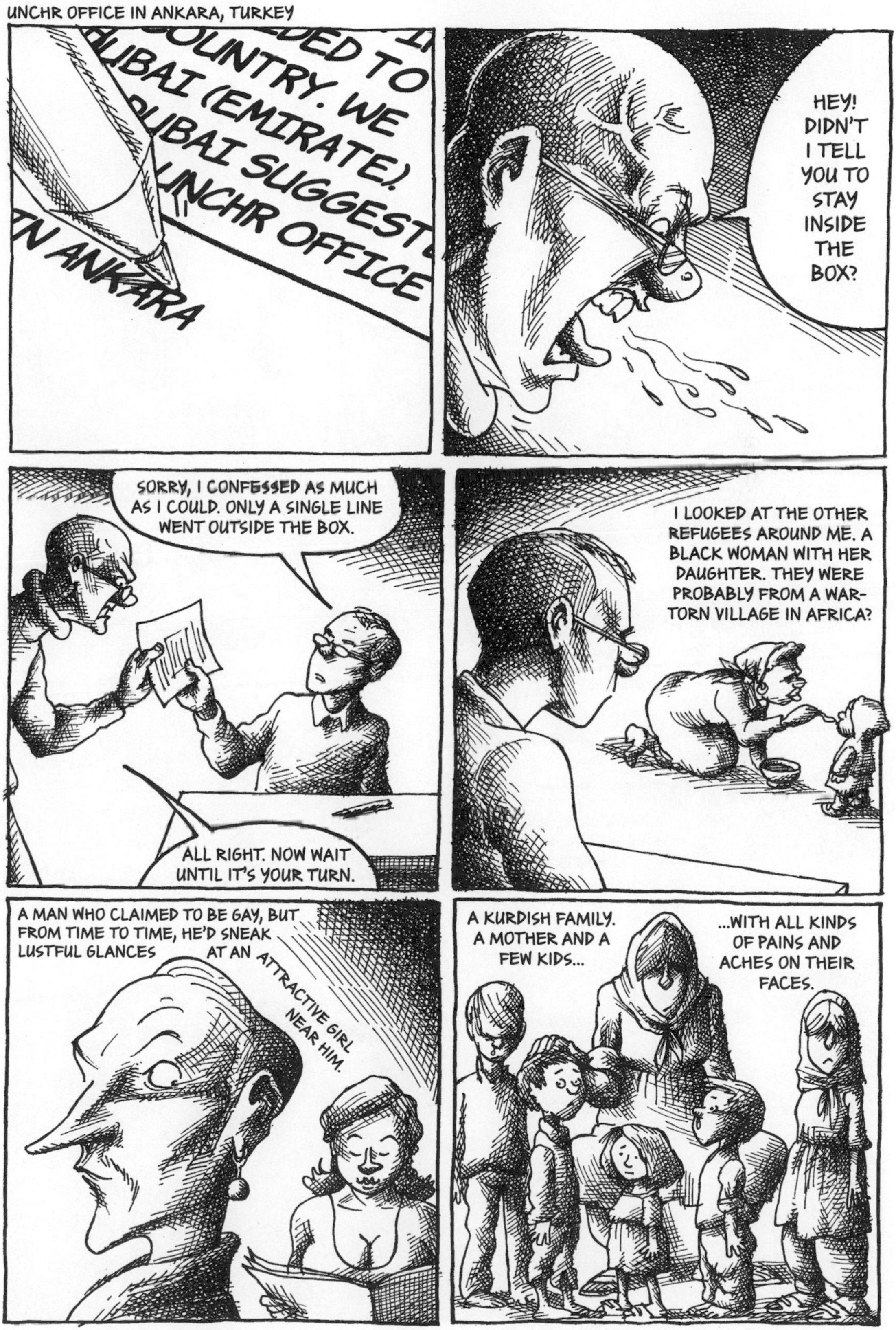
UNCHR OFFICE IN ANKARA, TURKEY
DED TO
COUNTRY. WE
UBAI (EMIRATE).
UBAI SUGGEST
UNCHR OFFICE
N ANKARA
HEY! DIDN'T I TELL YOU TO STAY INSIDE THE BOX?
SORRY, I CONFESSED AS MUCH AS I COULD. ONLY A SINGLE LINE WENT OUTSIDE THE BOX.
ALL RIGHT. NOW WAIT UNTIL IT'S YOUR TURN.
I LOOKED AT THE OTHER REFUGEES AROUND ME. A BLACK WOMAN WITH HER DAUGHTER. THEY WERE PROBABLY FROM A WAR-TORN VILLAGE IN AFRICA?
A MAN WHO CLAIMED TO BE GAY, BUT FROM TIME TO TIME, HE'D SNEAK LUSTFUL GLANCES AT AN ATTRACTIVE GIRL NEAR HIM.
A KURDISH FAMILY. A MOTHER AND A FEW KIDS...
...WITH ALL KINDS OF PAINS AND ACHES ON THEIR FACES.

A YOUNG COUPLE SPEAKING AZERI.

PERHAPS THEY TOOK REFUGE FROM RECENT CRACKDOWNS.

NEYESTANI! COME IN!

MR. NEYESTANI. I AM, OF COURSE, FAMILIAR WITH YOUR CASE.

UNFORTUNATELY, WE HAVE A LONG BACKLOG OF OTHER APPLICATIONS.

TAKE THIS DOCUMENT AND SHOW IT TO THE POLICE.

YOU'LL HAVE TO LIVE IN A SMALL TOWN, FOR 10 MONTHS, UNDER POLICE SUPERVISION, UNTIL IT'S YOUR TURN.

TEN MONTHS? WHERE?

ISPARTA!

YAAAAAAA

*ISPARTA IS A SMALL TOWN IN WESTERN TURKEY.

WE WENT BACK TO OUR MOTEL IN THE ULUS NEIGHBORHOOD.

EKMEK, FRESH EKMEK!

ULUS

ISPARTA IS SMALL AND VERY COLD. HOW WILL WE SURVIVE THERE?

OUR MOTEL WAS NOT TOP OF THE LINE. IT WAS REALLY COLD.

WE TURNED OFF THE HEAT AT NIGHT BECAUSE ELECTRICITY WAS EXPENSIVE. WE DIDN'T HAVE A FRIDGE BUT WE DIDN'T NEED ONE...

THE BALCONY WORKED JUST FINE.

WE WERE CHARGED AN ARM AND A LEG FOR THAT ROOM.

WE'RE STAYING FOR ANOTHER WEEK.

FORANOTHER? VAT IZ FORANOTHER?

155

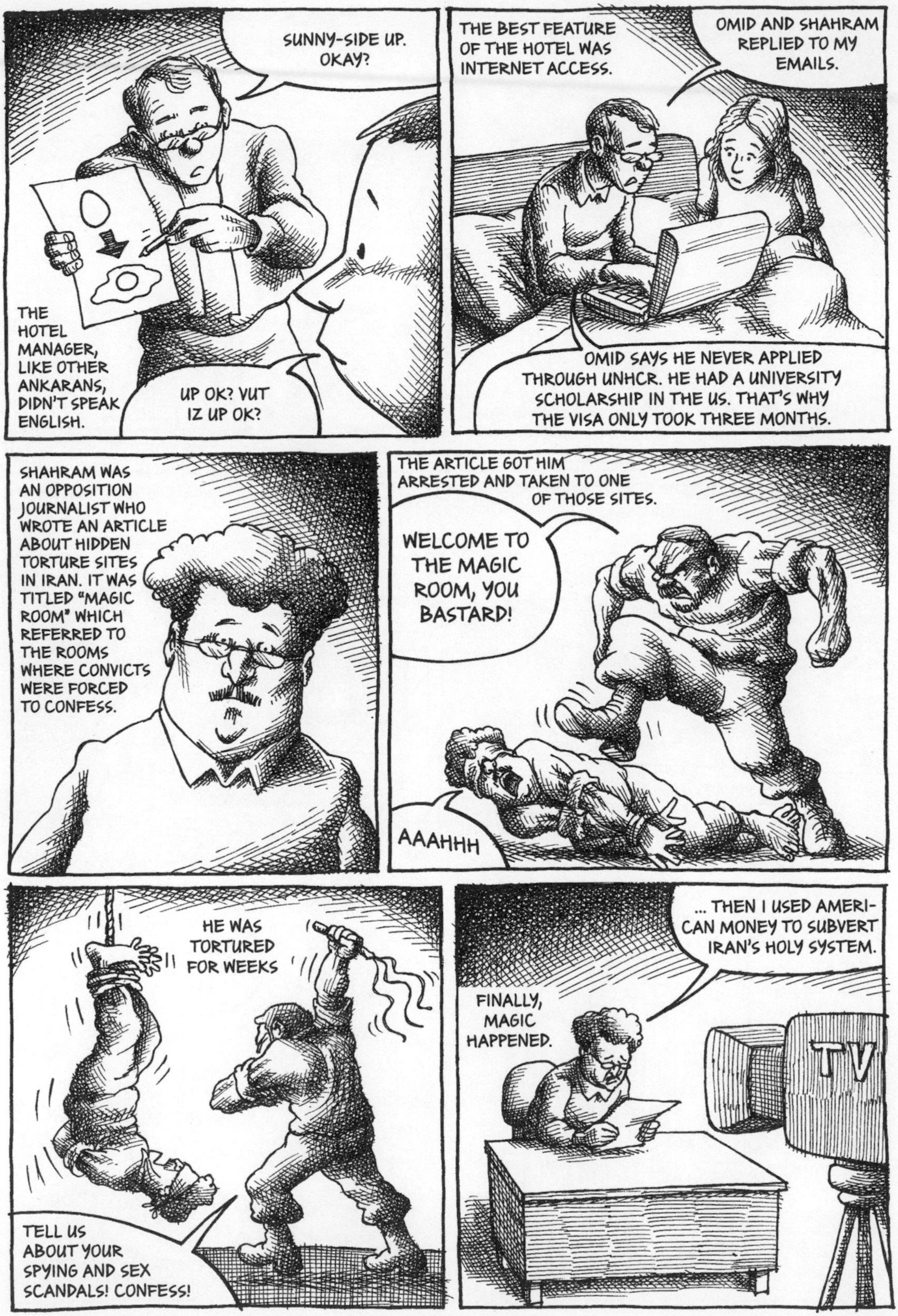
SUNNY-SIDE UP. OKAY?
THE HOTEL MANAGER, LIKE OTHER ANKARANS, DIDN'T SPEAK ENGLISH.
UP OK? VUT IZ UP OK?
THE BEST FEATURE OF THE HOTEL WAS INTERNET ACCESS.
OMID AND SHAHRAM REPLIED TO MY EMAILS.
OMID SAYS HE NEVER APPLIED THROUGH UNHCR. HE HAD A UNIVERSITY SCHOLARSHIP IN THE US. THAT'S WHY THE VISA ONLY TOOK THREE MONTHS.
SHAHRAM WAS AN OPPOSITION JOURNALIST WHO WROTE AN ARTICLE ABOUT HIDDEN TORTURE SITES IN IRAN. IT WAS TITLED "MAGIC ROOM" WHICH REFERRED TO THE ROOMS WHERE CONVICTS WERE FORCED TO CONFESS.
THE ARTICLE GOT HIM ARRESTED AND TAKEN TO ONE OF THOSE SITES.
WELCOME TO THE MAGIC ROOM, YOU BASTARD!
AAAHHH
HE WAS TORTURED FOR WEEKS
TELL US ABOUT YOUR SPYING AND SEX SCANDALS! CONFESS!
FINALLY, MAGIC HAPPENED.
... THEN I USED AMERI-CAN MONEY TO SUBVERT IRAN'S HOLY SYSTEM.
TV

SHAHRAM WAS FREED ON BAIL. HE ESCAPED TO TURKEY WITH HIS FAMILY AND ASKED FOR REFUGEE STATUS THROUGH UNHCR IN ANKARA. NOW HE'S FIGHTING COLD AND POVERTY IN A RURAL TOWN WHILE WAITING FOR HIS APPLICATION TO BE CONSIDERED.

HIS INTERVIEW WAS ONLY A MONTH AFTER APPLYING, BUT HE'S BEEN HERE FOR MORE THAN TWO YEARS! WE COULD BE STUCK HERE FOR FIVE YEARS!

I GOT AN EMAIL FROM AZZI.

SHE SAYS HER FRIEND AGAH WAS REJECTED FROM US AND CANADIAN EMBASSIES SO MANY TIMES, HE SPENT 20 MILLION TOOMANS ON A SMUGGLER. NOW HE'S SAFE AND SOUND IN CANADA!

20 MILLION? WE DON'T HAVE THAT KIND OF MONEY.

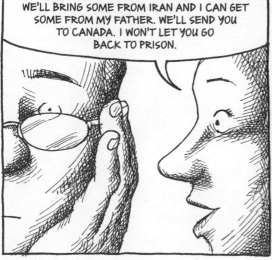

WE'LL BRING SOME FROM IRAN AND I CAN GET SOME FROM MY FATHER. WE'LL SEND YOU TO CANADA. I WON'T LET YOU GO BACK TO PRISON.

FORGET IT. I DON'T WANT TO GO ANYWHERE ALONE. WE FLED TO BE TOGETHER.

I'LL CALL THE NEW LAWYER. HE'S TRYING TO NEGOTIATE MY CASE. MAYBE WE CAN GO BACK TO IRAN.

DADZAAD, MY NEW LAWYER HAD TONS OF EXPERIENCE IN POLITICAL CASES.

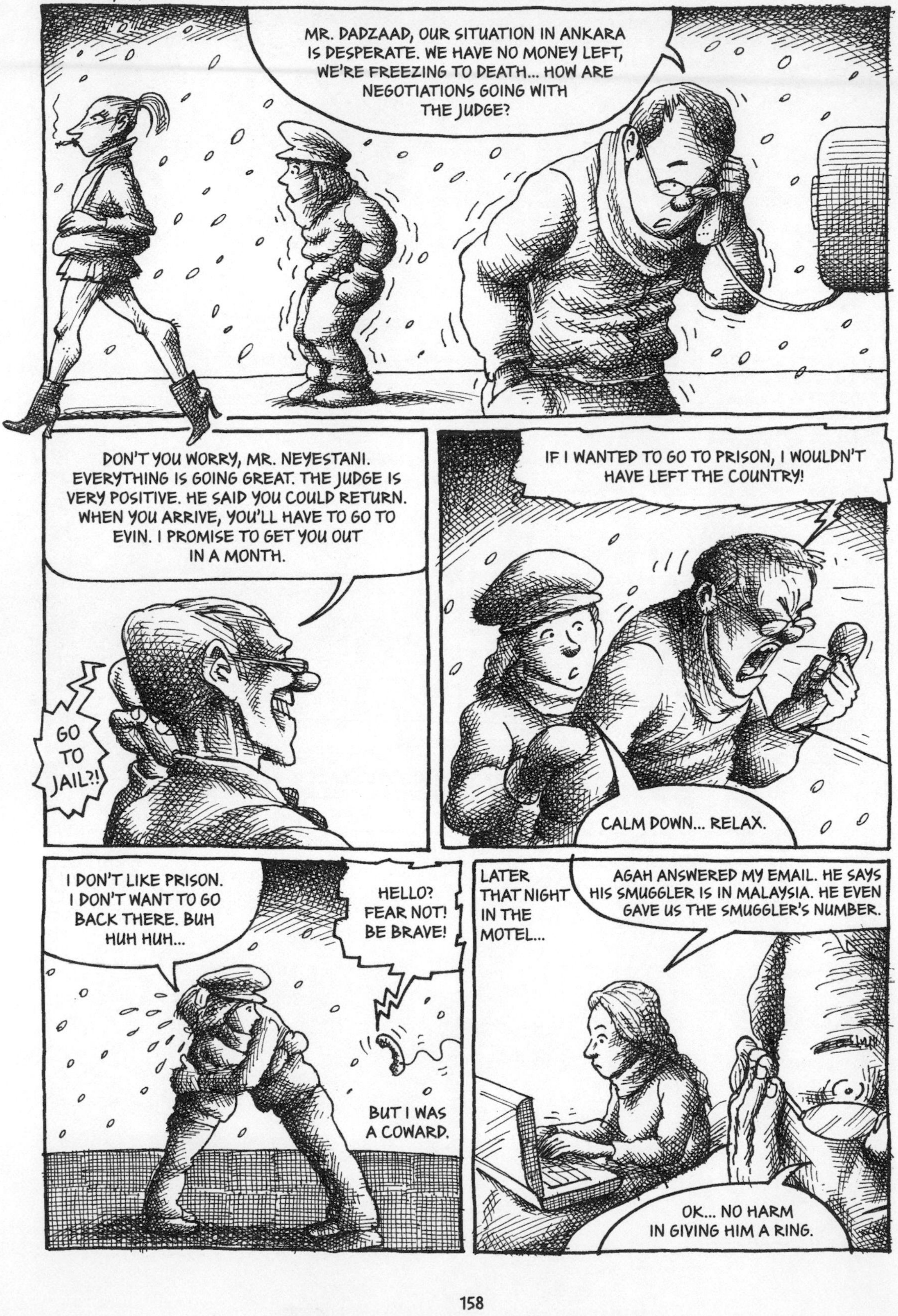
MR. DADZAAD, OUR SITUATION IN ANKARA IS DESPERATE. WE HAVE NO MONEY LEFT, WE'RE FREEZING TO DEATH... HOW ARE NEGOTIATIONS GOING WITH THE JUDGE?
DON'T YOU WORRY, MR. NEYESTANI. EVERYTHING IS GOING GREAT. THE JUDGE IS VERY POSITIVE. HE SAID YOU COULD RETURN. WHEN YOU ARRIVE, YOU'LL HAVE TO GO TO EVIN. I PROMISE TO GET YOU OUT IN A MONTH.
GO TO JAIL?!
IF I WANTED TO GO TO PRISON, I WOULDN'T HAVE LEFT THE COUNTRY!
CALM DOWN... RELAX.
I DON'T LIKE PRISON. I DON'T WANT TO GO BACK THERE. BUH HUH HUH...
HELLO? FEAR NOT! BE BRAVE!
BUT I WAS A COWARD.
LATER THAT NIGHT IN THE MOTEL...
AGAH ANSWERED MY EMAIL. HE SAYS HIS SMUGGLER IS IN MALAYSIA. HE EVEN GAVE US THE SMUGGLER'S NUMBER.
OK... NO HARM IN GIVING HIM A RING.

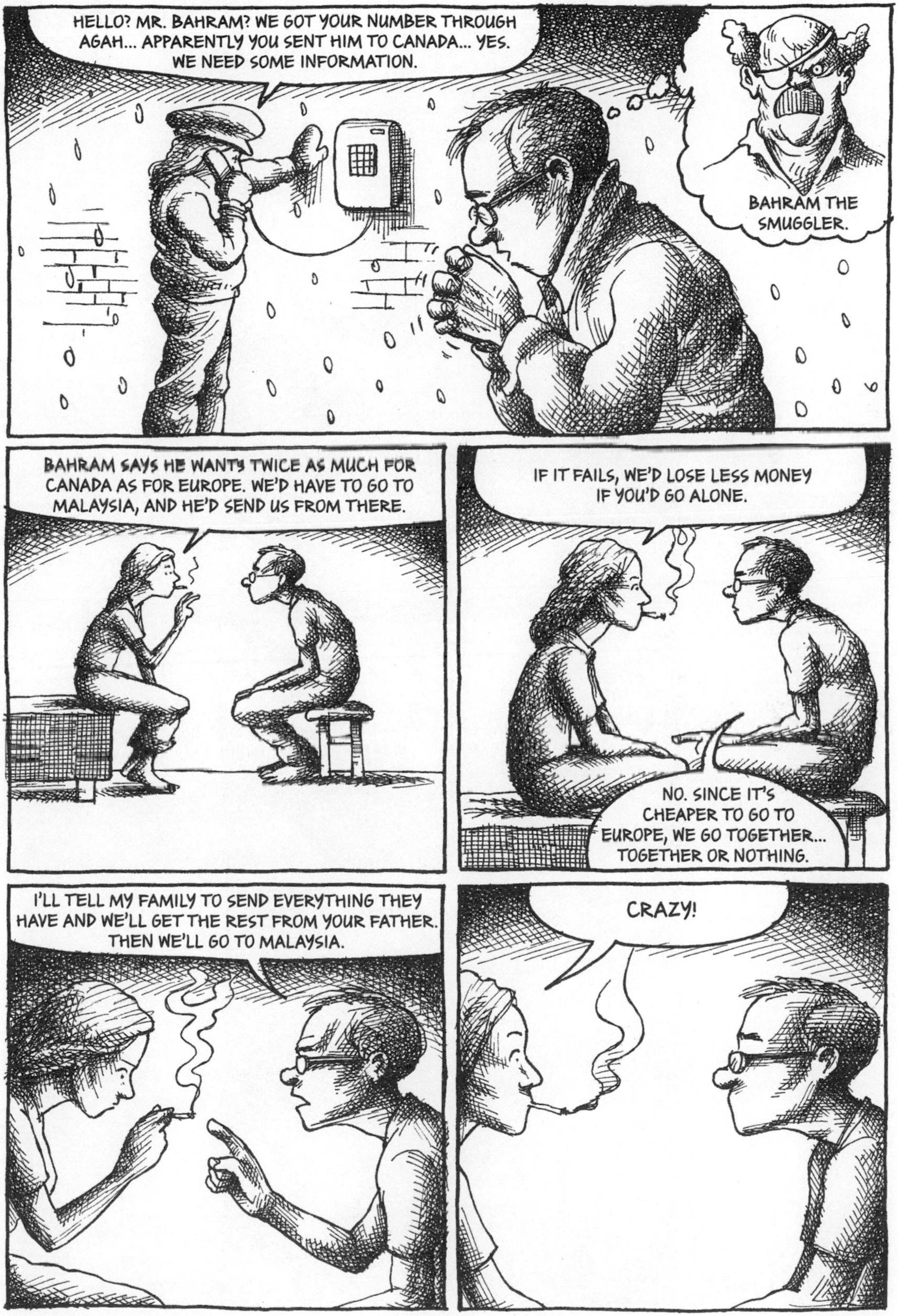

HELLO? MR. BAHRAM? WE GOT YOUR NUMBER THROUGH AGAH... APPARENTLY YOU SENT HIM TO CANADA... YES. WE NEED SOME INFORMATION.
BAHRAM THE SMUGGLER.
BAHRAM SAYS HE WANTS TWICE AS MUCH FOR CANADA AS FOR EUROPE. WE'D HAVE TO GO TO MALAYSIA, AND HE'D SEND US FROM THERE.
IF IT FAILS, WE'D LOSE LESS MONEY IF YOU'D GO ALONE.
NO. SINCE IT'S CHEAPER TO GO TO EUROPE, WE GO TOGETHER... TOGETHER OR NOTHING.
I'LL TELL MY FAMILY TO SEND EVERYTHING THEY HAVE AND WE'LL GET THE REST FROM YOUR FATHER. THEN WE'LL GO TO MALAYSIA.
CRAZY!

LET'S DO SOMETHING CRAZY!

CHAPTER FOURTEEN:

THE POSSESSED (2)

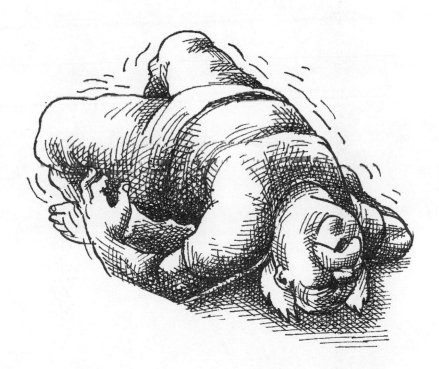

CHINA, THE START OF TANG LU'S GOOD DAY.
ENOUGH IS ENOUGH! MY BAD LUCK ENDS TODAY!
IT WAS 7 A.M. TANG LU KISSED HIS SEVEN-YEAR-OLD SON.
XIANG, YOU'LL BE PROUD OF YOUR DAD!
HE RODE HIS BIKE TO WORK.
HE FELT GREAT; TOP OF THE WORLD!
I'LL BEAT CHANG TODAY! ... AND PISS HIM OFF TOO !
FEBRUARY 14TH, 8 A.M., TANG LU GOT TO HIS OFFICE.

ON JAN 22, WE LANDED IN MALAYSIA.

DURING THE WHOLE TRIP I COULDN'T STOP THINKING ABOUT BAHRAM.

GATE 9

MR. SINGH

AKBAR

HE WAS WAITING FOR US AT GATE 9. I RECOGNIZED HIM INSTANTLY. HE LOOKED JUST AS I PICTURED HIM.

MR. BAHRAM?

BAHRAM, IT'S ME MR. NEYESTANI!

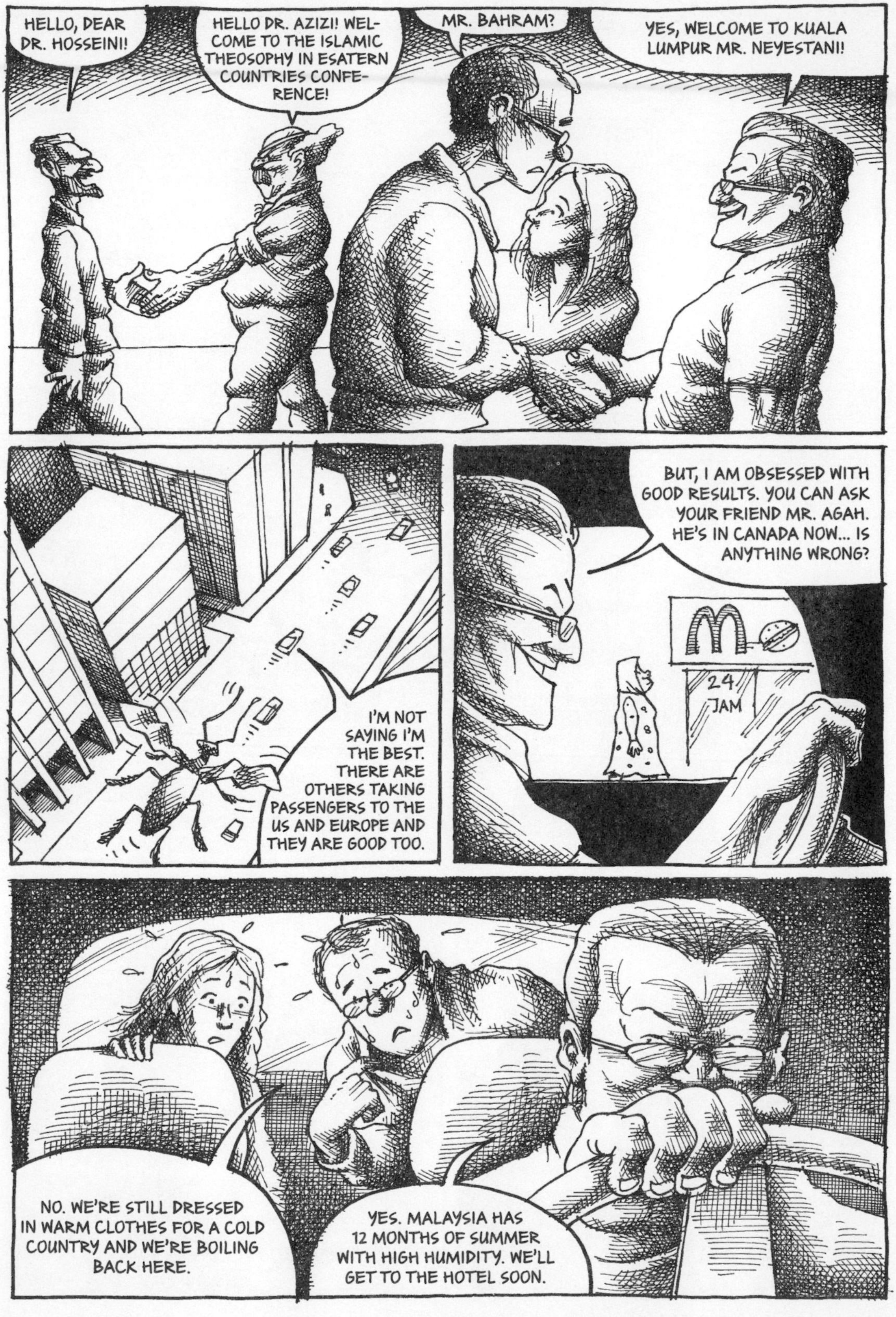
HELLO, DEAR DR. HOSSEINI!
HELLO DR. AZIZI! WEL-COME TO THE ISLAMIC THEOSOPHY IN ESATERN COUNTRIES CONFE-RENCE!
MR. BAHRAM?
YES, WELCOME TO KUALA LUMPUR MR. NEYESTANI!
I'M NOT SAYING I'M THE BEST. THERE ARE OTHERS TAKING PASSENGERS TO THE US AND EUROPE AND THEY ARE GOOD TOO.
BUT, I AM OBSESSED WITH GOOD RESULTS. YOU CAN ASK YOUR FRIEND MR. AGAH. HE'S IN CANADA NOW... IS ANYTHING WRONG?
24 JAM
NO. WE'RE STILL DRESSED IN WARM CLOTHES FOR A COLD COUNTRY AND WE'RE BOILING BACK HERE.
YES. MALAYSIA HAS 12 MONTHS OF SUMMER WITH HIGH HUMIDITY. WE'LL GET TO THE HOTEL SOON.

SEE? IT'S COMFOR-TABLE.

YOU HAVE A GOOD REST TONIGHT. LET'S MEET FOR BREAKFAST TOMORROW MORNING TO TALK ABOUT THE FIRST STEPS.

FROM OUR HOTEL WINDOW I COULD SEE THE NEW HIGH-RISES OF THE SEEMINGLY MODERN CITY.

BUT, WHEN WE WENT FOR A WALK,

THE OLDER PARTS OF TOWN FELT AS IF WE HAD ENTERED LAT'S COMIC BOOKS*.

*LAT IS A PROMINENT MALAYSIAN CARTOONIST.

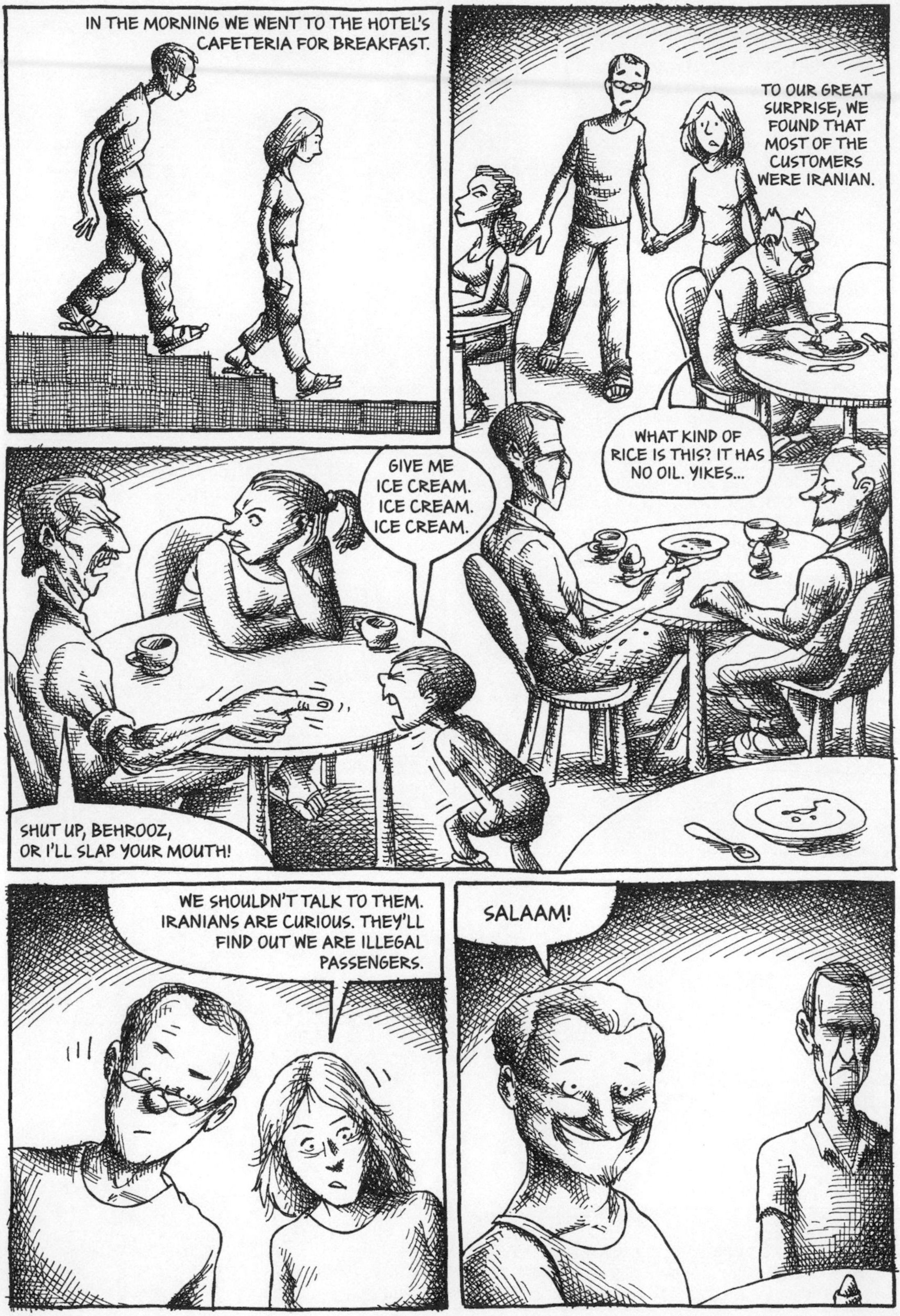
IN THE MORNING WE WENT TO THE HOTEL'S CAFETERIA FOR BREAKFAST.
TO OUR GREAT SURPRISE, WE FOUND THAT MOST OF THE CUSTOMERS WERE IRANIAN.
WHAT KIND OF RICE IS THIS? IT HAS NO OIL. YIKES...
GIVE ME ICE CREAM. ICE CREAM. ICE CREAM.
SHUT UP, BEHROOZ, OR I'LL SLAP YOUR MOUTH!
WE SHOULDN'T TALK TO THEM. IRANIANS ARE CURIOUS. THEY'LL FIND OUT WE ARE ILLEGAL PASSENGERS.
SALAAM!

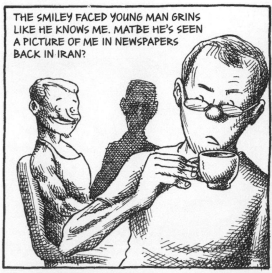

THE SMILEY FACED YOUNG MAN GRINS LIKE HE KNOWS ME. MATBE HE'S SEEN A PICTURE OF ME IN NEWSPAPERS BACK IN IRAN?

IN THE AFTERNOON, BAHRAM CAME TO OUR ROOM.

WE'LL GET YOU FRENCH PASSPORTS. THEY'LL MATCH YOUR FEATURES BETTER.

YOU'LL GO TO CHINA FIRST AND YOU'LL STAY THERE FOR A COUPLE OF WEEKS. YOUR NEW PASSPORTS WILL BE STAMPED THERE. WE CALL IT BEING "REVIVED." THEN YOU'LL FLY TO ENGLAND.

BUT WE DON'T SPEAK FRENCH.

DON'T WORRY, THE CHINESE BORDER OFFICIALS CAN'T SPEAK A BIT OF ENGLISH LET ALONE FRENCH. THEY WON'T GIVE YOU A HARD TIME. YOUR APPEARANCE IS PERFECT AND I CAN GUARANTEE SUCCESS. 100 PERCENT.

I REALLY HOPE YOU'RE RIGHT. HERE, 16 THOUSAND EUROS. IT'S ALL THE MONEY WE HAVE.

DON'T WORRY MR. NEYESTANI...

AGAH WAS WORRIED TOO, BUT NOW HE'S HAVING FUN IN CANADA. I CARE FOR THE SAFETY OF MY CLIENT MORE THAN MONEY.

WE MADE A MISTAKE. WE SHOULDN'T HAVE GIVEN ALL THE MONEY UP FRONT. IT WAS ALL WE HAD.

WE HAD NO CHOICE. AGAH SAID BAHRAM WOULDN'T START BEFORE HE HAD ALL THE MONEY.

A COUPLE DAYS LATER.

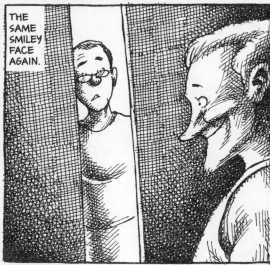

THE SAME SMILEY FACE AGAIN.

HELLO! HOW ARE YOU?

SORRY, DO WE KNOW EACH OTHER?

AREN'T YOU BAHRAM'S PASSENGERS?

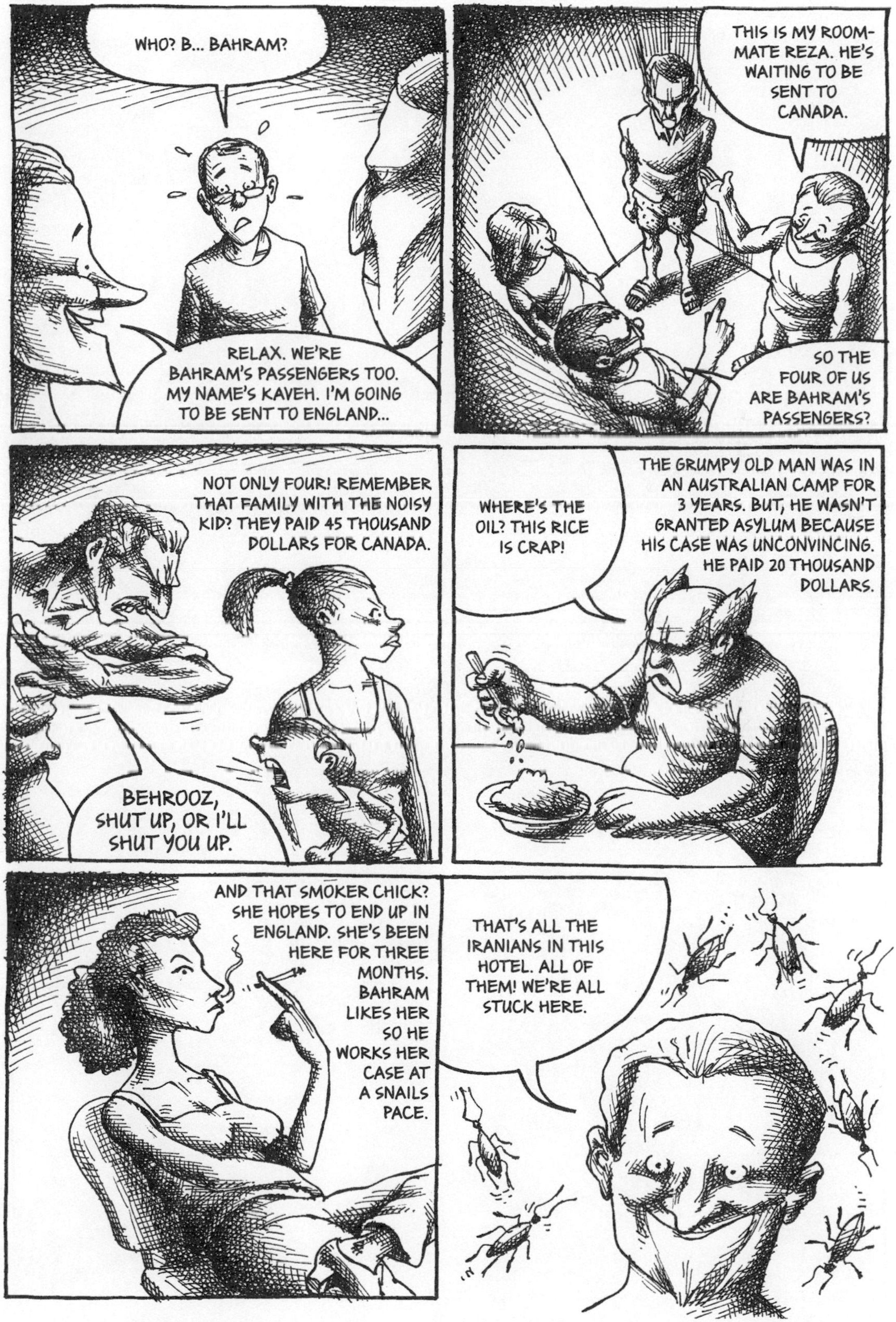
WHO? B... BAHRAM?
RELAX. WE'RE BAHRAM'S PASSENGERS TOO. MY NAME'S KAVEH. I'M GOING TO BE SENT TO ENGLAND...
THIS IS MY ROOMMATE REZA. HE'S WAITING TO BE SENT TO CANADA.
SO THE FOUR OF US ARE BAHRAM'S PASSENGERS?
NOT ONLY FOUR! REMEMBER THAT FAMILY WITH THE NOISY KID? THEY PAID 45 THOUSAND DOLLARS FOR CANADA.
BEHROOZ, SHUT UP, OR I'LL SHUT YOU UP.
THE GRUMPY OLD MAN WAS IN AN AUSTRALIAN CAMP FOR 3 YEARS. BUT, HE WASN'T GRANTED ASYLUM BECAUSE HIS CASE WAS UNCONVINCING. HE PAID 20 THOUSAND DOLLARS.
WHERE'S THE OIL? THIS RICE IS CRAP!
AND THAT SMOKER CHICK? SHE HOPES TO END UP IN ENGLAND. SHE'S BEEN HERE FOR THREE MONTHS. BAHRAM LIKES HER SO HE WORKS HER CASE AT A SNAILS PACE.
THAT'S ALL THE IRANIANS IN THIS HOTEL. ALL OF THEM! WE'RE ALL STUCK HERE.

I HAD A STRANGE DREAM THAT NIGHT.
I WAS BACK IN EVIN QUARANTINE BUT THE PRISONERS WERE REPLACED BY BAHRAM'S PASSENGERS.

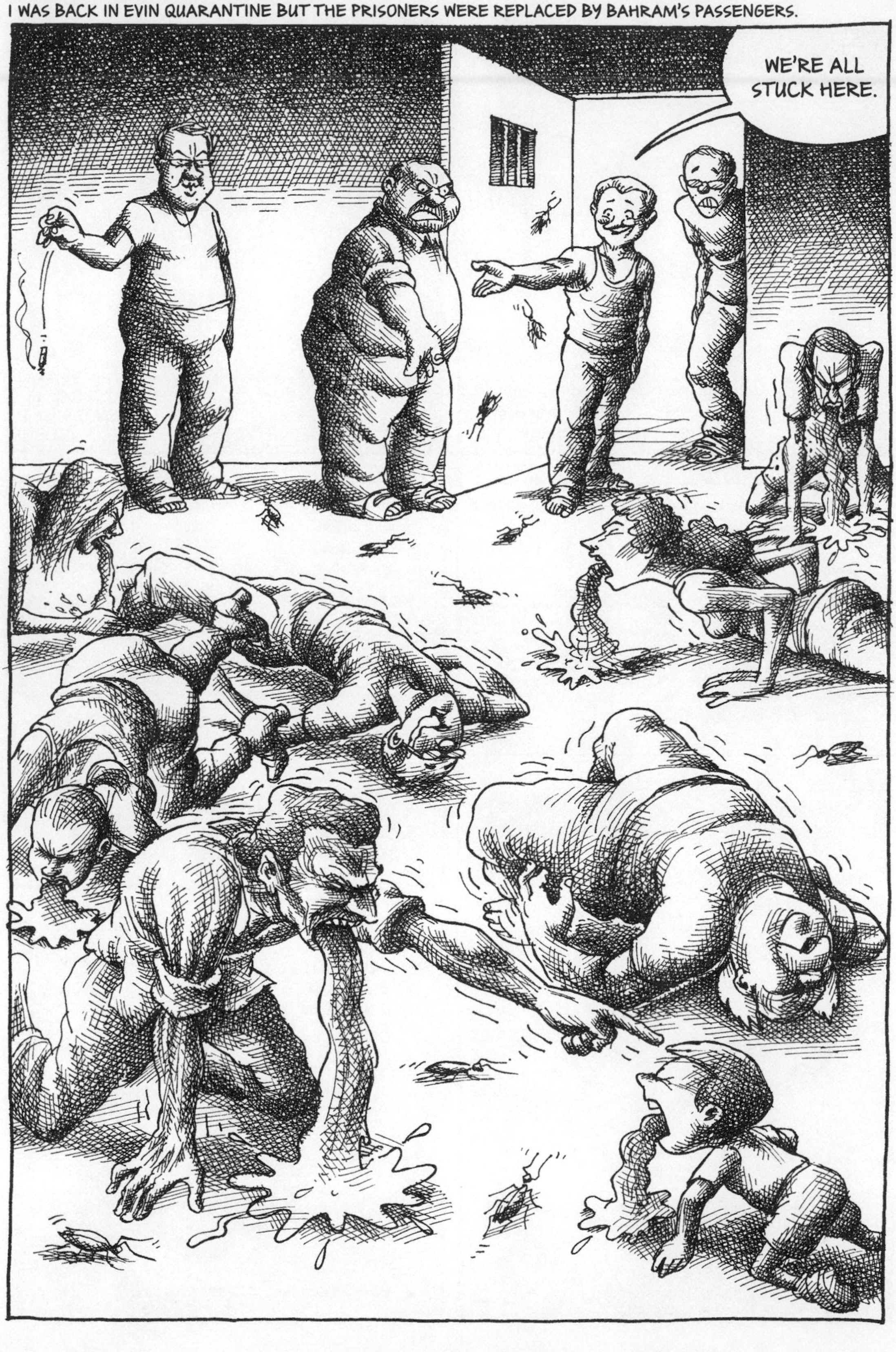
WE'RE ALL STUCK HERE.

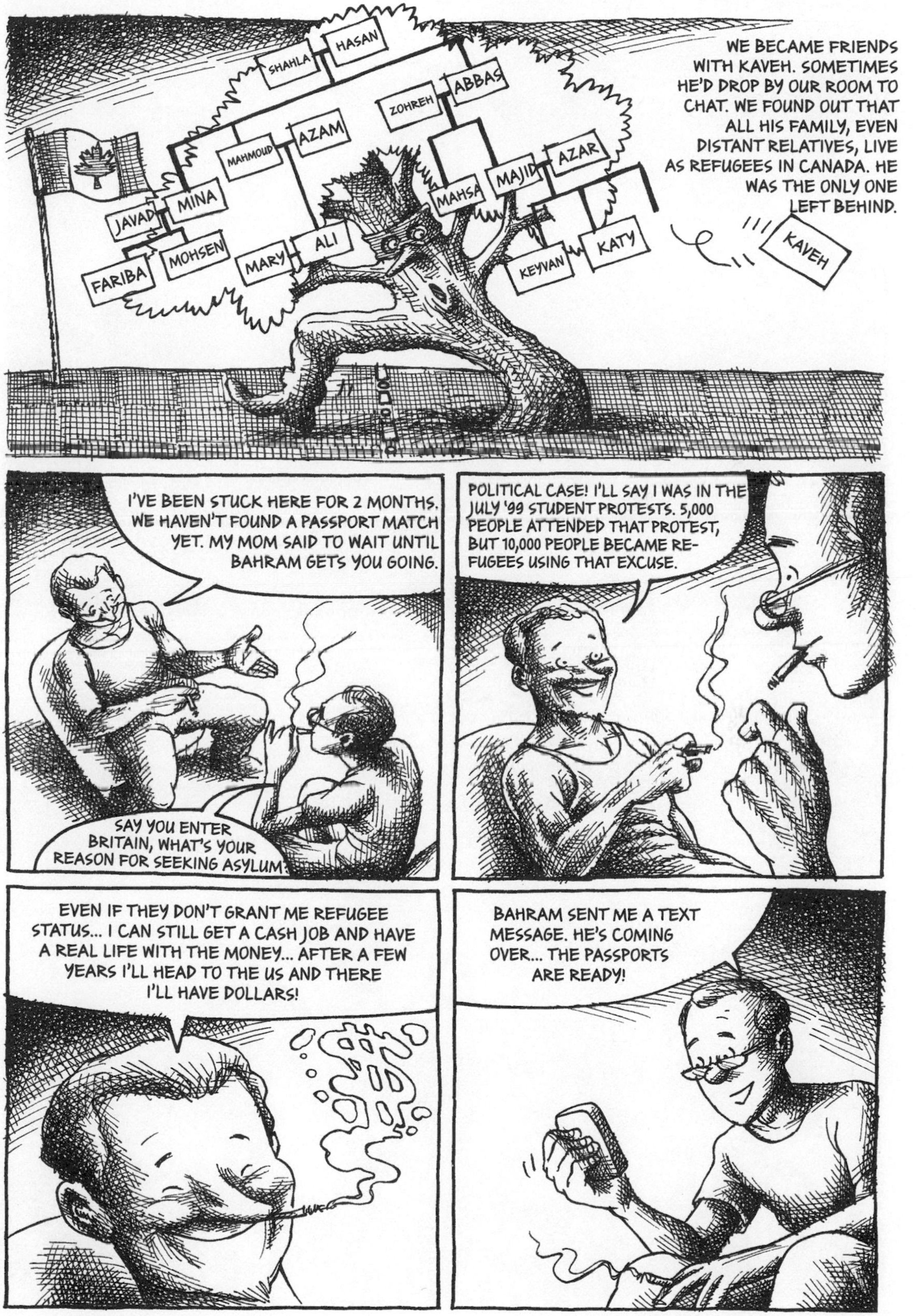
WE BECAME FRIENDS WITH KAVEH. SOMETIMES HE'D DROP BY OUR ROOM TO CHAT. WE FOUND OUT THAT ALL HIS FAMILY, EVEN DISTANT RELATIVES, LIVE AS REFUGEES IN CANADA. HE WAS THE ONLY ONE LEFT BEHIND.
SHAHLA
HASAN
ZOHREH
ABBAS
MAHMOUD
AZAM
JAVAD
MINA
FARIBA
MOHSEN
MARY
ALI
MAHSA
MAJID
AZAR
KEYVAN
KATY
KAVEH
I'VE BEEN STUCK HERE FOR 2 MONTHS. WE HAVEN'T FOUND A PASSPORT MATCH YET. MY MOM SAID TO WAIT UNTIL BAHRAM GETS YOU GOING.
SAY YOU ENTER BRITAIN, WHAT'S YOUR REASON FOR SEEKING ASYLUM?
POLITICAL CASE! I'LL SAY I WAS IN THE JULY '99 STUDENT PROTESTS. 5,000 PEOPLE ATTENDED THAT PROTEST, BUT 10,000 PEOPLE BECAME REFUGEES USING THAT EXCUSE.
EVEN IF THEY DON'T GRANT ME REFUGEE STATUS... I CAN STILL GET A CASH JOB AND HAVE A REAL LIFE WITH THE MONEY... AFTER A FEW YEARS I'LL HEAD TO THE US AND THERE I'LL HAVE DOLLARS!
BAHRAM SENT ME A TEXT MESSAGE. HE'S COMING OVER... THE PASSPORTS ARE READY!

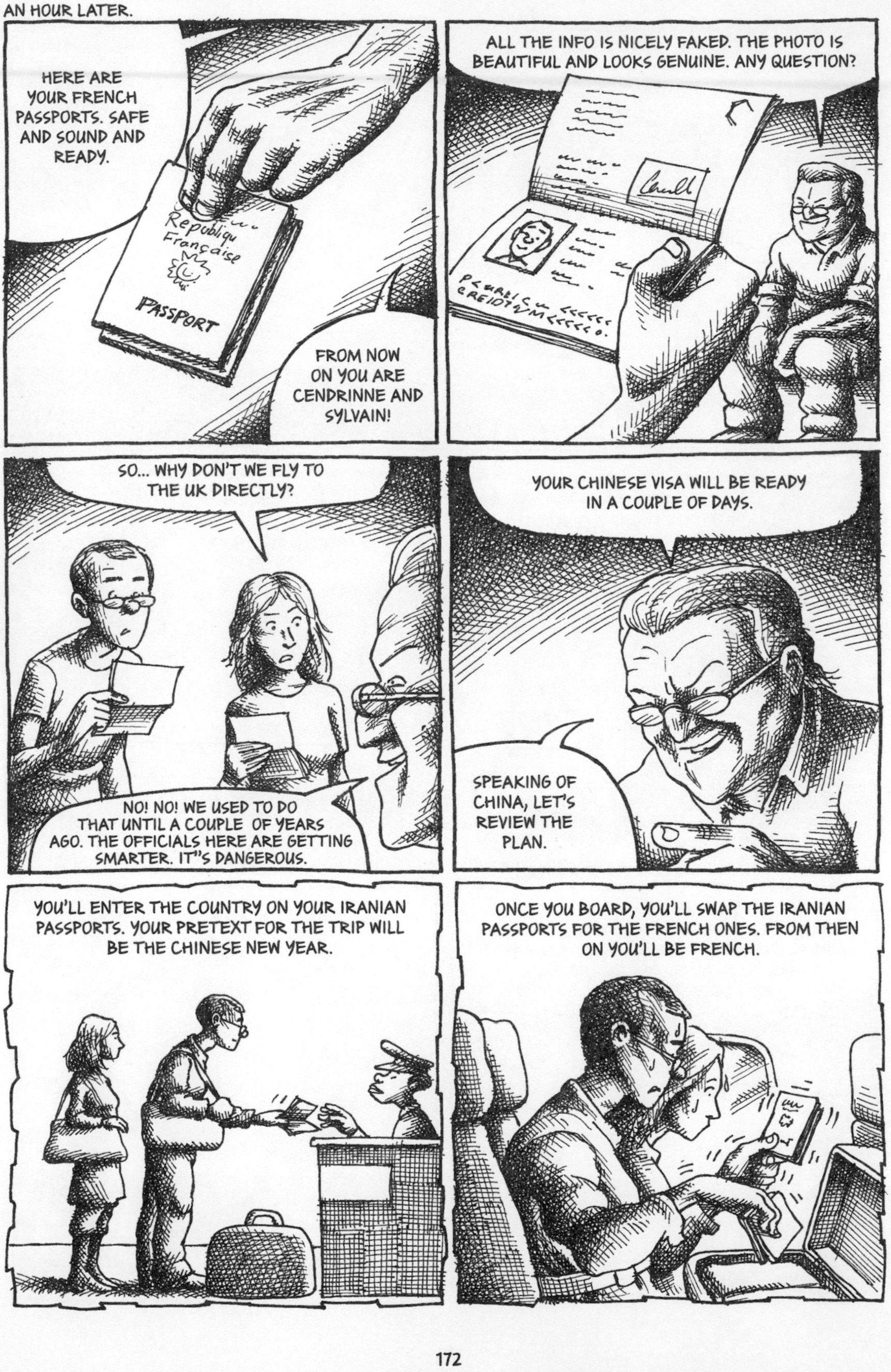
AN HOUR LATER.
HERE ARE YOUR FRENCH PASSPORTS. SAFE AND SOUND AND READY.
Republiqu Française
PASSPORT
FROM NOW ON YOU ARE CENDRINNE AND SYLVAIN!
ALL THE INFO IS NICELY FAKED. THE PHOTO IS BEAUTIFUL AND LOOKS GENUINE. ANY QUESTION?
SO... WHY DON'T WE FLY TO THE UK DIRECTLY?
NO! NO! WE USED TO DO THAT UNTIL A COUPLE OF YEARS AGO. THE OFFICIALS HERE ARE GETTING SMARTER. IT"S DANGEROUS.
YOUR CHINESE VISA WILL BE READY IN A COUPLE OF DAYS.
SPEAKING OF CHINA, LET'S REVIEW THE PLAN.
YOU'LL ENTER THE COUNTRY ON YOUR IRANIAN PASSPORTS. YOUR PRETEXT FOR THE TRIP WILL BE THE CHINESE NEW YEAR.
ONCE YOU BOARD, YOU'LL SWAP THE IRANIAN PASSPORTS FOR THE FRENCH ONES. FROM THEN ON YOU'LL BE FRENCH.

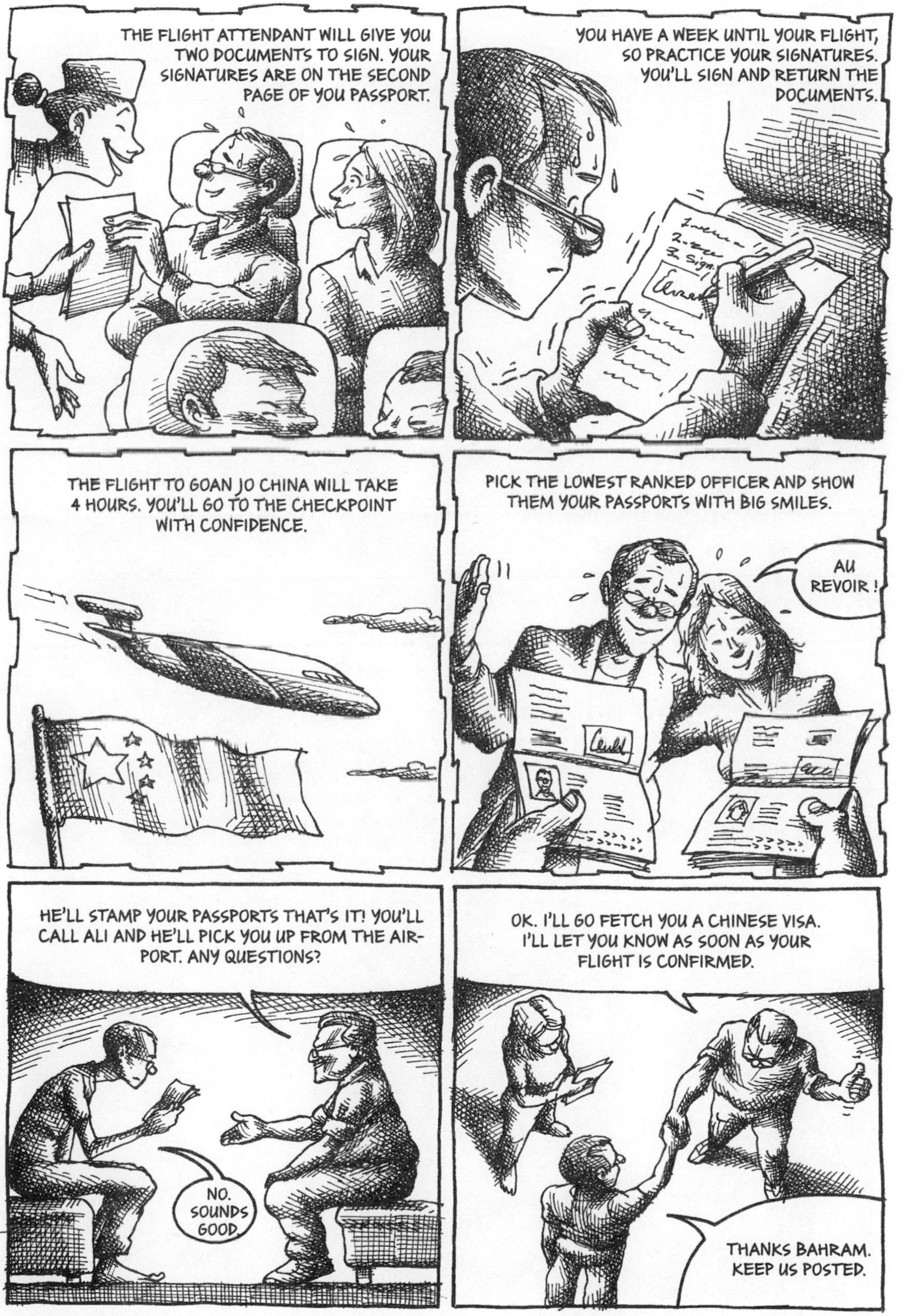

THE FLIGHT ATTENDANT WILL GIVE YOU TWO DOCUMENTS TO SIGN. YOUR SIGNATURES ARE ON THE SECOND PAGE OF YOU PASSPORT.
YOU HAVE A WEEK UNTIL YOUR FLIGHT, SO PRACTICE YOUR SIGNATURES. YOU'LL SIGN AND RETURN THE DOCUMENTS.
THE FLIGHT TO GOAN JO CHINA WILL TAKE 4 HOURS. YOU'LL GO TO THE CHECKPOINT WITH CONFIDENCE.
PICK THE LOWEST RANKED OFFICER AND SHOW THEM YOUR PASSPORTS WITH BIG SMILES.
AU REVOIR !
HE'LL STAMP YOUR PASSPORTS THAT'S IT! YOU'LL CALL ALI AND HE'LL PICK YOU UP FROM THE AIR-PORT. ANY QUESTIONS?
NO. SOUNDS GOOD.
OK. I'LL GO FETCH YOU A CHINESE VISA. I'LL LET YOU KNOW AS SOON AS YOUR FLIGHT IS CONFIRMED.
THANKS BAHRAM. KEEP US POSTED.

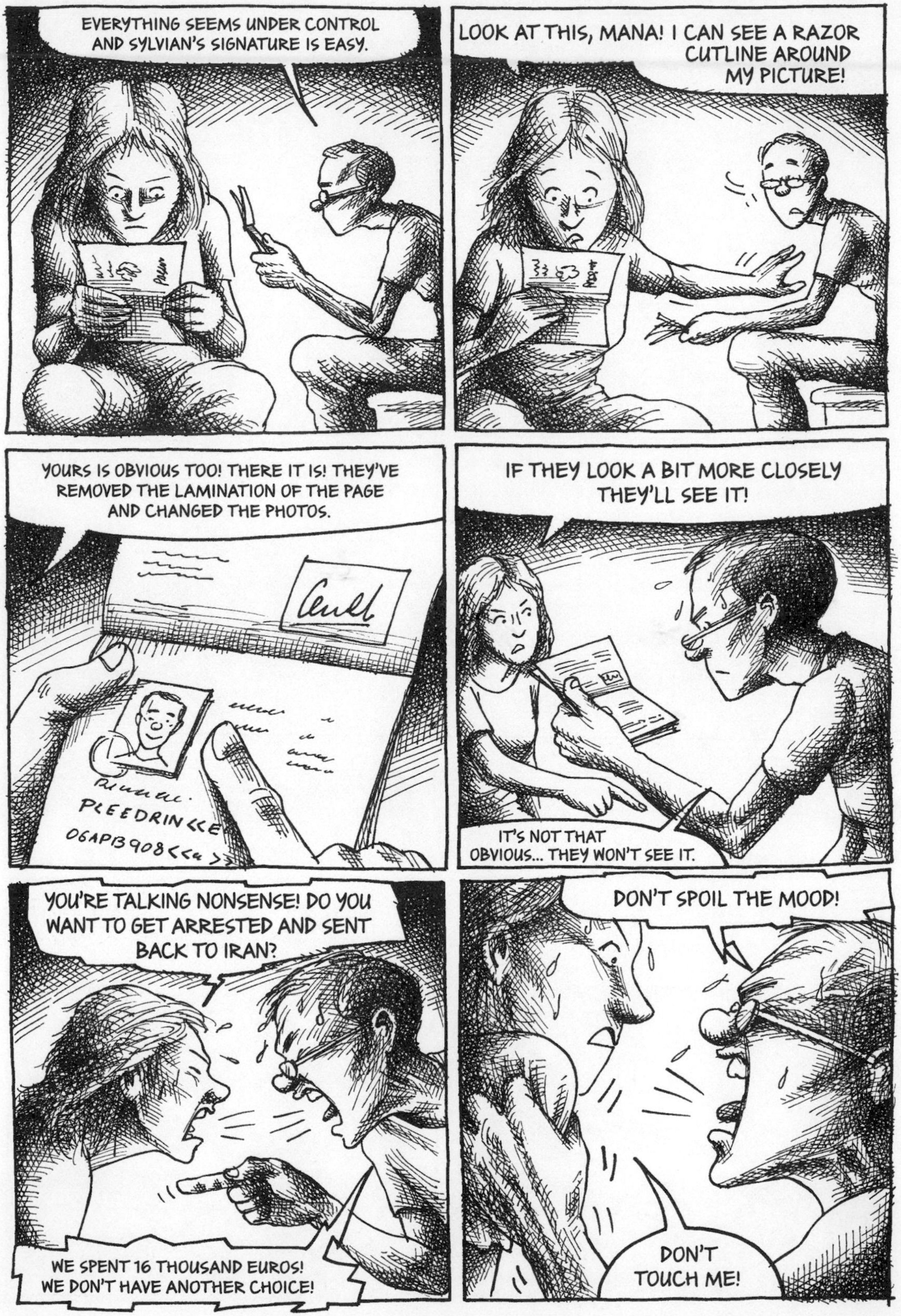
EVERYTHING SEEMS UNDER CONTROL AND SYLVIAN'S SIGNATURE IS EASY.
LOOK AT THIS, MANA! I CAN SEE A RAZOR CUTLINE AROUND MY PICTURE!
YOURS IS OBVIOUS TOO! THERE IT IS! THEY'VE REMOVED THE LAMINATION OF THE PAGE AND CHANGED THE PHOTOS.
IF THEY LOOK A BIT MORE CLOSELY THEY'LL SEE IT!
IT'S NOT THAT OBVIOUS... THEY WON'T SEE IT.
YOU'RE TALKING NONSENSE! DO YOU WANT TO GET ARRESTED AND SENT BACK TO IRAN?
WE SPENT 16 THOUSAND EUROS! WE DON'T HAVE ANOTHER CHOICE!
DON'T SPOIL THE MOOD!
DON'T TOUCH ME!

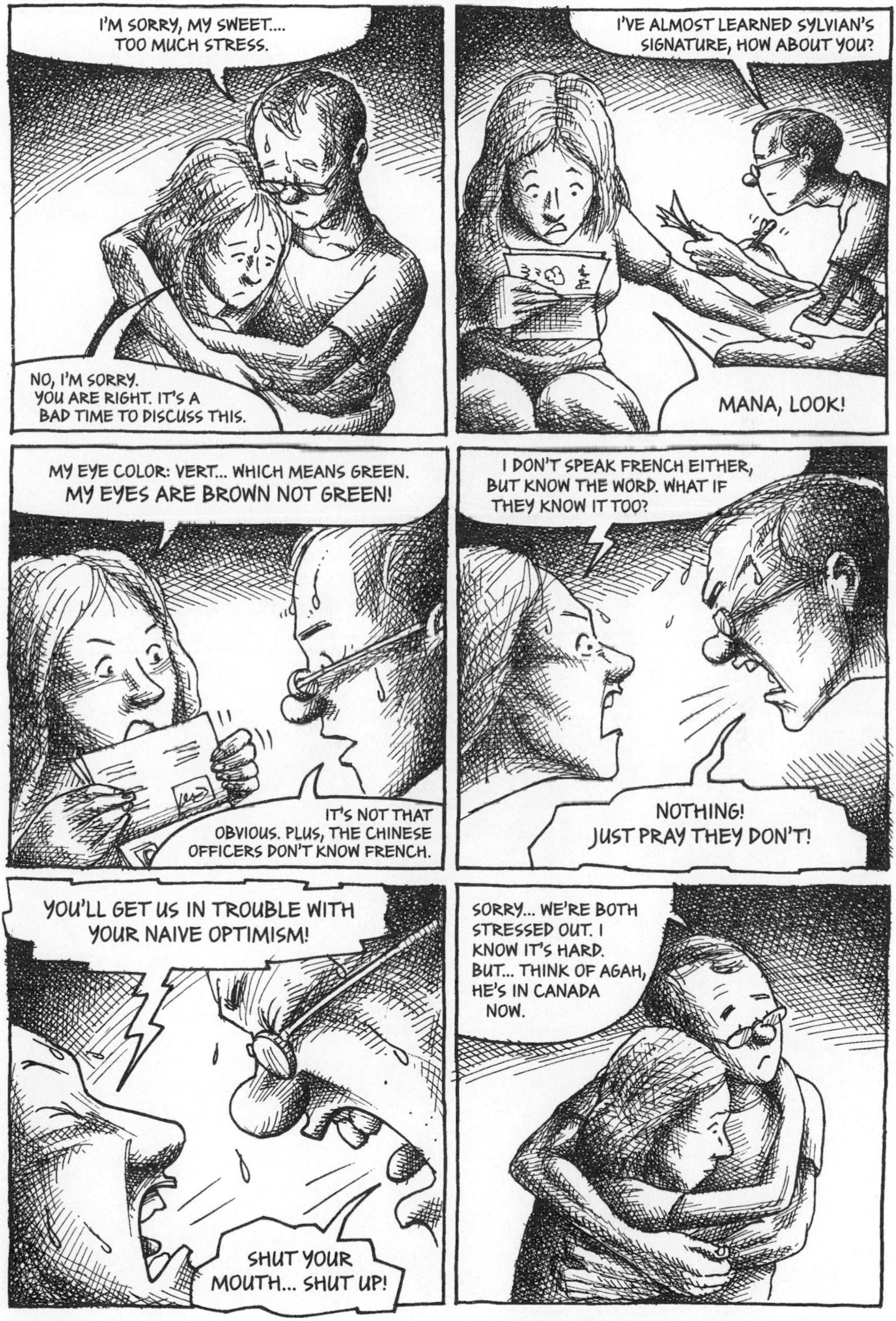
I'M SORRY, MY SWEET....
TOO MUCH STRESS.
NO, I'M SORRY.
YOU ARE RIGHT. IT'S A
BAD TIME TO DISCUSS THIS.
I'VE ALMOST LEARNED SYLVIAN'S
SIGNATURE, HOW ABOUT YOU?
MANA, LOOK!
MY EYE COLOR: VERT... WHICH MEANS GREEN.
MY EYES ARE BROWN NOT GREEN!
IT'S NOT THAT
OBVIOUS. PLUS, THE CHINESE
OFFICERS DON'T KNOW FRENCH.
I DON'T SPEAK FRENCH EITHER,
BUT KNOW THE WORD. WHAT IF
THEY KNOW IT TOO?
NOTHING!
JUST PRAY THEY DON'T!
YOU'LL GET US IN TROUBLE WITH
YOUR NAIVE OPTIMISM!
SHUT YOUR
MOUTH... SHUT UP!
SORRY... WE'RE BOTH
STRESSED OUT. I
KNOW IT'S HARD.
BUT... THINK OF AGAH,
HE'S IN CANADA
NOW.

I LOOKED IN THE MIRROR. ONCE AGAIN MANA
NEYESTANI CEASED TO EXIST. INSTEAD, I SAW
SYLVAIN DUBRE, BORN IN A PARISIAN SUBURB.

A FEW DAYS LATER I TALKED ABOUT OUR PASSPORT PROBLEMS WITH KAVEH.

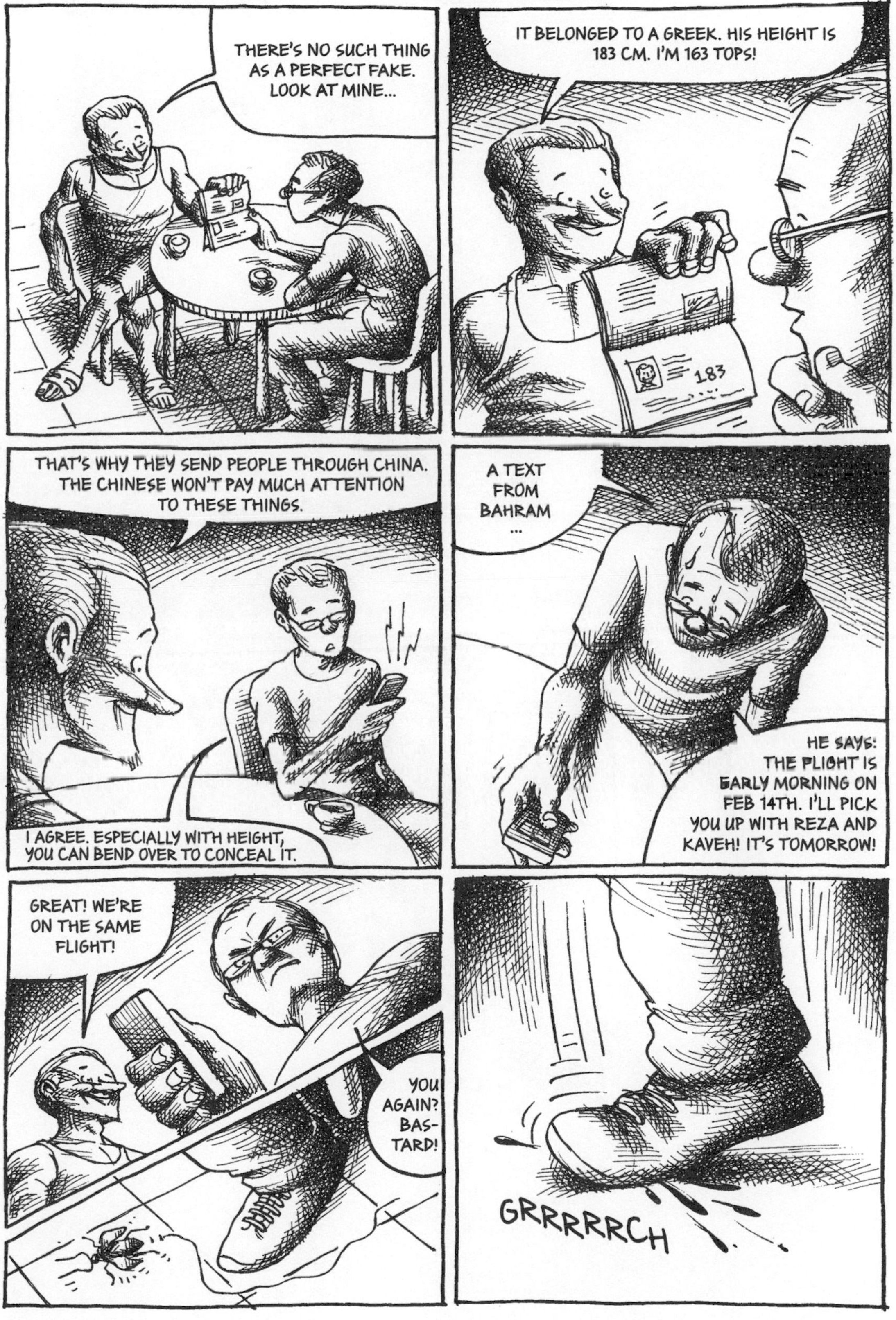
THERE'S NO SUCH THING AS A PERFECT FAKE. LOOK AT MINE...
IT BELONGED TO A GREEK. HIS HEIGHT IS 183 CM. I'M 163 TOPS!
183
THAT'S WHY THEY SEND PEOPLE THROUGH CHINA. THE CHINESE WON'T PAY MUCH ATTENTION TO THESE THINGS.
I AGREE. ESPECIALLY WITH HEIGHT, YOU CAN BEND OVER TO CONCEAL IT.
A TEXT FROM BAHRAM ...
HE SAYS: THE FLIGHT IS EARLY MORNING ON FEB 14TH. I'LL PICK YOU UP WITH REZA AND KAVEH! IT'S TOMORROW!
GREAT! WE'RE ON THE SAME FLIGHT!
YOU AGAIN? BAS-TARD!
GRRRRRCH

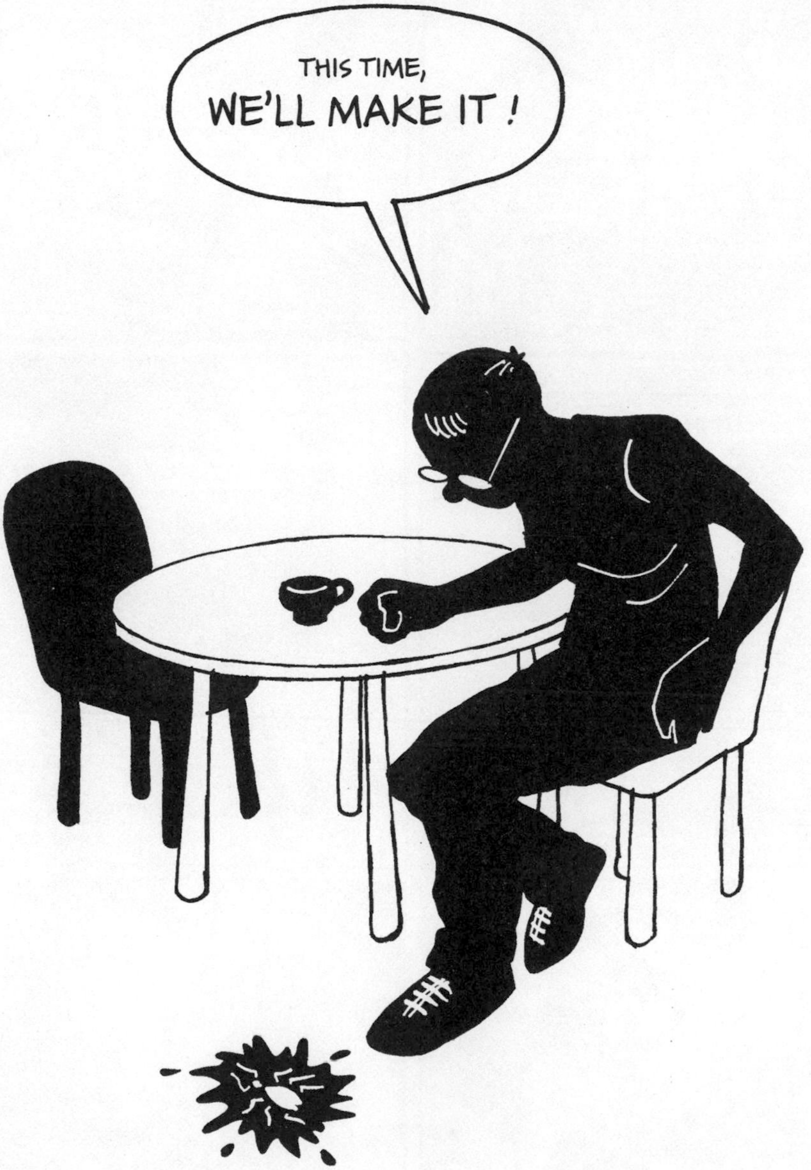
THIS TIME,
WE'LL MAKE IT!

CHAPTER FIFTEEN

DUEL

FEBRUARY 14TH AT 8AM TANG LU ARRIVED AT HIS OFFICE.

HE WENT TO HIS LOCKER AND CHANGED INTO WORK CLOTHES.

HE SAT DOWN AS HE DID EVERY DAY...

PASSPORT CONTROL

... AT THE PASSPORT CONTROL DESK AT THE GOAN JO AIRPORT

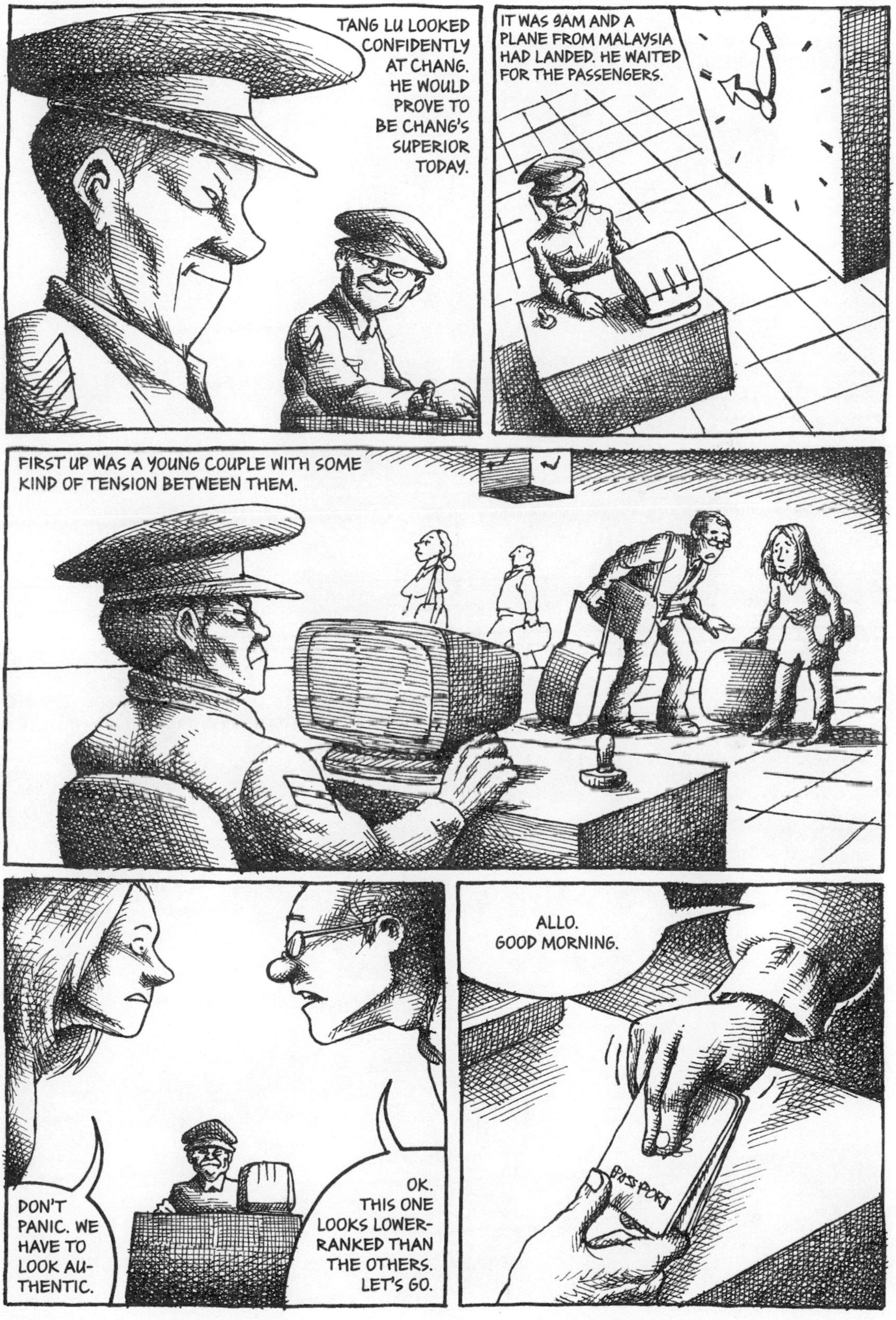
TANG LU LOOKED CONFIDENTLY AT CHANG. HE WOULD PROVE TO BE CHANG'S SUPERIOR TODAY.
IT WAS 9AM AND A PLANE FROM MALAYSIA HAD LANDED. HE WAITED FOR THE PASSENGERS.
FIRST UP WAS A YOUNG COUPLE WITH SOME KIND OF TENSION BETWEEN THEM.
OK. THIS ONE LOOKS LOWER-RANKED THAN THE OTHERS. LET'S GO.
DON'T PANIC. WE HAVE TO LOOK AU-THENTIC.
ALLO. GOOD MORNING.
PASSPORT

THE MAN'S FACE WAS VERY FAMILIAR. TANG LU THOUGHT HE MIGHT BE THE MIDDLE EASTERN CARTOONIST FROM LAST NIGHT'S DREAM...

BONJOUR!

...BUT THE PASSPORT WAS FRENCH.

FRENCH

WHY IS THE YOUNG MAN SWEATING SO MUCH? MAYBE IT'S THAT THICK JACKET HE'S WEARING.

WHY IS HE LOOKING AT ME LIKE THIS?

HE PROBABLY HEARD CHINA IS COLD... THE PLACE WHERE MY FATHER WAS IMPRISONED WAS VERY COLD.

HE MUST HAVE NOTICED THE CUT BENEATH MY PHOTO.

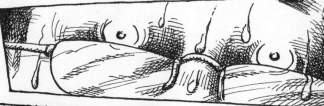

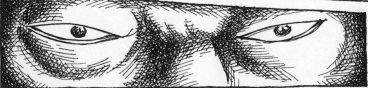

TODAY THE BAD LUCK OF THE LU FAMILY WILL END.

182

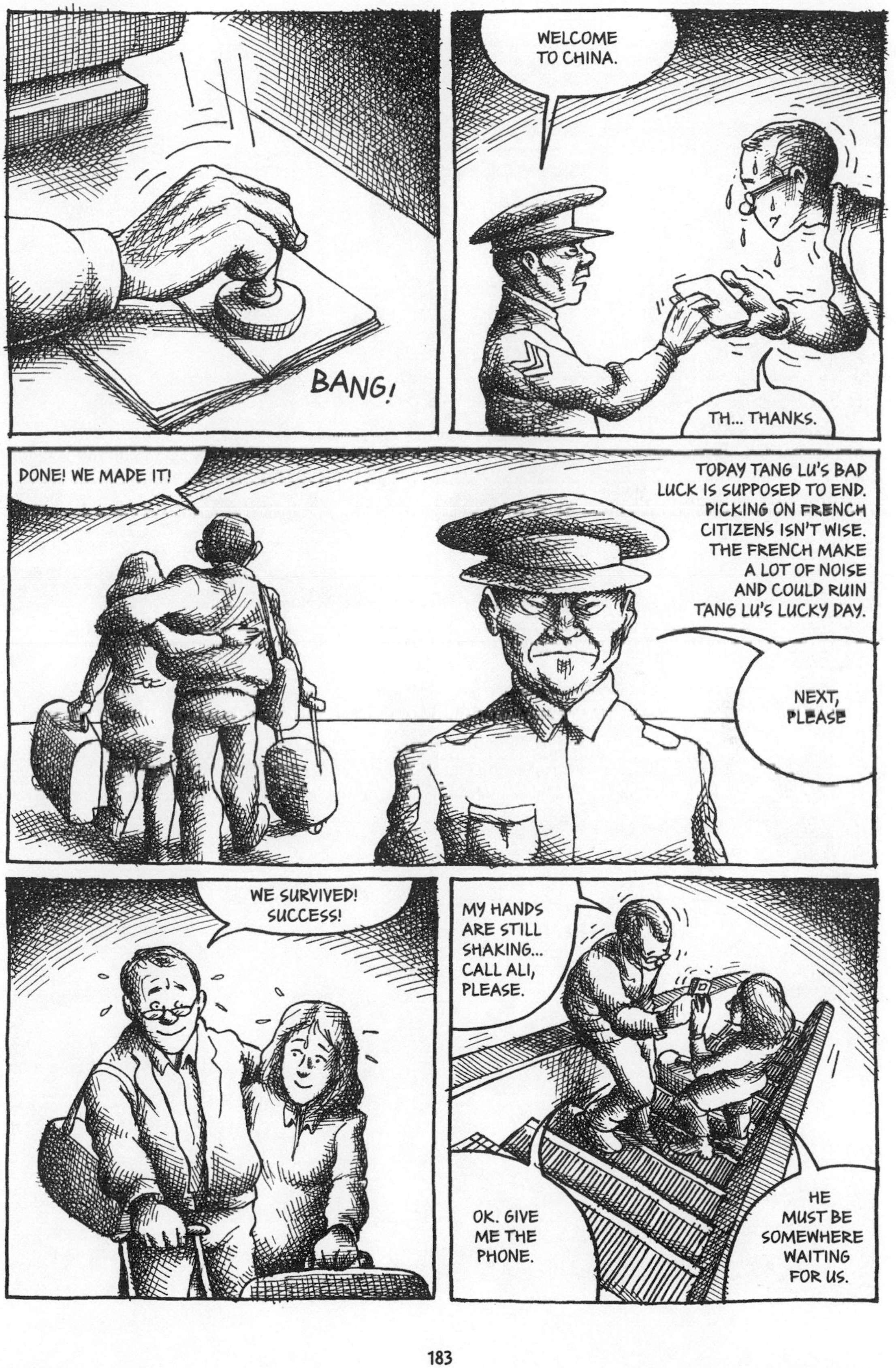
BANG!
WELCOME TO CHINA.
TH... THANKS.
DONE! WE MADE IT!
TODAY TANG LU'S BAD LUCK IS SUPPOSED TO END. PICKING ON FRENCH CITIZENS ISN'T WISE. THE FRENCH MAKE A LOT OF NOISE AND COULD RUIN TANG LU'S LUCKY DAY.
NEXT, PLEASE
WE SURVIVED! SUCCESS!
MY HANDS ARE STILL SHAKING... CALL ALI, PLEASE.
OK. GIVE ME THE PHONE.
HE MUST BE SOMEWHERE WAITING FOR US.

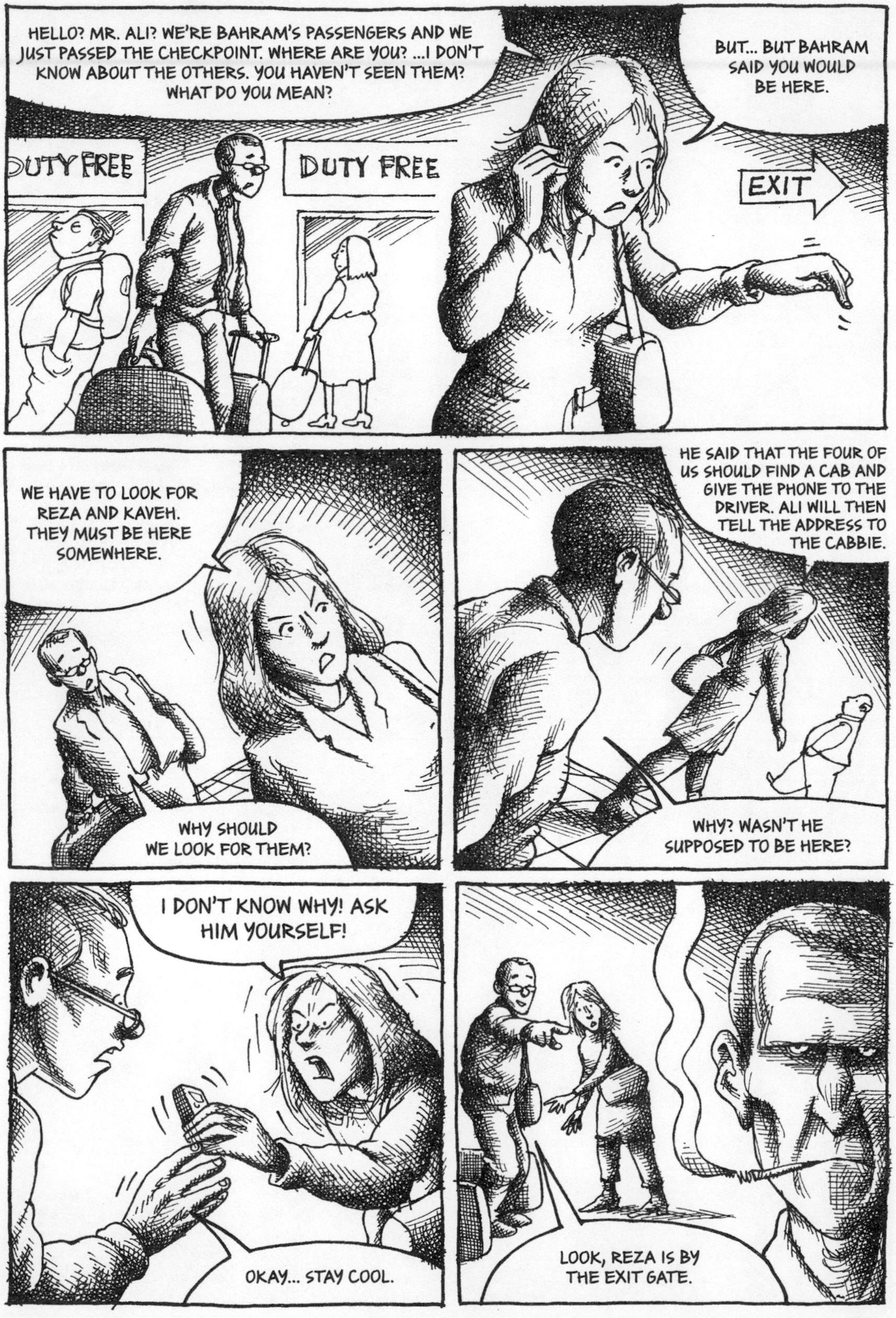
HELLO? MR. ALI? WE'RE BAHRAM'S PASSENGERS AND WE JUST PASSED THE CHECKPOINT. WHERE ARE YOU? ...I DON'T KNOW ABOUT THE OTHERS. YOU HAVEN'T SEEN THEM? WHAT DO YOU MEAN?
DUTY FREE
DUTY FREE
BUT... BUT BAHRAM SAID YOU WOULD BE HERE.
EXIT
WE HAVE TO LOOK FOR REZA AND KAVEH. THEY MUST BE HERE SOMEWHERE.
WHY SHOULD WE LOOK FOR THEM?
HE SAID THAT THE FOUR OF US SHOULD FIND A CAB AND GIVE THE PHONE TO THE DRIVER. ALI WILL THEN TELL THE ADDRESS TO THE CABBIE.
WHY? WASN'T HE SUPPOSED TO BE HERE?
I DON'T KNOW WHY! ASK HIM YOURSELF!
OKAY... STAY COOL.
LOOK, REZA IS BY THE EXIT GATE.

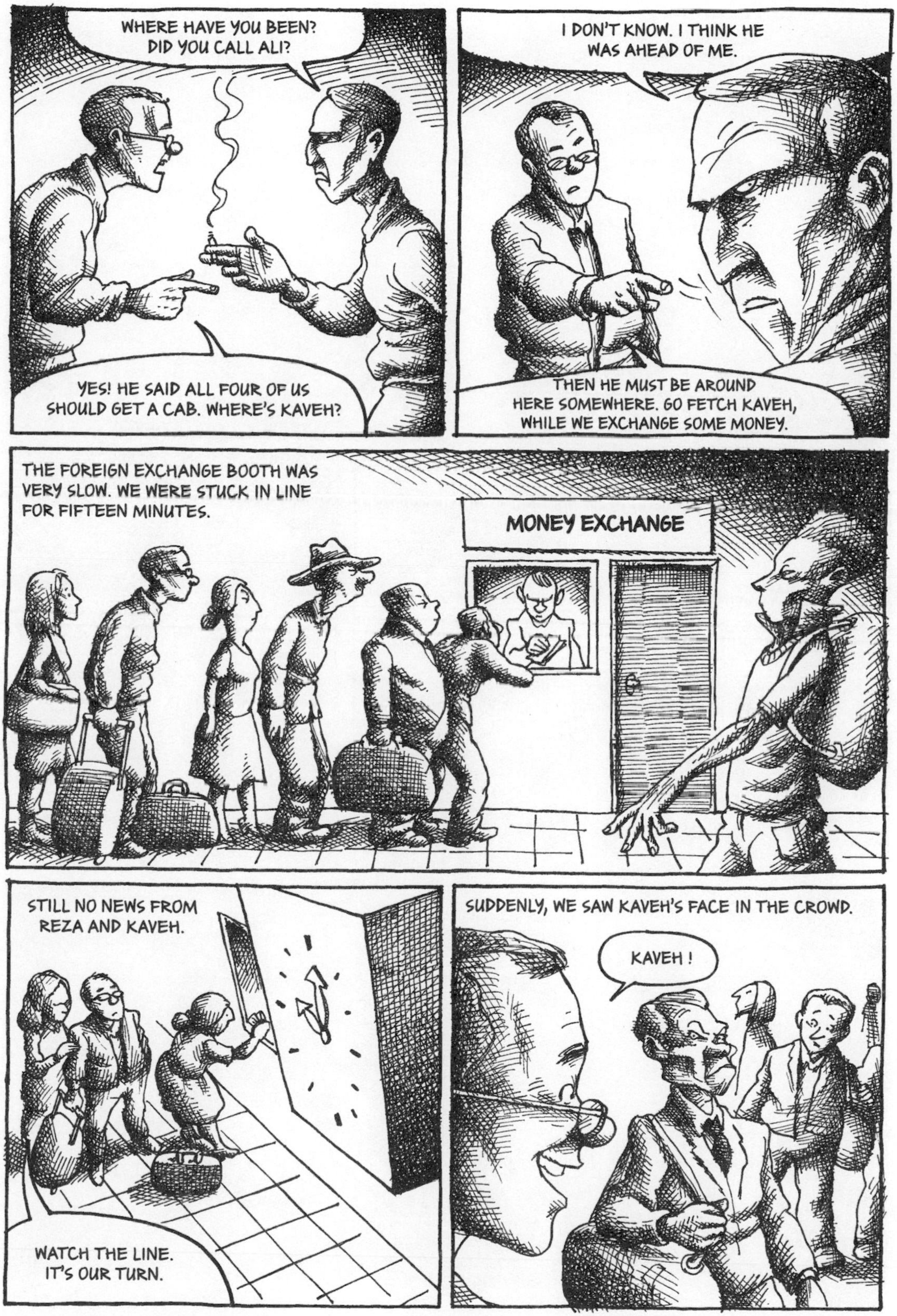
WHERE HAVE YOU BEEN? DID YOU CALL ALI?
YES! HE SAID ALL FOUR OF US SHOULD GET A CAB. WHERE'S KAVEH?
I DON'T KNOW. I THINK HE WAS AHEAD OF ME.
THEN HE MUST BE AROUND HERE SOMEWHERE. GO FETCH KAVEH, WHILE WE EXCHANGE SOME MONEY.
THE FOREIGN EXCHANGE BOOTH WAS VERY SLOW. WE WERE STUCK IN LINE FOR FIFTEEN MINUTES.
MONEY EXCHANGE
STILL NO NEWS FROM REZA AND KAVEH.
WATCH THE LINE. IT'S OUR TURN.
SUDDENLY, WE SAW KAVEH'S FACE IN THE CROWD.
KAVEH !

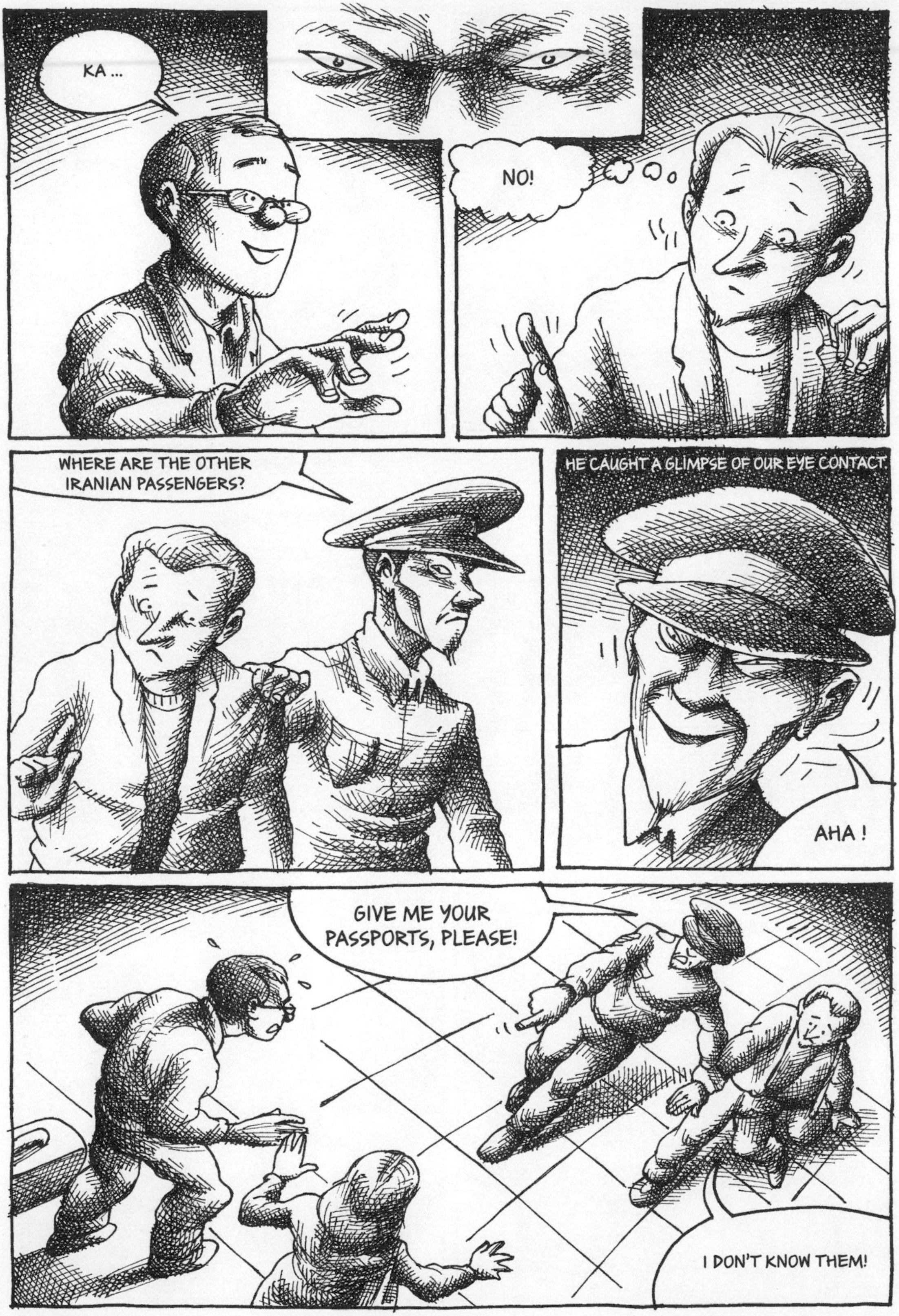
KA ...
NO!
WHERE ARE THE OTHER IRANIAN PASSENGERS?
HE CAUGHT A GLIMPSE OF OUR EYE CONTACT.
AHA !
GIVE ME YOUR PASSPORTS, PLEASE!
I DON'T KNOW THEM!

OK THEN. FOLLOW ME.
WHY?
IS ANYTHING WRONG? WE ARR FRRENCH! OUI?
JUST FOLLOW ME.
SIT IN THIS ROOM FOR US TO CHECK YOUR LUGGAGE.
WE'RE DONE FOR.
ONLY
PERSONNES
AS SOON AS I LEFT YOU, I WAS AR-RESTED AND BROUGHT HERE.
WHAT HAPPENED? DIDN'T YOU GET THROUGH PASSPORT CONTROL?
NO !

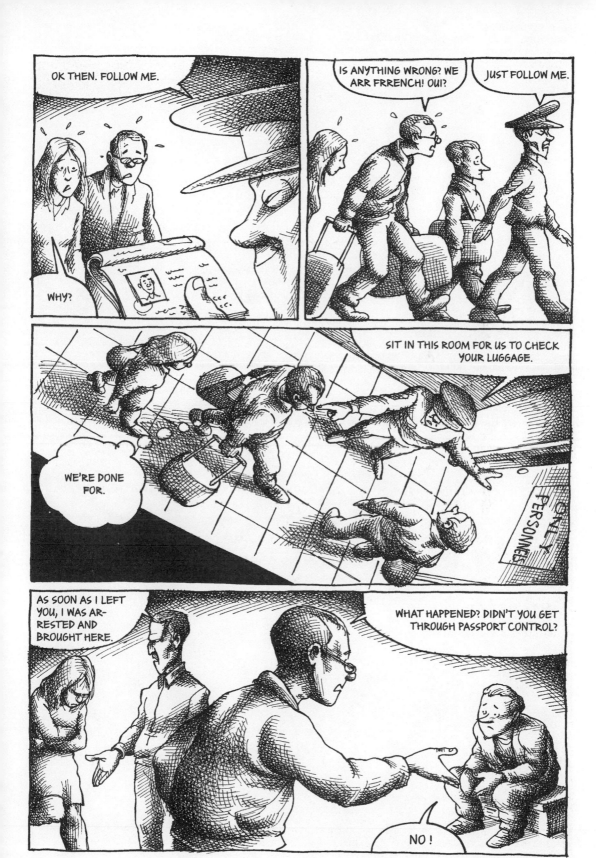

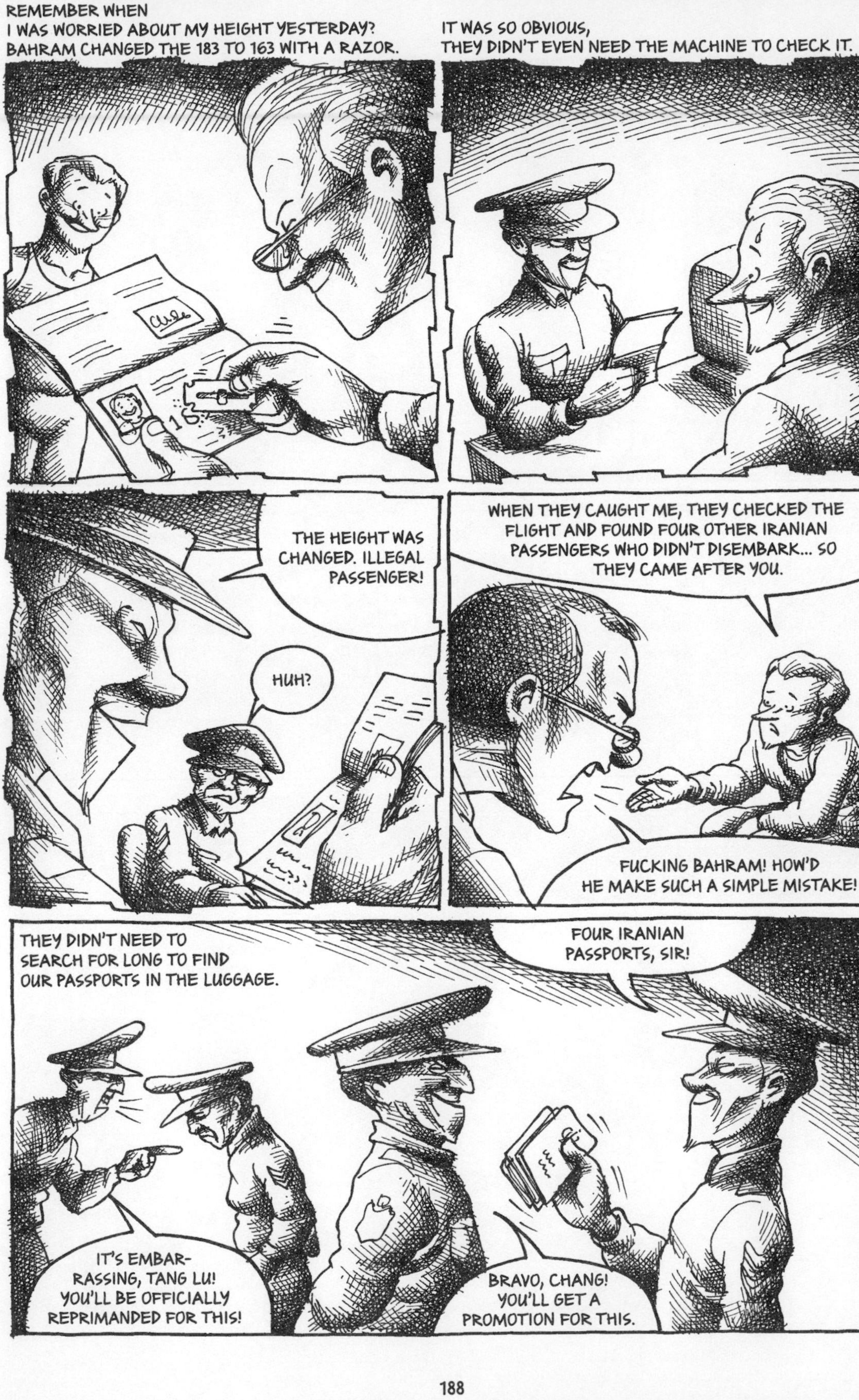

REMEMBER WHEN
I WAS WORRIED ABOUT MY HEIGHT YESTERDAY?
BAHRAM CHANGED THE 183 TO 163 WITH A RAZOR.
IT WAS SO OBVIOUS,
THEY DIDN'T EVEN NEED THE MACHINE TO CHECK IT.
THE HEIGHT WAS CHANGED. ILLEGAL PASSENGER!
HUH?
WHEN THEY CAUGHT ME, THEY CHECKED THE FLIGHT AND FOUND FOUR OTHER IRANIAN PASSENGERS WHO DIDN'T DISEMBARK... SO THEY CAME AFTER YOU.
FUCKING BAHRAM! HOW'D HE MAKE SUCH A SIMPLE MISTAKE!
THEY DIDN'T NEED TO SEARCH FOR LONG TO FIND OUR PASSPORTS IN THE LUGGAGE.
FOUR IRANIAN PASSPORTS, SIR!
IT'S EMBARRASSING, TANG LU! YOU'LL BE OFFICIALLY REPRIMANDED FOR THIS!
BRAVO, CHANG! YOU'LL GET A PROMOTION FOR THIS.

CHAPTER SIXTEEN

THE ARRESTED

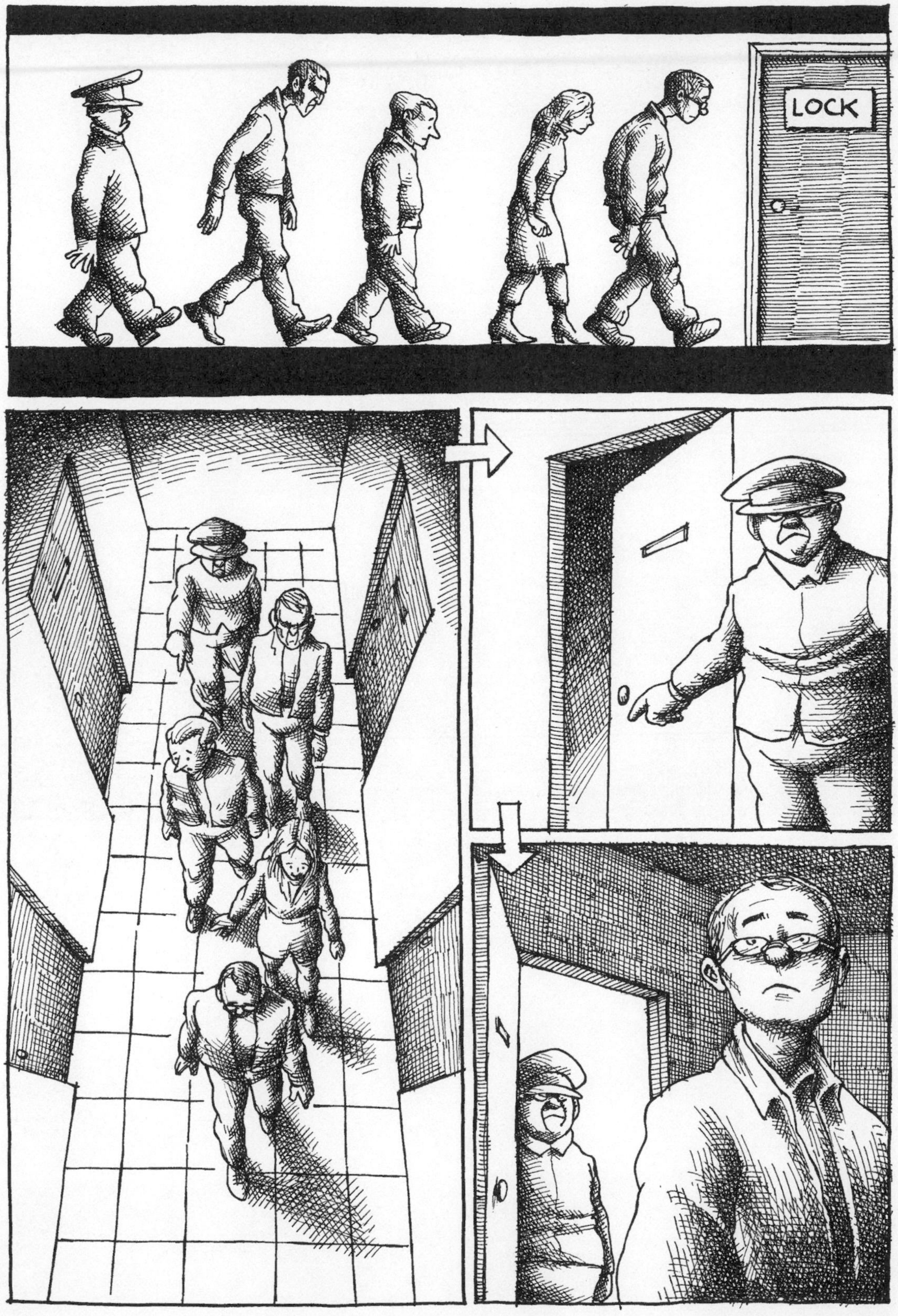
LOCK

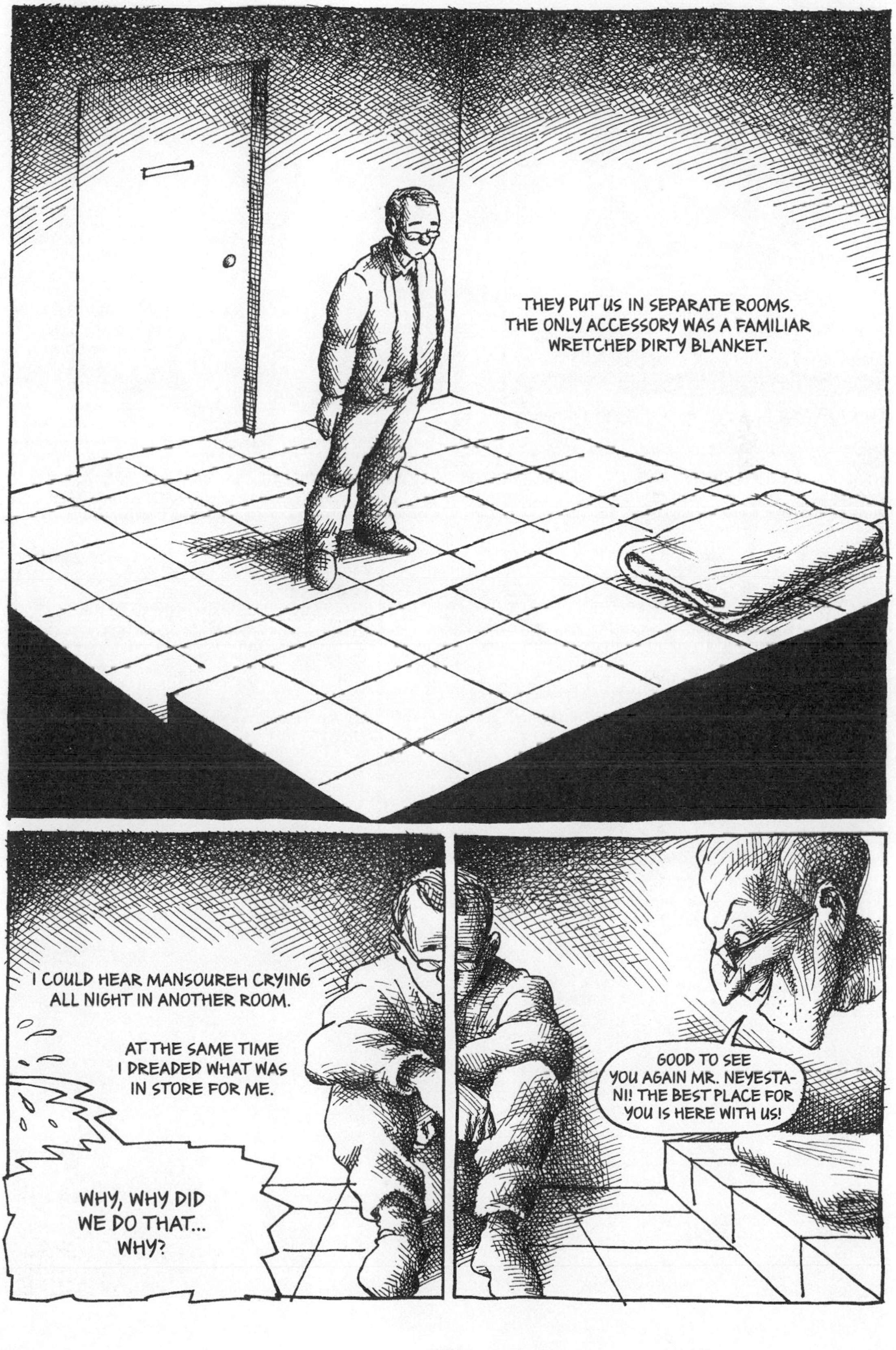
THEY PUT US IN SEPARATE ROOMS. THE ONLY ACCESSORY WAS A FAMILIAR WRETCHED DIRTY BLANKET.
I COULD HEAR MANSOUREH CRYING ALL NIGHT IN ANOTHER ROOM.
AT THE SAME TIME I DREADED WHAT WAS IN STORE FOR ME.
WHY, WHY DID WE DO THAT... WHY?
GOOD TO SEE YOU AGAIN MR. NEYESTA-NI! THE BEST PLACE FOR YOU IS HERE WITH US!

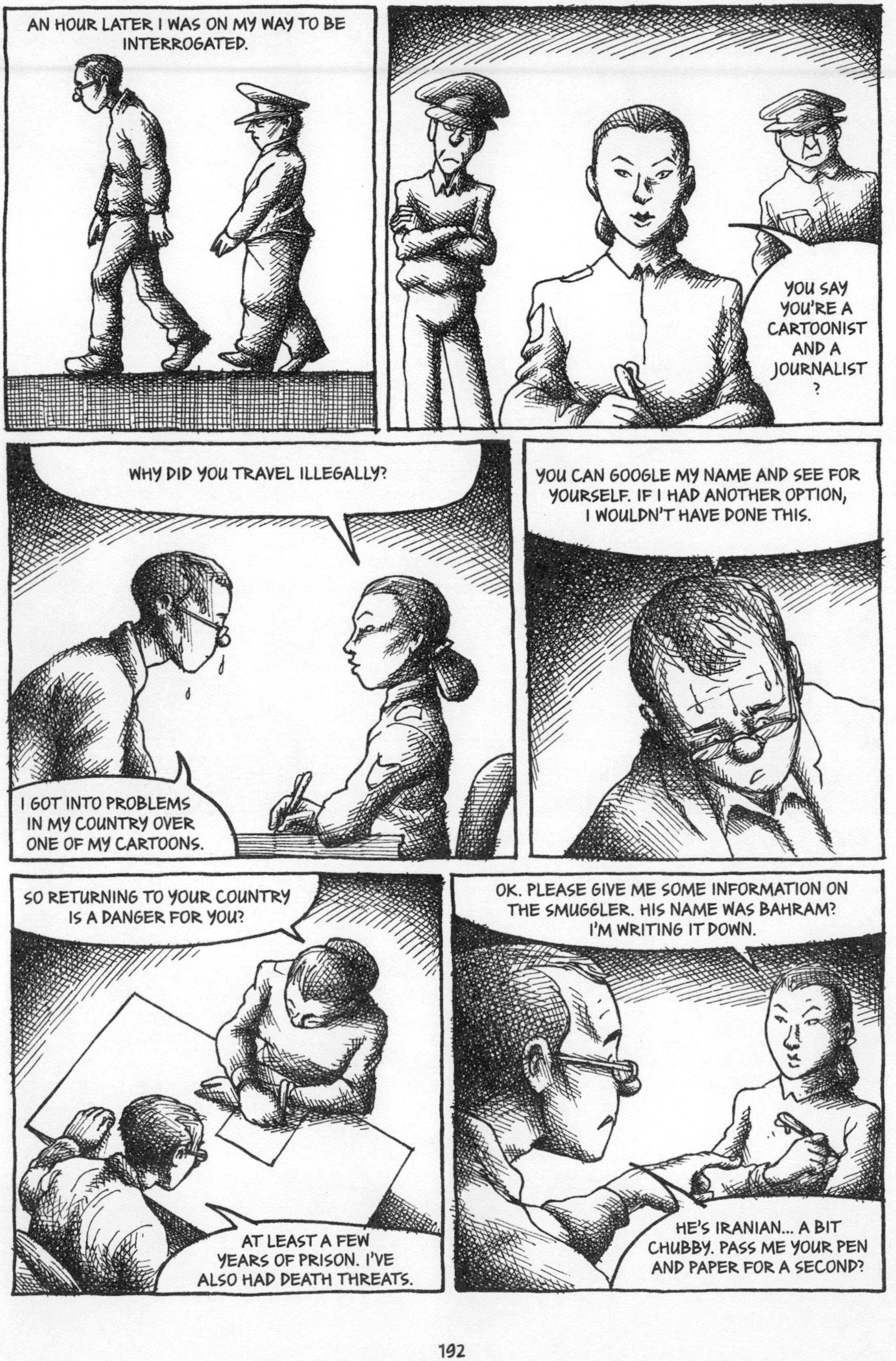
AN HOUR LATER I WAS ON MY WAY TO BE INTERROGATED.
YOU SAY YOU'RE A CARTOONIST AND A JOURNALIST ?
WHY DID YOU TRAVEL ILLEGALLY?
I GOT INTO PROBLEMS IN MY COUNTRY OVER ONE OF MY CARTOONS.
YOU CAN GOOGLE MY NAME AND SEE FOR YOURSELF. IF I HAD ANOTHER OPTION, I WOULDN'T HAVE DONE THIS.
SO RETURNING TO YOUR COUNTRY IS A DANGER FOR YOU?
AT LEAST A FEW YEARS OF PRISON. I'VE ALSO HAD DEATH THREATS.
OK. PLEASE GIVE ME SOME INFORMATION ON THE SMUGGLER. HIS NAME WAS BAHRAM? I'M WRITING IT DOWN.
HE'S IRANIAN... A BIT CHUBBY. PASS ME YOUR PEN AND PAPER FOR A SECOND?

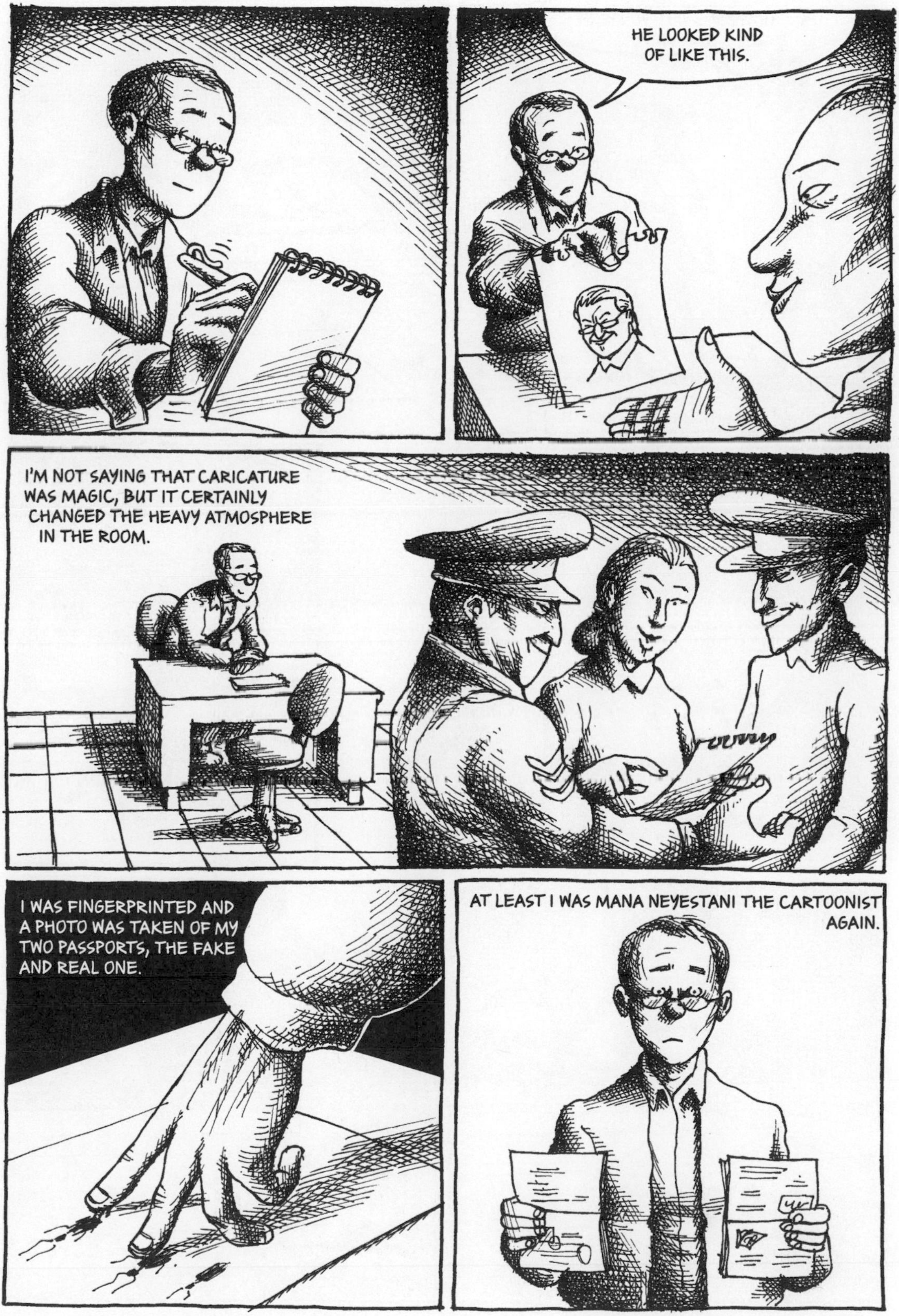
HE LOOKED KIND OF LIKE THIS.
I'M NOT SAYING THAT CARICATURE WAS MAGIC, BUT IT CERTAINLY CHANGED THE HEAVY ATMOSPHERE IN THE ROOM.
I WAS FINGERPRINTED AND A PHOTO WAS TAKEN OF MY TWO PASSPORTS, THE FAKE AND REAL ONE.
AT LEAST I WAS MANA NEYESTANI THE CARTOONIST AGAIN.

HOW LONG WILL YOU KEEP US HERE?
MAYBE ONE NIGHT... MAYBE A MONTH.
YOU BASTARD!
GRRCH
WHY?
WHY, WHAT?

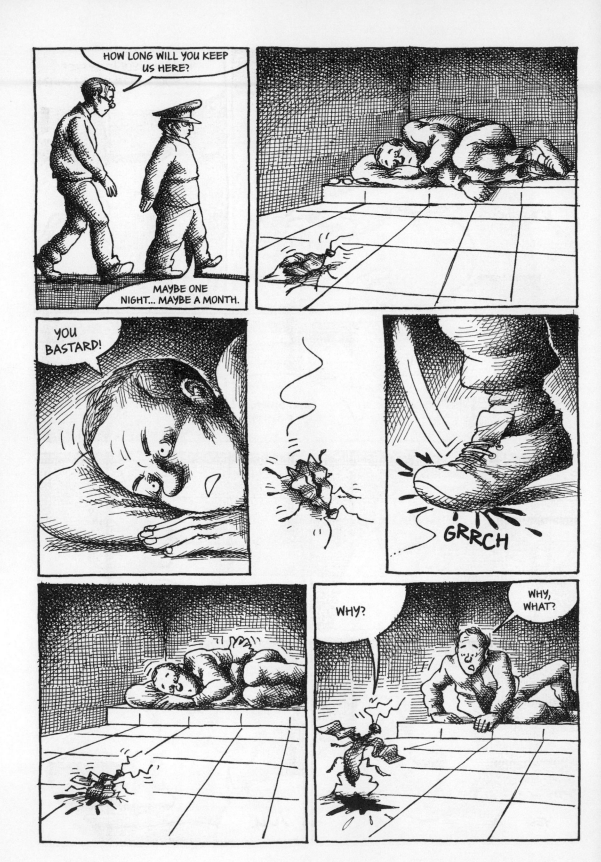

WHY DO YOU KEEP KILLING ME?
WHAT DO YOU WANT FROM ME?
LOOK CLOSELY AT MY FACE... DO YOU KNOW WHO I AM?
YES!
I AM YOU!

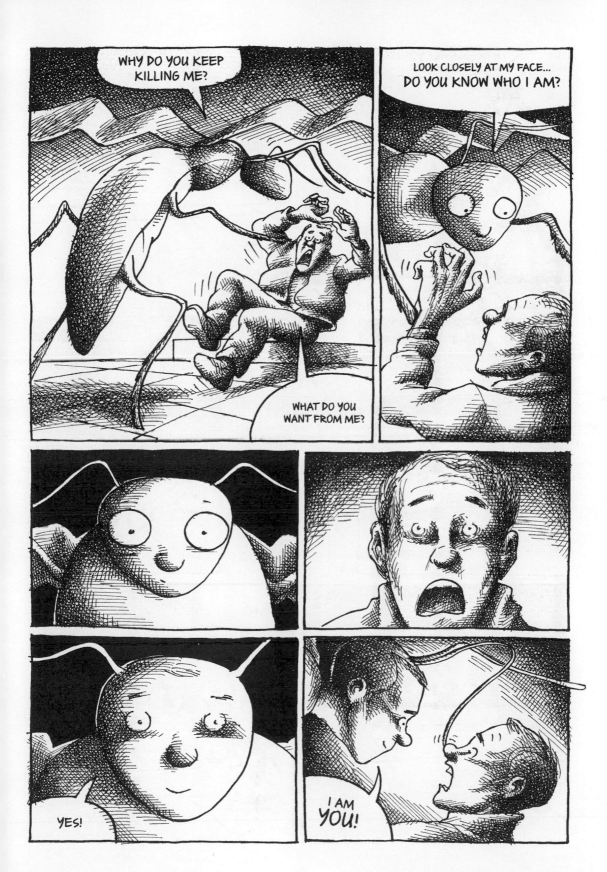

NOOO!
DON'T MAKE SO MUCH NOISE. WAKE UP! BREAKFAST TIME!
WHERE AM I?
小声点。起床。早饭时间 ！
THE GOAN JO AIRPORT DETENTION CENTER.

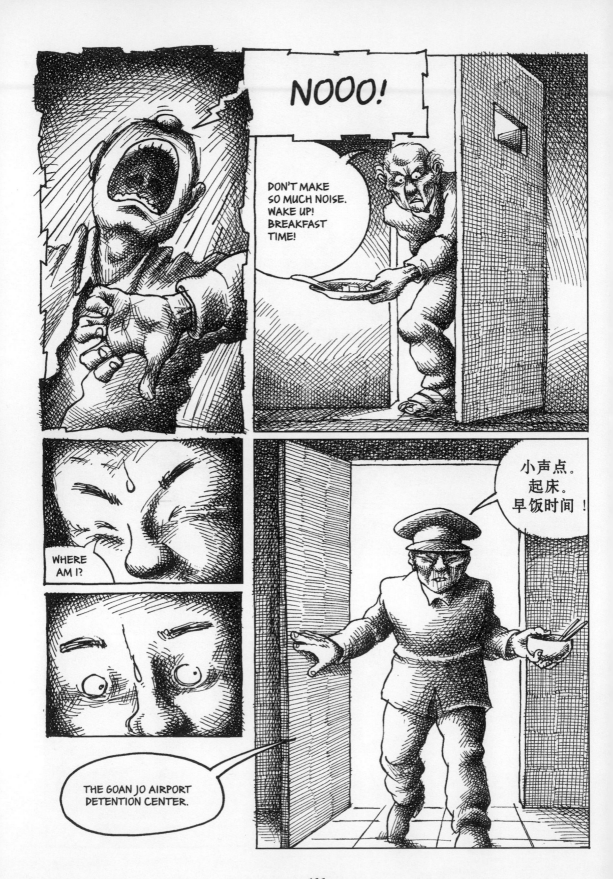

FINAL CHAPTER

LIMBO

AN HOUR LATER THE GUARD CAME IN.
GET READY FOR THE 2PM FLIGHT.
TWO PLAIN-CLOTHES OFFICERS ESCORTED US TO THE GATE.
KAVEH, WHAT'S NEXT?
SHUT UP AND GO FASTER!
OH, TO HAVE ONE CIGARETTE... JUST ONE!
NOTHING. THEY'LL GIVE OUR PASSPORTS TO THE PILOT WHICH MEANS WE'RE UNDER ARREST.
WHEN WE LAND IN MALAYSIA THE PILOT WILL HAND US OVER TO THE POLICE. THEY'LL INTERROGATE US FOR A COUPLE OF NIGHTS AND THEN SEND US PACKING TO IRAN WITH THE NEXT FLIGHT.
HOME SWEET HOME!
I ONLY WISH THEY'D GIVE US THE LUGGAGE BACK, SO I COULD DESTROY THE LETTER IN WHICH I EXPLAINED MY POLITICAL SITUATION. WHAT DO I HAVE TO DO WITH POLITICS ANYHOW!

HALF AN HOUR BEFORE BOARDING.

DON'T LEAVE MY SIGHT!
OK! TEIK EET EEZY!
KEEP THIS ENVELOPE WITH YOU!
?!
WE'RE LEAVING NOW, BUT YOU ARE UNDER SURVEILLANCE. MAKE SURE YOU GET ON YOUR FLIGHT.
OUR PASSPORTS!

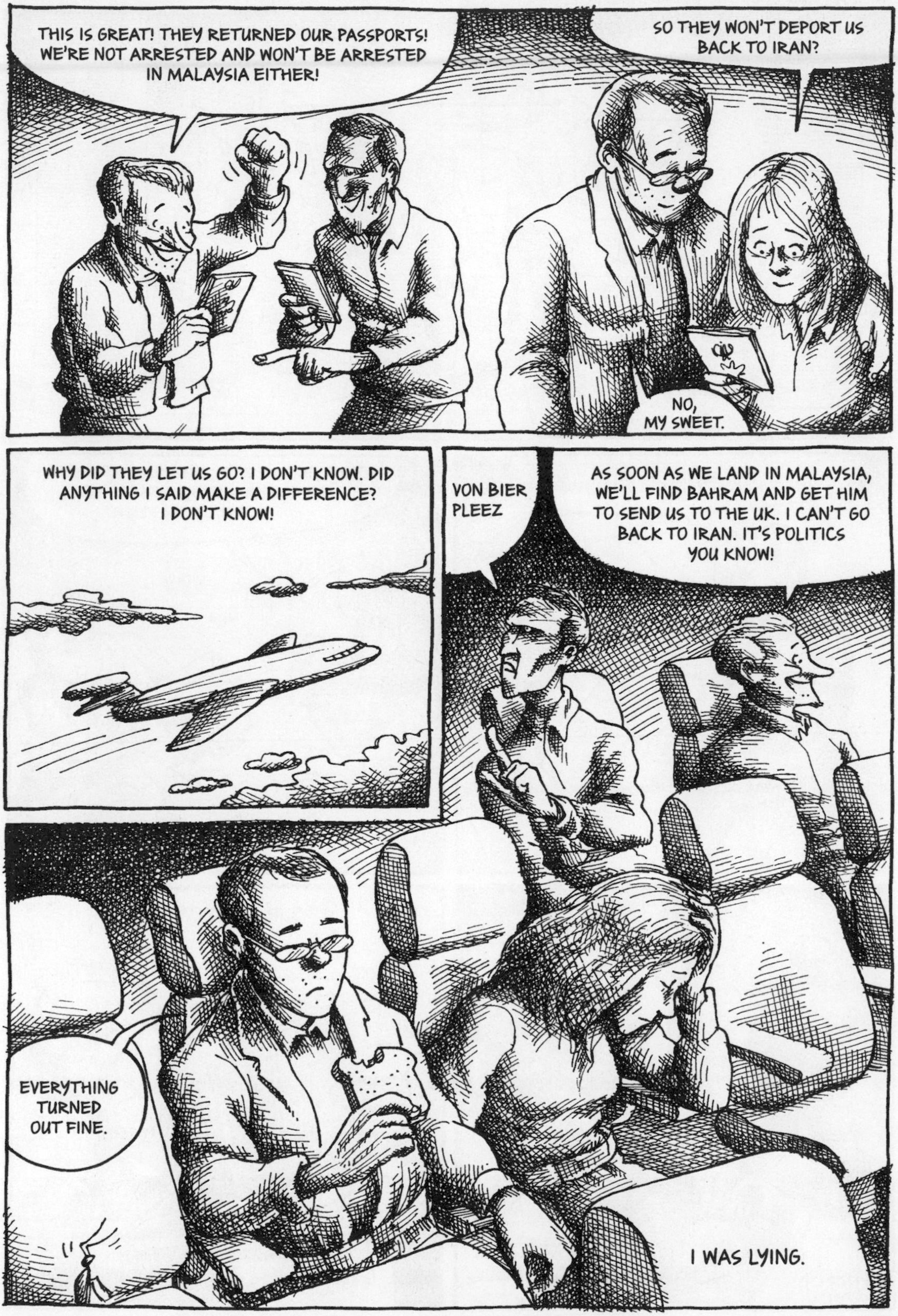
THIS IS GREAT! THEY RETURNED OUR PASSPORTS! WE'RE NOT ARRESTED AND WON'T BE ARRESTED IN MALAYSIA EITHER!
SO THEY WON'T DEPORT US BACK TO IRAN?
NO, MY SWEET.
WHY DID THEY LET US GO? I DON'T KNOW. DID ANYTHING I SAID MAKE A DIFFERENCE? I DON'T KNOW!
VON BIER PLEEZ
AS SOON AS WE LAND IN MALAYSIA, WE'LL FIND BAHRAM AND GET HIM TO SEND US TO THE UK. I CAN'T GO BACK TO IRAN. IT'S POLITICS YOU KNOW!
EVERYTHING TURNED OUT FINE.
I WAS LYING.

WE LOST EVERYTHING IN OUR CHINESE GAMBLE.

IT'D BE IMPOSSIBLE TO GET THE MONEY BACK FROM BAHRAM. WE STILL DIDN'T HAVE A SAFE PLACE TO GO TO.

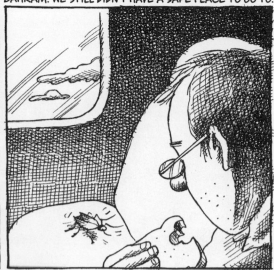

WHAT SHOULD WE DO IN MALAYSIA? I DON'T KNOW. HOW LONG COULD WE STAY THERE? I DON'T KNOW!

WHAT WILL HAPPEN TO US?

THANKS!

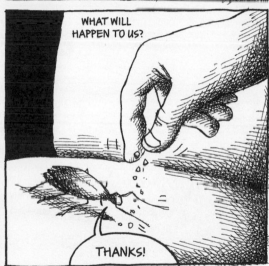

AT LEAST WE'RE STILL TOGETHER.

FREEDOM MEANS BEING WITH MANSOUREH. I WISH THIS MOMENT WOULD LAST FOREVER!

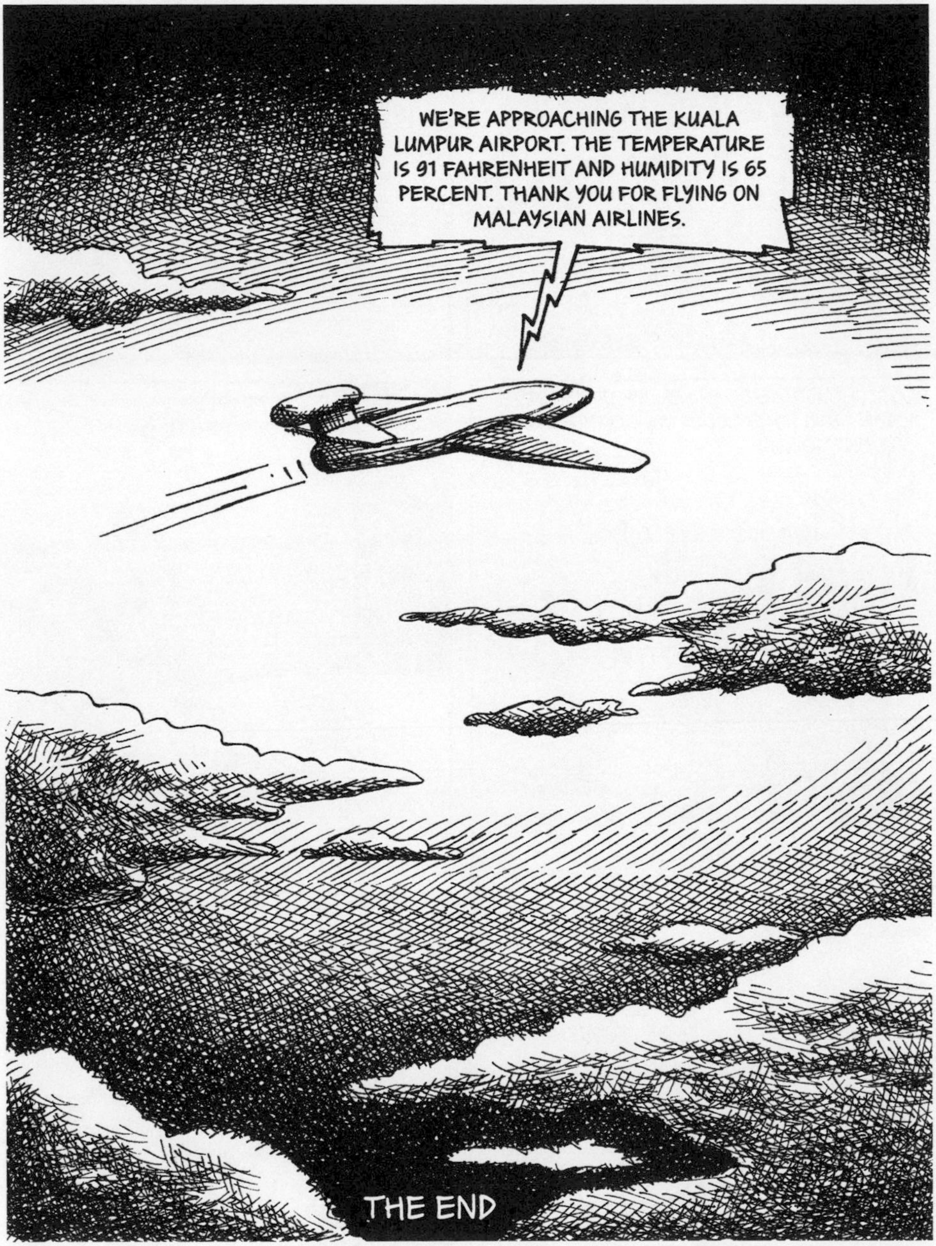
WE'RE APPROACHING THE KUALA LUMPUR AIRPORT. THE TEMPERATURE IS 91 FAHRENHEIT AND HUMIDITY IS 65 PERCENT. THANK YOU FOR FLYING ON MALAYSIAN AIRLINES.
THE END

EPILOGUE

Upon my return to Malaysia, I registered as an English student in Kuala Lumpur. That allowed me to remain in the country for another year. The following year, I was accepted at the University of Malaya for a Masters in Visual Arts. That guaranteed me another four years of student status in Malaysia. Mansoureh was with me through that time.

Several times, we applied for student visas to the US, Canada and Europe. We were rejected every time.

I continued drawing cartoons, but now it was for various anti-Iranian regime websites hosted in the States and Europe. My work during this time reflected on Iran's political situation, and included a series of cartoons that depicted subversive points of view. When I spoke out against the 2009 election fraud in my work, Malaysia became unsafe. Due to strong ties between Malaysia and Iran, I was at risk of being extradited to Iran. Thanks to "Reporters Without Borders," I got protection from ICORN (International Cities of Refuge Network). Soon after, I received an invitation from The City of Paris for a cultural residency. Monsoureh and I moved to France in February 2011, where we still live today.

Mehrad Ghasemfar, the editor-in-chief of *Iran Jomeh* and my cellmate at Evin, still works as a radio producer and host of Radio Farda in Prague.

Saïd Mortazavi, the judge, was the prime suspect in the torture case at the notorious Kahrizak prison. He was never convicted or sentenced.

After serving his sentence, **The 'Engineer,'** emigrated to Canada with his family. He's working for a reputable Canadian company and has a good life. I'm still in touch him.

A few years ago, while I was still in Malaysia, I received an email from **Shoghie**, the Azeri protester who shared my cell for a few days. He's been studying in Germany.

I learned that **Kaveh**, made a second attempt to smuggle himself out of Malaysia. Last I heard he entered England on an Irish passport and now works as a bartender.

Many of the **Azeri demonstrators** have been jailed and tortured. On every anniversary of that first protest, the cities are heavily monitored by armed militias to prevent any potential unrest. Each year they arrest several people.

Immediately after stepping down as the publisher of Iran newspaper, **Gholamhosein Eslami Far** was appointed to another government position. After a while, he returned to Iran newspaper, where he carries on publishing supplements on weekend and other occasions for INRA (Islamic Republic News Agency), a government institution.